Racism after 'race relations'

The book examines the scope of the concept of racism in the light of the problematic status of the idea of 'race' and of the histories of migration and nationalism. It takes issue with the emphasis in recent writing which links (often exclusively) racism with colonialism, an argument that typically concludes that only black people can be the victims of racism. By means of an exploration of nation formation within Europe and its relationship with migration, it argues that a number of interior racisms have existed in Europe. These are in addition to exterior, colonial racisms, and their victims have included various populations, including other Europeans. This analysis is premised on a reconsideration of the debate about the status of concepts of 'race' and 'race relations'. Against the background of this conceptual and historical survey the book concludes with an analysis of the current interrelationships between migration, nationalism and racism in the European Community, at a time when it is seeking to renegotiate its position in the capitalist world economy.

The book will be of interest to students concerned with the nature and history of racism and nationalism, as well as with the interrelationship between the formation of nation states and migration. Academics specializing in these matters will also find the book relevant because it contributes to the international debate about racism and migration.

Robert Miles is Reader in Sociology at the University of Glasgow and Visiting Professor at Glasgow Caledonian University. He has authored and co-authored a series of books on racism and migration, and has published widely in academic journals and in edited books. He lectures regularly in Europe and North America and he has held visiting positions in Montreal and Paris.

Racism after 'race relations'

Robert Miles

London and New York

First published 1993
by Routledge
11 New Fetter Lane, London EC4P 4EE

Simultaneously published in the USA and Canada
by Routledge
29 West 35th Street, New York, NY 10001

© 1993 Robert Miles

Typeset in Times by
NWL Editorial Services, Langport, Somerset

Printed and bound in Great Britain by
Mackays of Chatham PLC, Chatham, Kent

British Library Cataloguing in Publication Data
A catalogue record for this book is available from the British
Library

Library of Congress Cataloging in Publication Data
A catalog record for this book is available from the
Library of Congress

ISBN 0–415–07453–3
ISBN 0–415–10034–8 (pbk)

But from the ruins of Sheikh Dahr came not a sound of protest, not even the bark of a dog. Nothing but the silence of the earth and another, more subtle silence that seemed to blow down from the mountains, the silence of deeds that cannot be undone and of wrongs that no one can right.

(Oz 1986: 127)

The opposition to Nazism shaped in a dramatic fashion the refutation of racism as a legitimate intellectual stance. Politics mobilised many respectable intellectuals and scientists, who showed their eagerness to participate in the political discourse – and even more so, disclosed commitment and initiative.

(Barkan 1992: 345)

For Michael Banton and Colette Guillaumin

Contents

Acknowledgements

It is fortunate that knowledge and books are socially produced. It would have been rather dull to have sat alone for months on end in order to write these chapters. I have learnt a great deal from my European colleagues and friends, either with whom I have discussed the arguments presented here at different times since the mid-1980s or whose writing has been a special stimulus. I owe special debts of gratitude to: Etienne Balibar, Frank Bovenkerk, Phil Cohen, Kristin Couper, Diana Kay, Helma Lutz, Marco Martiniello, Gérard Noiriel, Jan Rath, Nora Räthzel, John Schüster, Max Silverman, Daniel Singer, Jean Singer-Kérel, John Solomos, Dietrich Thränhardt, Gilles Verbunt, Rob Witte, Catherine Wihtol de Wenden and Michel Wieviorka. Thanks also to Danielle Juteau and her colleagues at the Université de Montréal. From them, I learnt that Québec is the site of a very particular set of historical articulations, between Europe and the Americas, between competing colonialisms and strategies of civilisation, between indigenous peoples and colonisers, between classes, between nationalisms and racisms, between all these (and more) and sexism.

The essays collected here are revisions of papers that have been published previously. Several are published in English for the first time. All have been revised extensively, partly to reflect new thinking, partly to take account of new literature and partly in order to articulate and develop a series of problems and themes which have interested me in recent years and which are used to create and structure the book.

Chapter 1 was first published in Germany as 'Die marxistische Theorie und das Konzept "Rasse" ' in E.J. Dittrich and F.-O. Radtke (eds) *Ethnizität: Wissenschaft und Minderheiten*, Opladen: Westdeutscher Verlag, 1990. An earlier revision has been published in Canada as 'Analysing structured inequalities: Marxism and the idea of "race" ' in L. Samuelson (ed.) *Social Problems: Thinking Critically*, Toronto: Garamond Press, 1993. Chapter 2 was first published as 'Recent Marxist theories of nationalism and the issue of racism' in the *British Journal of Sociology*, 1987, 38(1): 24–43. Chapter 3 was first published in Germany as 'Die Idee der "Rasse" und Theorien über Rassismus: Überlegungen zur britischen Diskussion' in U. Bielefeld (ed.) *Das Eigene und das Fremde: Neuer Rassismus in der Alten Welt?*, Hamburg: Junius Verlag, 1991. Chapter 4 was first published as a review article with the title 'Whatever happened to the sociology of migration?' in *Work, Employment and Society*, 1990, 4(2): 281–98. Chapter 5 was first published as 'Nationality, citizenship and migration to Britain, 1945–1951' in the *Journal of Law and Society*, 1989, 16(4): 426–42. Chapter 6 was first published as 'Migration to Britain: the significance of a historical approach' in *International Migration*, 1991, 29(4): 527–43. Chapter 7 was first published in France as 'La politique et l'idéologie de l'integration en Europe' in a book by the Agence pour le Dévelopment des Relations Interculturelles with the title *L'Intégration des Minorités Immigrées en Europe Tome 1: Problématiques*, Paris: Centre National de la Fonction Publique Territoriale, 1991. And Chapter 8 was first published in Canada as 'Migration, racism and the nation state in contemporary Europe' in V. Satzewich (ed.) *Deconstructing a Nation: Immigration, Multiculturalism and Racism in 90s Canada*, Toronto: Garamond Press, 1992. Thanks to all those who granted permission for the revised versions of these papers to be published here.

Some of these papers began life or were nurtured as contributions to conferences or seminars in Bielefeld, Belgrade, Hamburg, Paris, Montréal, Saskatoon and Toronto. I gratefully acknowledge the award of grants by the British Academy, the British Council and the University of Glasgow which made it possible for me to participate in these events. The book was finished in the course of exercising the not too onerous duties incumbent upon a visiting academic at the Ecole des Hautes Etudes en Sciences Sociales in Paris. I am especially grateful to Michel Wieviorka and Didier Lapeyronnie, who invited me, who made me very welcome, and who provided productive stimulation (and not only because we disagree about some important theoretical matters).

The book is dedicated to two people whose writing has been, in very different ways, an important influence on my own thinking. But neither they, nor my other colleagues and friends, should feel in any way responsible for the consequences of their influence.

Robert Miles

May 1992, Paris and Glasgow

Introduction

Adam Garde had never quite bought the fantasy Oskar had been pushing all evening. For Hitler was more than a man: he was a system with ramifications. Even if he died, it was no guarantee the system would alter its character. Besides, it was not in the nature of a phenomenon such as Hitler to perish in the space of an evening.

(Keneally 1986: 292)

The idea that 'race' is a contemporary problem is a customary observation in Britain, North America, Australasia and beyond. Newspaper headlines report that 'Race riots hit Los Angeles', that there is a 'Race bias in employment' and that an 'MP plays the race card'. In Britain, the Commission for Racial Equality comments annually on the state of 'race relations'. Social workers are taught 'race awareness' and university academics in the social sciences are expected to include a 'race component' in many of their courses.

If 'race relations' are a feature of contemporary society, it seems obvious that academics should study them. But the casual observer could equally well conclude from personal observation that it is 'obvious' that the sun circulates around the earth. In order to believe otherwise, it is necessary to confront personal experience with analytical reasoning and forms of rational measurement. In other words, 'obviousness' is a condition which depends upon the location of the observer and the set of concepts employed to conceive and interpret the object.

Some social scientists have sought to construct a theory of 'race relations'. Others have criticised their efforts and have proposed that the more appropriate object of analysis is *racism* (although they often disagree about the analytical status of the idea of 'race'). The argument offered here is that, after 'race relations', there is indeed another way of looking at social relations, a way that does not need to employ the idea of 'race' as an analytical concept. But, by substituting racism as the focus of study, we take on another set of analytical problems, several of which are discussed in this book: there are different ways of conceptualising and theorising racism. After the 'race relations' paradigm, we have also to confront the problems of the racism paradigm.

Three main themes shape this book: each theme is discussed in a separate part but they also interlock across these three parts. The structural division of the book therefore designates broad arenas of analysis, arenas within which particular arguments recur throughout, constituting threads which seek to establish a wider coherence. The first theme continues the debate about the analytical status of the notion of 'race' and the parameters of the concept of racism in the social sciences. The second theme advocates the analytical importance of a historical perspective on the central role of migration in the development of capitalist social formations and on the expression of racism within those formations. And the third theme presents certain issues prominent in the analysis of the interrelationship between immigration and the economic, political and ideological integration of the European Community (EC).

THE CONCEPT OF RACISM

The title of this book suggests that there are reasons to define a field of study and a theoretical perspective that transcend that identified by the interrelated notions of 'race' and 'race relations'. These notions continue to carry a complexity of meanings within everyday (political and academic) discourse in the English-speaking world. This continuity is worthy of explanation, but the task of explanation is complicated by the tendency within academic analysis not only to use them to define a field of study, but also as if they were *explanans*. Within academic work, it is often claimed, for example, that 'Unemployment is determined by race', and that 'The riots in Brixton (or Los Angeles) demonstrate that race is a central determinant of inequality in British (or United States) society.' Most writers (although certainly not all, e.g. Riggs 1991) deny that they are using the idea of 'race' as if it referred to a biological hierarchy of fundamentally different groups of people who possess a variable capacity for 'civilisation'. Nevertheless, the manner of their use of the notion commonly implies an acceptance of the existence of biological differences between human beings, differences which express the existence of distinct, self-reproducing groups.

Indeed, it is difficult to avoid such an implication. The idea of 'race' evolved in such a way that its object became the supposed existence of biological types of human being. When, during the first half of the twentieth century, scientific knowledge demonstrated conclusively that the world's population could not be legitimately categorised in this way, the idea of 'race' no longer had a 'real' object. What remained was the common-sense idea that 'races' existed, an idea sustained by the unquestionable reality of somatic and cultural differences between people. If social scientists retain the idea of 'race' as an analytical concept to refer to the social reproduction and consequences of this belief, it necessarily implicitly carries the meaning of its use in the everyday world.

The critique of the use of the idea of 'race' as an analytical concept in the social sciences now has a long history (Barzun 1938, Guillaumin 1972, 1980). Drawing on this work, more than a decade ago I published a critique of the 'race relations' problematic which had dominated British sociology during the 1960s and 1970s (Miles 1982, see also 1984a, 1987a, 1988a, Miles and Phizacklea 1984). I also offered an alternative paradigm for the study of the determinants and effects of the expression of racism in the capitalist social formations of western Europe after the end of the Second World War, a paradigm founded on the political economy of labour migration.

In response, some writers have rejected the use of the notion of 'race' as an analytical concept and it has become increasingly common to find the use of the word problematised by being placed in inverted commas as a sign of renunciation. There have been two other responses. On the one hand, some writers, whose work is broadly grounded in either the Marxist tradition or other critical anti-capitalist perspectives, have defended the use of the notion of 'race' as an analytical concept in the study of racism while simultaneously rejecting the 'race relations' paradigm (e.g. Gilroy 1987, Anthias 1990, Solomos 1990, Small 1991a, 1991b). I discuss some of this latter work in the broader context of the evolution of a Marxist theory of 'race' in Chapter 1 but some preliminary comments are useful here in order to introduce this debate.

Perhaps the strongest case made in favour of the retention of the notion of 'race' as an analytical concept arises from the fact that it has been used by the victims of racism to fashion a strategy and practice of resistance to their subordination. The idea of 'race' can then be regarded as open to conflicting interpretations and uses: it can become an idea offering the potential of liberation because it provides a focus for political organisation and practice against exclusion effected and legitimated through a repressive discourse of 'race'. But the radical notion of 'race struggle' is not without contradictory consequences and these lead to further problems for those seeking to attribute the idea of 'race' with analytical meaning.

During the 1980s, limits to the mobilisation of the 'race' struggle became increasingly apparent in Britain. Throughout the decade, the idea of 'race' was closely associated with the idea of 'black', to the extent that the notions of 'race struggle' and 'black struggle' were synonymous. It has been argued that use of the notion 'black' as a means of political mobilisation embodies a specific rather than a universal tradition of resistance, one which is expressive of the colonial subordination of people of exclusively African origin. The attempt to generalise the 'black' struggle to all those whose lives are influenced by racism therefore disavows the specific cultural and historical origins of non-African peoples. Thus, so the argument continues, the idea of 'black' has been of little or no significance in the mobilisation of Muslims in Britain to protest against the publication of Salman Rushdie's book *The Satanic Verses*. All attempts to 'force' the struggles of people of south Asian origin into the 'black' or 'race perspective' therefore entail making them subservient to another culture and strategy of resistance, one which neglects their distinct origins and cultural symbols (Modood 1988, 1990, 1991, see also James 1989).

There is another example. Throughout much of the 1980s, there has been a struggle by a group of activists within the Labour Party to establish an autonomous Black Section within the organisation. The history of that struggle also reveals some of the difficulties entailed in any attempt to organise a 'black' struggle around the idea of 'race'. In 1989, a Labour MP of Caribbean origin argued that, because those people demonstrating against the publication of *The Satanic Verses* were 'black', then the Black Sections movement should support them. Jeffers comments (1991: 75):

> Yet these demonstrators were out on the streets not as blacks, but as outraged Muslim fundamentalists. Not all Muslims are black, and not all Muslims take the fundamentalist position. Why then should black socialists give support to hardline religious leaders?

The danger of always explaining the practice and situation of 'black' people as being the result of racism is inherent in the initial classification as 'black', for it is a classification that reproduces the extant racist dichotomy as in a mirror image, but with an alternative value content. The primary issue at stake for the Muslims demonstrating against the publication of *The Satanic Verses* was that the book was blasphemous. While there was scope (and perhaps with good reason) to argue also that racism was one determinant of a situation which permitted blasphemy against Islam, it remains the case that support for the demonstrators required an acknowledgement of their particular religious beliefs but not that many of them were 'black'. What both of these examples demonstrate is that the related ideas of 'race' and 'black' are now contested to an extent that their use as analytical concepts is even more problematic.

There has been another response to my critique of the 'race relations' paradigm: one of its original architects, Michael Banton, has defended its continued use (1991). This defence substantiates my original objections. Banton notes that 'racial relations' are 'identified by the subjective meaning attached to differences' (1991: 129) in order to distance his conception from one which treats such relations as being between really existing biological 'races'. Nevertheless, ambiguity arises from the proposal that the subject matter of the 'race relations' problematic should be 'an examination of the changing significance of colour, descent, national and ethnic origins as well as race, and as one set among the many kinds of grounds on which people draw distinctions' (1991: 129). But if 'race' is *something* that has a changing significance, that is used by people to make distinctions, what is it? Banton suggests (1991: 118) that social scientists should adopt legal definitions (unless there is good reason not to) and so, presumably, we can find an answer to the question in law and the legal process.

Banton claims that British law has developed an adequate (and by implication superior) vocabulary to deal with discrimination. Yet, by Banton's own admission, this is drawn not from a more sophisticated or theorised comprehension of the reality of social relations but rather from everyday meanings: both the British House of Lords and the Court of Appeal agree that the notions of 'colour, race, nationality or ethnic or national origins' are to be interpreted in the light of public definitions (Banton 1991: 125). In other words, the legal category of 'race' is formally defined and given legal sanction in accordance with the everyday definition of 'race'. Banton's 'race relations' paradigm therefore entails a truly hegemonic reification in which the circularity of meaning in social relations is sanctioned by the sociology of 'race relations', whose concepts are to be drawn from the meanings generated by, and the practices of, the state itself in the form of the legal process.

The problem originates in the law itself, and not in the practice of the courts *per se*. British law defines a 'race' or 'racial group' as 'a group of persons defined by reference to colour, race, nationality or ethnic or national origins' (cited in Banton 1991: 118). And Banton notes that the three Race Relations Acts suggest that 'each individual could be assigned to a race, and that relations between persons of different race were necessarily different from relations between persons of the same race' (Banton 1991: 115). The definition is (necessarily) circular: a 'race' is a group of people defined by 'their race': this formulation assumes and legitimates as a reality that each human being 'belongs' to a 'race'. This assumption is reproduced throughout Banton's advocacy of the 'race relations' paradigm. For example, in a discussion of those medical conditions which result in 'white' people developing a darker skin colour, Banton suggests that all that has changed is the colour of their skin but not their 'race' (1991: 120, see also 1991: 122): the implication can only be that each human being is 'really' a member of one or another 'race'.

Banton's defence of the 'race relations' problematic is an excellent example of Guillaumin's critique of the way in which the law, and therefore the state, can reify the idea of 'race' (1980). By incorporating into the law and the legal process the idea that there are 'races' whose relations, one to another in a situation of inequality, must be regulated, the state validates the beliefs of the phenomenal world and orders social relations in such a way that they are structured and reproduced in a racialised form. Unlike the situation in Nazi Germany during the 1930s or in South Africa during the era of apartheid, British 'race relations' law is not intended to enforce the subordination of particular 'races', but rather to make certain forms of discrimination illegal. Viewed in terms of egalitarian values, while this is progressive because it not only sanctions a certain kind of moral order but also imposes formal penalties on those who act in ways contrary to the law, it does nothing to stigmatise the false idea of 'race' (cf. Banton 1991: 129). Rather, British 'race relations' law legitimates the belief in the existence of 'races' in an attempt to eliminate a particular practice of discrimination. The circularity can only be broken by means of theoretical intervention which defines an alternative construction and a set of practices which transcend extant social relations.

I have advocated a theoretical intervention which prioritises the concept of racism (1982, 1989a). Here, I am in agreement with those writers referred to above who reject the 'race relations' problematic but who retain the idea of 'race' as an analytical concept. Collectively, we share the terrain of the alternative problematic of racism (Banton 1991: 118, 129). This problematic has dominated academic and political debate since the late 1970s. Banton's rejection of the concept of racism (1987: ix) has resulted in much of his work being considered tangential to the main direction of this European debate during this period. More recently, his defence of the 'race relations' paradigm, alongside his active commitment to the elimination of racist discrimination via his membership of the United Nations Committee on the Elimination of Racial Discrimination, has led him to engage again with the concept of racism (1991, 1992). This engagement serves to highlight the significance of the other two essays that appear in Part I of this book.

Banton believes that the racism problematic has its own legitimacy (1991: 118) but his reservations about the use of the concept, and therefore about the analytical value of the racism problematic, are profound. While recognising that the concept of racism has considerable rhetorical power in international relations, he concludes that it is problematic because it neglects interpersonal relations, because it homogenises practices that should be analysed separately, and because it reifies the phenomenon to which it refers (1991: 118). As a result, he remains committed to working within the 'race relations' problematic although he acknowledges that the two could usefully develop in parallel.

In the course of evaluating my advocacy of racism as a central analytical concept to define a field of study, Banton presents my work as representative of the racism problematic. Not all would agree with this prioritisation and he does not recognise, nor seek to engage with, the diversity of positions found within the racism paradigm. The boundary and meaning of the concept of racism is the site of theoretical struggle: I have delineated some of the more important positions in this struggle elsewhere (1989a), and I continue this exploration in Part I and elsewhere in this book. One of the important issues around which debate has developed concerns the proposition that the concept of racism refers to an ideology with a historically specific origin in colonialism. This position sometimes leads to the conclusion that racism is a 'white ideology' created exclusively to dominate 'blacks'.

In my original critique of the 'race relations' problematic (1982), I argued that an explanation for the origin and reproduction of racism should take account of the influence of colonialism on the determination of racist ideologies. Subsequently, I have expressed reservations about an explanation for the nature and origin of racism which focuses exclusively on the colonial situation and I have suggested that, in part, the origins of racism can be traced back to pre-capitalist social relations within and beyond Europe and that its reproduction is as much determined by the rise of the nation state as by colonialism (1989a: 38–40, 99–100, 111–121). It is unfortunate that Banton overlooks these arguments which, while critical of others writing within the racism paradigm, demonstrate that the debate about the nature and scope of the concept of racism has moved beyond the parameters that he identifies.

Moreover, I am not the only writer to have sought to transcend the colonial paradigm of racism. Some recent contributions to the debate have suggested that the origin of racism can be traced in part to the categories of thought invented by the European Enlightenment, thereby at least mediating the link between racism and colonialism (Goldberg

1990b) by proposing a more culturalist account of origins. Others have suggested that the invention of racism took place in medieval feudal Europe, using categories and ways of thinking which, in turn, have their origin in 'antiquity', in the 'classical civilisations' of Greece and Rome (Delacampagne 1983).

Yet, the view that racism is a historically specific ideology, in the sense that its invention paralleled the rise of capitalism, continues to have its advocates. Wallerstein states boldly that 'le capitalisme, en tant que système, engendre le racisme' (1988: 50). In so doing, he reiterates a long-established Marxist argument, although with a more novel reasoning. For Wallerstein, the increasing prevalence of the ideology of universalism necessarily parallels the rise of the capitalist world economy. But, because capitalism inevitably generates social inequality, and so a structure of social relations that openly contradicts the principles of equality and universalism that legitimate capitalism, the ideology of racism was invented to explain the subordination of specific populations whose position of inequality results from the fact that their labour power is exploited by the payment of low wages (1988: 44–50). For Wallerstein, it follows from the fact that the capitalist world system requires the exploitation of this labour power (and therefore the inclusion of the people that supply it within the world system) that the capitalist epoch is historically unique. Prior to the rise of the capitalist world system, formally similar discourses had the consequence of expulsion or exclusion rather than a subordinate form of inclusion. Wallerstein uses the concept of xenophobia to refer to these equally historically specific ideologies of exclusion (1988: 47–8).

The issue of whether these two arguments can be reconciled is not addressed in this book. They are noted here to demonstrate that the debate about the nature and scope of the concept of racism is multifaceted and that not all who have contributed to it would accept the contention that the concept refers to an ideology that is specific to colonialism and to the epoch dominated by the capitalist mode of production. They are also noted in order to respond to another common argument, that which suggests that the debate about the meaning of the concept of racism is formal and arid, and therefore of little interest or consequence (Castles *et al.* 1984: 194). I disagree.

Because the concept has an evaluative content, it should not be used with impunity. While I doubt that the notion is 'beginning to lose its force as an epithet' (Banton 1992: 72) (because it is only a very small number of politicians on the far right of the political spectrum who are prepared to declare themselves as racists), the possibility of such an outcome is real. Furthermore, the historicity or otherwise of racism is an issue which has practical implications for policy formulation and for the organisation of anti-racist struggle: it certainly matters as to whether or not racism has its origin exclusively in the interwoven histories of capitalism and colonialism (and can perhaps be expected to be eradicated in due course) or whether it has a more universal character and reality (and is therefore less likely to be neutralised by policy or political struggle). Finally, to marginalise the matter of definition is to grant to the racists an autonomy to deny their avowal of racism. For if we 'retreat' to the position that racism is whatever we define it to be at any time, we concede to the racists the opportunity to argue (with justification) that the notion is no more than an item in the arsenal of 'left-wing' rhetoric.

MIGRATION THEORY AND HISTORY

For some readers, it may seem a self-indulgent luxury to write a book about racism which does little to document the contemporary consequences of racism for its victims. A catalogue of everyday racism could indeed be compiled and others have contributed to such a task in different ways (e.g. Brown 1984, Essed 1991). Vital though this work is, it is not the only matter that is worthy of attention. There is an important contribution to be made by academic research which has a *historical* focus, not least because it permits an assessment of the extent to which contemporary realities may be specific to the contemporary conjuncture, or to a particular epoch (feudalism, capitalism, etc.), or alternatively are universal attributes of all social relations. As Part I demonstrates, a historical perspective on the evolution of the concept and numerous subjects of racism is necessary if we are to comprehend the specificity (or otherwise) of contemporary racisms. In Part II, I suggest that such a focus can be stimulated further by reflecting on the theory and history of migration.

It has become common for France to be described, like the USA, as a 'melting pot' for different populations of migrant origin: both can be seen as nation states consciously constructed from the diverse populations that migrated into these territories during the nineteenth and twentieth centuries (e.g. Noiriel 1988). Given the scale of migration into France over the past one hundred and fifty years, there are good reasons to make such a comparison. But this is a comparison which tends to suppress the significance of the history of migration into other western European nation states (including Britain) because, in comparative terms, the scale of immigration has been much less than that into France.

While this is factually true, there are reasons not to leave the matter there. The analytical dichotomy between social formations constructed through immigration (e.g. the USA, France) and those not so constructed (e.g. Britain, Germany) has the potential to legitimate the view that the latter nation states have evolved as an expression of a 'unitary people' whose specific character has been 'undiluted' by the immigration of 'foreign elements'. This is an argument that leads towards the conclusion that immigration is therefore necessarily undesirable because 'our own people' will 'naturally' resist such a 'dilution' of their 'timeless traditions and way of life'.

There are two senses in which the historical analysis of migration is relevant to the discussion of such an assertion. First, the long transition from feudalism to capitalism in Europe, a transition that was inseparable from the creation of the nation state as a political reality, was effected by means of a revolutionary and ongoing transformation of social relations, including an uprooting and moving of people from one spatial location to another. The creation of the proletariat, the emergence of towns and cities, the transformation of the domestic unit so that it became solely a site for reproduction, the development of industrial production, the evolution of market relations, all of these processes were effected through the migration of people. There is a sense in which the historical evolution of the British or German nation state, as one historical instance of capitalist development, is as much a product of migration as that of France or the USA.

There may be a difference in the extent to which the migrants originated beyond the boundary of the nation state, but this does not detract from the reality of nineteenth-century European towns and cities as 'melting pots', into which flowed, from far and near, millions of rural peasant producers, speaking different languages and dialects and expressing specific cultural practices and values. The idea of late-twentieth-century cities as uniquely 'multicultural' has, therefore, little historical validity. Furthermore, the migration process was mediated by capital investment in, and technological advancement of, systems of transportation which made it increasingly possible for larger and larger numbers of people to move greater and greater distances at faster and faster speeds. It was also mediated by the state as it increasingly sought to regulate migration by policing the boundary of the nation using the principle of nationality (which was, in turn, often shaped by racism). Ironically, the former mediation increased the salience of the latter: formalised systems of immigration control, organised by the state, were unnecessary when material realities ensured that fewer people had the ability to move great distances, and therefore across state-defined national borders.

Irrespective of the level of capital and technological investment in systems of transportation, throughout history human beings have found it necessary to migrate from their place of birth, and have found the means to do so. The reasons why they continue to do so are of contemporary significance because immigration is now ranked high on national and international political agendas: immigration is a social process that is widely considered to require state regulation (especially by governments otherwise ideologically committed to 'rolling back the state'). It is therefore an object of the policy-making process. The formulation of policies presumes an account of the determinants of the process that is to be regulated. When government ministers and state officials throughout Europe claim that new laws are required to deal with the 'immigration crisis' caused by 'bogus refugees' who are really only economic migrants in disguise, they are in effect proposing a theory of migration, or at least a theory of one particular migration. If their claims are to be the subject of critical scrutiny, a theory of migration is imperative. Some of the problems and possibilities of such a theory are discussed in Chapter 4.

There is a second reason why the study of the history of migration is relevant to an evaluation of the claim that certain nation states have been built on the foundation of a 'homogeneous people'. A critical evaluation of the nationalist myth of the 'homogenous people' requires research on the evolution of the myth itself and on the Others against whom the myth has been created and reproduced. The history of immigration (understood here in the sense of spatial mobility across national boundaries) is an important dimension of such a critical examination because immigration inserts into the nation state a population that potentially may be defined as an unacceptable Other. And, while research on the history of immigration to Britain is in its infancy (Holmes 1988, Pooley and Whyte 1991), what we already know demonstrates not only that the scale of immigration has been considerable at certain times, but also that political agitation for 'strict immigration control' has a history which extends back over the past one hundred years.

During the 1960s, there was a flurry of interest in this history, and a number of studies drew parallels between the political reaction to the then ongoing migration to Britain from the New Commonwealth and the reaction to east European migration to Britain during the late nineteenth and early twentieth centuries (e.g. Garrard 1971, Gainer 1972). Sociological interest in such a comparison has since waned. For some, there is no reason to take account of earlier migrations, and of the political reaction to them, because they did not give rise to a 'race relations' situation. For others who define racism exclusively as an ideology created by 'white people' to exploit 'blacks', the fact that the immigrants were 'white' is sufficient to exclude these historical events from consideration: by definition, racism could not have been an active political force in these earlier periods.

Both arguments imply or argue that immigration to Britain from the New Commonwealth since the Second World War, and its social consequences, are unique. In so far as a historical perspective on this migration has evolved, it seeks to recover the 'hidden history' of the 'black presence' in Britain, and the state's attempts to prohibit 'black immigration' or to expel 'blacks' from Britain. The result is an analysis in which everything is always the same: history reveals a continuity from past to present, a continuity in which 'blacks' are the sole and perpetual victim of racism. This is an analysis which carries the potential of mirroring and inverting racism itself: in so far as racist ideologies attribute to specific populations characteristics which confine them to permanent inferiority or difference, this is echoed in the conclusion that 'blacks' are destined to serve as the permanent victims of 'white society'. If there were any substance to such an analysis, it would be difficult to find a reason to believe that the situation could be any different now or in the future.

Much depends upon the adequacy of a concept of racism which, by definition, permits only 'blacks' to be the subject of racist ideology (cf. Cohen 1988, 1992). An evaluation of this definition is facilitated by the recovery of the history of migration to Britain that I offer in Chapters 5 and 6 (as well as of the analysis of racisms of the interior in Chapter 3). It is a historical recovery which emphasises the political significance of the scale of European migration to Britain from the end of the nineteenth century through to the 1960s, and of an ideological reaction to different migrant presences which warrants description as racism if we reject the a priori conception of racism as a 'white ideology' and take seriously the idea of historically specific *racisms* (cf. Kushner 1989, Kushner and Lunn 1989, Holmes 1991, Cesarani 1992).

While a certain modality of racism may predominate in one particular conjuncture, the history of racism is not exhausted by a focus on the trajectory of that single instance: 'older' modalities of racism may underlie or articulate with a dominant contemporary racism, and so the recovery of their history is necessary in order to comprehend not only their previous effects but also their potential contemporary significance. Furthermore, the effects of racisms are always mediated by and through other structures and social relations, the most important of which are class relations and the political reality of the nation state.

The proposed focus on the history of migration and its significance for an understanding of the nature and effects of racism is open to an interpretation which is not warranted and which should be rejected at the outset. It could be concluded from the argument of Part II that the occurrence of international migration is a precondition for the expression of racism within a social formation. Certainly, much of the recent discussion about the increasing influence of racism in Europe is expressive of what might be described as the migration/racism problematic. This is not without good reason: in most of the nation states of western Europe over the past three decades, there has been a political debate about the extent to which 'our nation' has been unacceptably transformed by 'alien' or 'Third World' or 'unassimilable' immigrants, of whom there are 'too many'. The logic of my argument advocating a historical perspective on migration, and on the ideological and political reactions to migration, suggests that such a debate is not in itself new (although the specificity of the conjuncture might mean that the debate has novel dimensions and effects), but rather has been stimulated by migrations of varying origin and character at different points in time.

However, analysis of the reactions to immigration does not exhaust the analysis of the different modalities of racism, neither historically nor contemporarily. Neither the racist imagination, nor the social forces that stimulate that imagination, depend upon immigration to provide a subject for its rational and not so rational (cf. Cohen 1992) constructions of an Other that is so different from Us that They should either 'belong' elsewhere or should be denied resources or rights available to the majority, or even the 'luxury' of being at all. Otherness can be equally successfully constructed by signifying a long-resident population as either a long-hidden 'bacterium' which has intentionally assimilated itself into all corners of the nation in order to effect its evil intent unobserved, or as a long-evident 'naturally' distinct alien force whose negative effects have, for some reason or another, been intensified at this or that particular moment.

At different times in the history of Europe, Jews and 'gypsies' have been amongst the populations that have been signified in these ways in a number of nation states (e.g. Chevalier 1988: 277–366, Burleigh and Wippermann 1991: 77–135, Pollak 1992: 77–107). These instances demonstrate that, contrary to those who argue that 'being black' makes 'black' people especially vulnerable to racism in a 'white society', it is because visibility is always the outcome of a process of signification in a historical context that one can conclude that those who cannot be seen by virtue of their really existing phenotypical features are equally vulnerable to being racialised: their 'non-visibility' can be constructed by the racist imagination as the proof of their 'real' and 'essential' (but 'concealed') difference, which is then signified by a socially imposed mark (as in the example of the Nazi requirement that Jews wear a yellow Star of David: Burleigh and Wipperman 1991: 93–6).

Otherness can also be constructed by means of a racism which signifies a wholly imaginary presence as real: the modality of racism that has Jews as its subject in central Europe today is an especially significant phenomenon in the light of the virtual 'success' of the Nazi state's 'final solution' to the 'Jewish problem' in this region during the 1930s and early 1940s (cf. Wieviorka 1991: 164–8). The very fact that there are so few living Jews can become socially accepted as proof of either the real extent of 'Jewish power' or of the continued success of Jews in assimilating themselves, of 'hiding' in order to continue their 'destructive' work. Ironically in this instance, the 'success' of the 'final solution' begets the idea, if not the possibility, of a repeat performance because it is not the presence of Jews (or any other Other) that ensures the reproduction of racism, but rather a particular conjuncture of social relations. The racist imagination can be made to do its work not only with a real population as its subject (but transmuted through signification into an Other), but also with an absent, wholly imagined, subject (transmuted through signification into a 'really existing' Other). Neither modality of racism is dependent upon a prior immigration to deliver a new subject which can be racialised.

EUROPEAN PERSPECTIVES

During the 1970s, most courses in British institutions of higher education that dealt in one way or another with racism were framed by the 'race relations' paradigm and usually included comparative material on 'race relations' in the USA and South Africa. The histories of colonialism and of slavery figured prominently in the syllabus. If the course had an especially radical or innovatory intent, there might also have been some discussion of the evolution of the migrant labour system in post-1945 western Europe, although there would have been some ambiguity about the relevance of this material for an analysis of British 'race relations'. This ambiguity was usually resolved by claiming that Britain was, of course, 'different' from the rest of western Europe because the British state had not sought to resolve the post-1945 problem of labour shortages by organising or regulating a migrant labour system. In fact this was not true, as the history of migration under the post-war Labour government reveals (see Chapter 6).

Moreover, in so far as analytical parallels were drawn in order to devise policies to eliminate discrimination or in order to inspire and give direction to radical strategies of resistance to racism, these were with 'race relations' and the 'race struggle' in the USA: events there were widely viewed, by both advocates and opponents of racism, as predictors of events that would surely follow in Britain. Rarely did anyone ask whether this was a comparison that made any analytical or, indeed, political, sense: it was simply self-evident that a comparison could be drawn because, during the 1960s, Britain had witnessed the creation of a 'race relations' situation, and 'race relations' was self-evidently a problem that had fractured social relations in the USA for a much longer period of time.

As the influence of the 'race relations' paradigm began to weaken, two analytical developments occurred during the 1980s (see Chapter 1). On the one hand there was an intensified focus on the expression of, and struggle against, racism in Britain (although, in practice, the subject matter was almost always limited to England: see Miles and Dunlop 1986, 1987, Evans 1991), an analysis which sought to explain racism as a central dimension of the crisis of British capitalism (e.g. Hall *et al.* 1978, CCCS 1982, Gilroy 1987). The crisis of the 1970s was an organic crisis, one which the Labour government proved incapable of solving and which demonstrated that fascism was very much alive, although confined to the fringes of national politics (even if it was a direct and powerful force in certain areas of English cities). The outcome was the election of a right-wing, authoritarian Conservative government which openly legitimated the racist fears of 'our own people'.

During the 1980s, comparative analysis was of little importance to those who interpreted these developments as a further sign of the need for Marxists to renew (or sometimes to reject) their theoretical armoury: Britain's 'race' problem was to be understood in its full specificity and the struggle against racism was given the highest priority. Yet, despite the formal recognition of the existence of a plurality of racisms, there was only one racism in Britain, that which oppressed British 'blacks'. While there was a validity to this emphasis when seen in the light of, for example, the actions of the British state in response to the migration and settlement of British subjects originating from the New Commonwealth, it also marginalised the significance of the expression and effects of other racisms experienced by, for example, the Irish, Jews and travelling people in Britain.

On the other hand, a new comparative interest germinated slowly during the second half of the 1980s, one which has racism in Europe as its object. Politically, this was shaped by the crisis over immigration that escalated elsewhere in Europe (especially in France and Germany) during this decade, by the increased political support for neo-fascism, and by the implications for immigration control of the renewed attempt to create a single market within the EC. Theoretically, it was shaped by the tradition of the political economy of labour migration. As a result, research on Europe became *de rigueur* for many working within the racism paradigm during the early 1990s. In developing this new research focus, there is much to be learnt from the work of those who analysed the role of racism in the evolution of the political crisis in Britain during the 1970s.

Irrespective of the particularity of the political and ideological form of each nation state, all of the social formations within the EC face a common set of problems in restructuring and restabilising the capitalist economy and civil society in a period dominated by a continuing reorganisation of the capitalist world economy. One of these problems concerns immigration, or rather the politics of immigration: there is a complex relationship between the continuing reality of immigration and the extent to which a politics of immigration becomes a major political force at any single point in time. While there are important differences between the nation states that comprise the EC concerning the extent to which a politics of immigration dominates the national political agenda, because immigration control has become a matter for EC debate and for intergovernmental action within the EC, its prominence as an issue in one nation state is now much more likely to have an impact on the political debate in other nation states.

Equally, all the member states of the EC in north-west Europe continue to regulate the political and ideological consequences of the large-scale labour migrations that occurred during the 1950s, 1960s and early 1970s. These consequences include the continuing political agitation to reduce or stop immigration, the need to respond to the conflicts that arise from the struggle against the racism and practices of exclusion that have an important influence on the social position of many populations of migrant origin, and the debate about the extent to which the rights of citizenship should be derived from the individual's national legal status. The difficulties are compounded by the continuing reality of immigration and the limits to the ability of the state to terminate immigration, for the reasons discussed in Chapter 8.

There is a further dimension to the configuration of political forces – nationalism. The political debate about the consequences of immigration has focused in part on the fragmentation of the alleged pre-existing unity of the nation which has occurred as a result of the migration and settlement of 'alien', culturally and 'racially' distinct populations. As a result, the national tradition and identity are perceived to be under threat: for the right and also sections of the left, this requires a reaffirmation and defence of the heritage of 'our own people' (and hence the renewal of nationalism), as well as the exclusion of those whose presence allegedly destroys the fabric of the nation. Viewed in historical perspective, there is nothing especially original about this development (see Chapters 2 and 5). But the effects are refracted through a novel international conjuncture, one in which the reality of the nation state, and the power of the individual state to regulate social relations within its 'sovereign territory', is being transformed in Europe as a result of the interplay between the power of international capital and the political reorganisation embodied in the evolution of the EC as a supranational political unit. The declining economic and political significance of the nation state can be measured by the rise of both unionist and separatist nationalisms which, in the face of the increasing power of the world market, seek either to preserve the boundaries of extant nation states or to reorganise those boundaries.

In this context, in most of the nation states of the EC, the state has formulated a similar response to the politics of immigration. The need for strict controls on future immigration is stressed, even though in reality there are limits on the ability of the state to effect the control promised. This policy is presented as being symbiotic with another, a policy that seeks the integration of at least certain populations of migrant origin who are now, in effect, permanently settled within the EC, even if they do not possess the nationality of the nation state in which they are resident. The justification offered claims, in one way or another, that the problems created by immigration (and therefore immigrants themselves) must now be solved by fully integrating them into the 'national community', one condition for which is that 'our own people' are satisfied that the problems will not be made more intense by the arrival of yet more immigrants. It is a justification which locates the source of the problem in the migrant presence and which legitimates the duality between 'our own people' and the intrusive migrant Other. The political and ideological significance of these state-initiated integration policies is discussed in Chapter 7.

But if the focus of comparative discussion about racism is now shifting away from the old British colonies of the USA and South Africa to Europe, Europe has become one of the important arenas for debate and therefore disagreement about the nature, origins and effects of racism. In other words, there are different perspectives on the developments described and on the expression of racism within Europe (cf. Miles 1991c, 1993). One influential position (at least on the left) claims that a radical 'race' perspective on Europe is now needed. It is argued that the creation of the new Europe at the end of the twentieth century entails the creation of a 'Fortress Europe' through policies which prevent 'black' people from entering its borders and which sustain a common 'white', Judaeo-Christian heritage by repelling or subordinating alien (non-European) cultural influences (such as Islam). The consequence is the creation of a new, European or Euro-centric racism: as a result, 'race' is a determining force not just with Britain, but throughout Europe (e.g. Sivanandan 1988, Webber 1991).

One does not have to advocate a 'race' perspective to agree that the consolidation of the single European market within the EC is leading to the creation of a common European policy on immigration control (Groenendijk 1989, 1992), although the path to that end is not without its diversions and culs-de-sac. Moreover, as I show in Chapter 8, this argument depends on an oversimplistic analysis of migration flows into the EC and of the economic, ideological and legal position of populations of migrant origin within the EC. If a Fortress Europe is in the making, it is not only 'black' people who are to be shut out. If it is a fortress that is being constructed, it is intended to deny entry to almost all of those seeking a buyer for their semi- and unskilled manual labour power, as well as those searching for a sanctuary from civil conflict and state repression (Zolberg *et al.* 1989). Because there is now only a very limited need for new migrant workers to fill semi- and unskilled positions in the manual labour market of the EC, there is a predominant class logic to the structure of exclusion, and racism is a secondary and contingent (although not unimportant) determinant.

Moreover, 'black' people do not occupy a common legal status within the EC. Again, much depends on the scope and boundary of 'blackness'. The majority of 'black' people resident in Britain are British citizens. Their legal status parallels that of other 'black' people in other EC countries: French residents born in Guadeloupe and Martinique (in the French Caribbean) are French citizens because these islands are included amongst the French *départements d'outre-mer* (Condon and Ogden 1991a, 1991b). Dutch residents who migrated from Surinam before Surinamese independence in 1975 are Dutch citizens because Dutch citizenship was granted to the population of Dutch colonies (NSCGP 1979: 69–70). Of course, this common legal status does not protect them from being the object of racism and of related exclusionary practices. But, as citizens, they have rights, including the right to full political participation, which are not accorded to the 'black' residents in Europe who remain, in law, foreign nationals.

This latter category is divided into those whose residence is recognised and permitted by the state and those who are 'illegal immigrants' (e.g. Layton-Henry 1990c, Rath 1990, Wihtol de Wenden 1990). These legal statuses constitute the terrain for practices of exclusion which are in addition to those that might arise from racism, and they make resistance to exclusion extremely hazardous if the migrants wish to remain resident within Europe. It is this considerable variation in political status, and in the sheer number of those people permanently resident in the EC who do not possess the full rights of citizenship, that constitutes something specific about Europe at the end of the twentieth century. To resort to the language of the 'race relations' problematic for one moment, this variation in legal status does not correlate with 'race'. Rather, a 'race' perspective (radical or otherwise) overrides this heterogeneity.

And what of the claim that a new European racism has been created, one that is either derived from a preceding modality of racism or shaped uniquely by the social relations that characterise late-twentieth-century capitalism in Europe (Sivanandan 1988, Balibar 1991)? Certainly, in the light of the creation of the EC as an economic and political unit which can compete successfully within the capitalist world economy with the USA and Japan, there is an ongoing reconstruction of the European identity and a renegotiation of its articulation with extant national identities within Europe. However, the result of this reconstruction and renegotiation is not yet easy to assess, and the advocates of the existence of this new modality of racism rarely offer any evidence as to the extent to which it has been embraced by the citizens of the new Europe. The reaction to the Maastricht Treaty suggests that nationalised identities remain a very powerful force. Moreover, the extent to which the racism is really new can only be determined by an analysis of its relationship with preceding modalities of racism (certain of which had an explicitly European content), and this remains an unfulfilled task (Miles 1992).

Approaching the analysis of racism in Europe with a 'race' perspective, radical or otherwise, misleads, not only because the idea of 'race' is itself profoundly ideological, but also because it has a specific origin within the British nation state. It has a set of meanings and resonances which derive from the particular constellation of political forces within that nation state. Applied to analyse the situation in other nation states, with their distinct histories of imagining and constructing the nation and therefore the Other, a 'race' perspective often does not have an object or, if it does, it is rather different from that in Britain. For example, the history of fascism in Germany, and the German occupation of France and the Netherlands (from which followed the deportation of Jews from French and Dutch territory), has resulted in a very different set of resonances attaching to the notion of 'race': a Race Relations Act (of which there have been three in Britain since the mid-1960s) is inconceivable in these three countries because it would be instantly and widely interpreted as legislation intended to regulate relations between different 'races' in a manner that echoes the 'final solution' to the 'Jewish problem'. Consequently, the comparative analysis of the history and contemporary expression of racism in Europe serves to demonstrate the limitations and contradictions of the 'race relations' paradigm.

At a more general level, the problem is not a peculiarly British one. If Marxist theory continues to bear the imprint of its Eurocentric origins, then it is likely that not only British but also French, German and Dutch analyses of racism within these individual nation states will import some kind of specificity into their respective analyses of the wider European situation. The ease with which many French researchers employ the analytical categories of *intégration* and *assimilation*, categories which have a specific resonance in the light of the French Revolution and the centralising tendencies of the French state, to comprehend the situation in other European nation states testifies to this. In the first instance, it is perhaps inevitable that the researcher approaching racism in Europe as his or her subject will employ an analytical framework derived from the specificities of the historical evolution of the nation state in which he or she works, but the attempt to employ it elsewhere will demonstrate the need of a critical reflection and re-evaluation.

The formulation of a theoretical framework at a more general level of abstraction is therefore a necessary task for those seeking to explain the influence of racism within Europe (Bovenkerk *et al.* 1990, 1991). It is for this reason that the attempt to explain the increasing influence of racism in France since the 1970s as a result of the decline of industrial society and the disappearance of the proletariat as a social movement (Wieviorka 1991, 1992) is important, because it is an argument that, potentially, applies to all social formations that exhibit what Wieviorka describes as *la grande mutation* (1992: 25–41). While I do not share his theoretical premises, Wieviorka's concepts and theoretical perspective have the virtue of being generally applicable to other European nation states and, therefore, of generating a general theory concerning the contemporary expression of racism in Europe. The same is true for the recent work of Balibar (1991, see also Balibar and Wallerstein 1988), who remains firmly in the tradition of historical materialism.

CONCLUSION

And so, after 'race relations', we are free to analyse the origin and consequences of the different modalities of racism in different conjunctures without the distorting prism implanted by the use of the idea of 'race' as an analytical concept. But if we do not study and theorise 'race' or 'race relations', what is our object? It is the study of the determination and effects of different modalities of racism within the historical matrix mapped by the evolution of the capitalist mode of production and by the associated rise of the nation state. And if the subject matter requires an analysis of the historical evolution of capitalism, it is also necessary to consider the extent to which the emergent capitalist social formations arose from contradictory social relations within feudalism. Hence, it is equally necessary to enquire whether the invention of racism is rooted in any way in those pre-capitalist social formations.

I refer specifically, in the first instance, to the articulation between the capitalist mode of production and the nation state, rather than between capitalism and colonialism, because (as will become apparent in Part I) this maps the primary set of social relations within which racism had its origins and initial effects. Colonialism was an integral moment of this articulation, but racism was not an exclusive product of colonialism: it did its work, had its effects, as much within the nation states at the centre of the evolving capitalist world economic system as in those social formations of the periphery which were constructed as dependent extensions of the former. It is the historical recovery of the racisms that were articulated in the course of the extension of commodity production and exchange within the evolving framework of the nation state within Europe that, I believe, constitutes one important new area for further investigation. We might then be able to better comprehend the historical significance of the articulation between not only racism and nationalism within Europe, but also between racisms and colonialism.

This programme of work needs to be a European programme, simply because north-west Europe became the centre of an expanding world trading network as well as (and more importantly) of the capitalist mode of production between the seventeenth and nineteenth centuries. The 'making of bourgeois Europe' (Mooers 1991) was an uneven and contradictory process, one in which different constellations of territorially specific class relations were mediated in different ways and at different times by the world economy, with the result that the centres of capitalism at the centre evolved at different times, at different speeds, and via different political interventions. It is widely accepted that the comparative analysis of capitalist development requires a comparison between Britain, France and Germany. Studies of the rise of nationalism and of the nation state in Europe also commonly compare and contrast these three social formations, two of which were major colonial powers. As a result, after 'race relations' the task of conducting a comparative historical analysis of the origin and consequences of racism in these three nation states can at least develop in the awareness that some of the relevant background material has already been assembled. Such an analysis would shift the focus of analysis away from that defined by the 'race relations' paradigm.

This historical analysis is not for its own sake: it provides a framework against which we can assess what is specific to (or 'new' in) the events of the past thirty years. Hence, the historical recontextualisation of the consequences of post-1945 migration to Britain that I propose here is a part of a wider European analysis of the continuities and discontinuities in the articulation of racism. Thereafter, the politics of immigration and racism in contemporary Europe return us (academically as well as politically) to two central issues that have arisen consistently from the analysis of the nature and consequences of the historical development of the capitalist mode of production and its domination of the world economic system.

The politics of immigration necessarily raises a series of questions concerning the uneven development of capitalism and the contradictions of nation state formation. If migration to Europe from the peripheries of the world system is fundamentally determined by, in varying combination, material deprivation and political conflict arising from a failure to establish stable political democracies, then the only effective long-term means of immigration control is the termination of uneven economic development and the creation of conditions that favour stable democratic systems, and not ever more technologically sophisticated systems of surveillance, administration and restraint at the external border of the EC.

Hungry and frightened people can also be very ingenious and determined people, and who can blame them for seeking entry, by any means necessary, to Europe when the leaders of the 'free world' proclaim the moral and technological superiority of capitalism: from the other side of the fence, it is not always easy to see the contradictions and uneven development that equally characterise the centre of the 'free' world. Yet when those same leaders repeat the call for 'strict immigration control', it is difficult to avoid the conclusion that the price of development and political stability at the centre is paid by those many Others who are said to belong naturally in another place as much as (if not more than) the excluded within. The politics of immigration control therefore directs us to an analysis of uneven political and economic development within the world system. This is at least as important as the debate about the multiple identities of the decentred subject created by consumption in 'post-modern' society, because many millions of people in the world do not have the luxury of thinking of themselves as such.

And the politics of racism raises the question of why it is that capitalist social formations cannot realise in practise the universal values and equality that advocates and apologists of capitalism proclaim. More specifically, it demonstrates that the struggle for, and over the nature of, citizenship has not ended. It is not only that there are several million permanent residents of the EC who continue to be denied several of the rights that are supposedly the sign of a 'civilised' society and a 'mature democracy'. But then it was only during the first half of the twentieth century that women were judged to be sufficiently 'civilised' and 'mature' to participate fully in the rights of citizenship won by the male proletariat during the nineteenth century in Europe. It is also that racism serves as one more mechanism to effect and legitimate the allocation of scarce resources (jobs, houses, welfare payments, justice, etc.) to those who are formally citizens of capitalist social formations. We do not need to articulate the struggle against these exclusions as a 'race struggle' when we can express them as specific instances of a wider and longer struggle for a universal citizenship. This does not necessarily entail obscuring the specificity of a form of exclusion and it does link it to one of the central contradictions that characterises the history of capitalism.

After 'race relations', we have no reason to debate the nature and meaning of 'race'. After 'race relations', there is no need to seek a 'race perspective' on Britain or Europe. The nation states of the EC are not confronted with a 'race problem', but rather with the problem of racism, a problem which requires us to map and explain a particular instance of exclusion, simultaneously in its specificity and in its articulation with a multiplicity of other forms of exclusion. Hence, we can now confront the fundamental issues concerning the character and consequences of inequality reproduced by and in contemporary capitalist social formations, freed from a paradigm which finds an explanation for that inequality within the alleged 'nature' of supposedly discrete populations rather than within historically and so humanly constituted social relations.

Part I
The concept of racism

Chapter 1

Apropos the idea of 'race' . . . again

The discourse promoting resistance to racism must not prompt identification with and in terms of categories fundamental to the discourse of oppression. Resistance must break not only with *practices* of oppression, although its first task is to do that. Resistance must oppose also the *language* of oppression, including the categories in terms of which the oppressor (or racist) represents the forms in which resistance is expressed.

(Goldberg 1990b: 313–4)

INTRODUCTION

Marxist theory has experienced difficulties in attempting to comprehend and explain the expression and consequences of racism in its articulation with the development of the world capitalist system. These difficulties originate not only in general problems 'internal' to Marxist theory (for example, the problems of economism and reductionism), but also from the uncritical incorporation of the idea of 'race' into Marxist theory, and from the related failure to separate analytically the idea of 'race' and the concept of racism. Additionally, they arise from the considerable influence of political and academic writing in the United States during the twentieth century. Consequently, British analyses of racism and of the consequences of post-1945 migration to Britain remained, until the late 1980s, relatively isolated from other European writing which, is characterised by a more critical approach to the use of the idea of 'race'. As a result, much British Marxist theory has reproduced many of the problems evident in non-Marxist analyses.

The problem discussed here is an epistemological one. It concerns the conceptual language that is used to explain certain facets of the historical development of social formations dominated by the capitalist mode of production. Marxist theory has, by virtue of its own epistemological assumptions, necessarily developed by means of a dialectic between historical and conceptual analysis, and has therefore critically (although not consistently) evaluated the ideas and concepts thrown up in the 'everyday world' in order to establish theoretically their analytical value. It is because the social world is not always as it presents itself that what Gramsci called 'common sense' must be subject to theoretical practice. The necessary task of theoretical analysis has been carried out only rarely by Marxist writers when dealing with the idea of 'race'.

It is not denied that the idea of 'race' has been and is employed (sometimes implicitly) in Britain (and elsewhere) as an ideological dimension of the exclusion of people from access to work, welfare services, housing and political rights, etc. Moreover, neither is it denied that the idea of 'race' has been and is utilised by those so excluded to construct an alternative, positive self-identity and a basis for political resistance to their exclusion (cf. Gilroy 1987: 27, Anthias 1990: 35, Small 1991a). For example, Jews in France embraced the idea of the existence of a distinct Jewish 'race' in the nineteenth century (Marrus 1971: 10–27). The sole issue addressed below concerns the framework used to analyse and contextualise these (and other) economic, political and ideological processes. I make no systematic attempt to confront related issues such as the reputed failure of Marxist writers to resolve adequately the (mistakenly formulated) class/'race' problem, a matter on which I have written elsewhere (1980, 1982, 1984a, 1987b, see also Fields 1982, Solomos 1986, Wolpe 1986, Anthias 1990), although I shall conclude with some comments relevant to this issue.

THE IDEA OF 'RACE' AND THE CONCEPT OF RACISM

The history of the construction and reproduction of the idea of 'race' has been analysed exhaustively (e.g. Barzun 1938, Montagu 1964, Jordan 1968, 1974, Guillaumin 1972, Stepan 1982, Banton 1987). As a result, it is well understood that the idea of 'race' first appeared in the English language in the early seventeenth century and began to be used in European and North American scientific writing in the late eighteenth century in order to name and explain certain phenotypical differences between human beings. By the mid-nineteenth century, the dominant theory of 'race' asserted that the world's population is constituted by a number of distinct 'races', each of which has a biologically determined capacity for cultural development. Although the accumulation of scientific evidence during the early twentieth century (e.g. Barkan 1992) challenged this theory, it was the use of 'race' theory by the National Socialists in Germany that stimulated a more thorough critical appraisal of the idea of 'race' in Europe and North America and the creation of the concept of racism in the 1930s.

The concept of racism is therefore a recent creation in the English language (Miles 1989a: 42–3). It was first used as a title for a book written in the German language by Magnus Hirschfeld in 1933/4 which was translated and published in English in 1938. In *Racism*, Hirschfeld refuted nineteenth-century arguments which claimed the mantle of science to sustain the notion of the existence of a hierarchy of biologically distinct 'races'. But he did so without offering any formal definition of racism and without clarifying how racism is to be distinguished from the concept of xenophobia (1938: 227). During the same decade, a number of other books were published which sought to demonstrate that the idea of 'race' employed in Nazi ideology lacked any scientific foundation, some of which also used the concept of racism to label these ideologies (Huxley and Haddon 1935, Barzun 1938, Montagu 1974, Benedict 1983).

But on one matter, these writers were divided, that of whether or not 'races' nevertheless existed. On the one hand, Benedict (1983) legitimated nineteenth-century biological and anthropological classifications of the human population into three 'races'. On the other hand, Montagu (1974) argued that, in so far as there were biological differences between human beings, they did not correspond to these earlier classifications and he therefore recommended that the term 'race' be excised completely from scientific discourse.

Hence, the scientific and political critique of fascist ideologies that resulted in the creation of the concept of racism was not accompanied by a consistent rejection of either the idea of 'race' or the belief that the human population was divided into biologically distinct 'races'. Indeed, the dispute about whether or not the term 'race' should be used within science to refer to populations characterised by particular genetic profiles continues to this day (Miles 1982: 15–19). Thereby, the basis for the continued confusion of the two terms was created and has been maintained. All the while that it is thought that 'races' exist then there is the possibility, indeed even the necessity, to constitute a theory of how different 'races' interact with one another. In so far as the ideology of racism is identified as one determinant of these 'race relations', a theory of racism becomes entangled in a theory of 'race relations'. And in so far as Marxist writers have incorporated an idea of 'race' as an analytical, or even a descriptive, concept into their theorising about racism, they too have become similarly entangled.

A MARXIST THEORY OF 'RACE RELATIONS'?

One of the earliest Marxist texts to analyse 'race relations' was O.C. Cox's *Caste, Class and Race* (1970). It was first published in the United States in 1948. Despite the existence of another tradition of Marxist writing in the USA which claimed to theorise 'race', Cox's book was cited for a long time by Marxists and non-Marxists alike (e.g. Castles and Kosack 1972: 16, Rex 1983: 15–16), as *the* seminal Marxist statement, and the work of the Frankfurt School (which was produced during its exile from Germany: see Outlaw 1990: 69–72) was largely ignored.

Now, it is referred to rarely in the British and North American literature (see, for example, the passing reference in Omi and Winant 1986: 31), although recently one of the original British architects of the 'race relations' problematic has shown a renewed interest in it (Banton 1991). This silence results partly from the fact that there is no longer any widespread interest in Cox's central theme, namely a comparison between caste and 'race' relations. It is also because Cox denied Afro-Americans any autonomous political role, a view that is contrary to more recent political philosophies of 'black' resistance which advocate auto-nomous political organisation on the part of 'black' people. Finally, as we shall see, Cox rejected the use of racism as an analytical concept, a concept that has in the past three decades become central to Marxist analysis and to critical analysis more generally.

Nevertheless, at the time of its publication, *Caste, Class and Race* was a work of some originality and it remains a work of considerable scholarship. Cox set out to construct a Marxist theory of 'race relations' (1970: ix). He attempted this largely by means of an extended critique of extant writing on 'race relations' in the USA, most of which defined its object of analysis as 'race relations' in the southern States. His central argument was that 'race relations' were not similar, or equivalent, to 'caste relations', as most writers claimed at the time. As a result, a large part of *Caste, Class and Race* sought to establish the nature of caste in Indian society and then to demonstrate that 'race relations' in the USA did not exhibit the defining features of 'caste relations'. The decline in the significance of the caste thesis means that much of this argument has little relevance to contemporary concerns.

But Cox's alternative theorisation is of interest because of the way in which it incorporated the ideas of 'race' and 'race relations' and attributed them with analytical status within the framework of Marxism. As a result, Marxists could claim, *contra* 'bourgeois' theorists, that they too had a theory of 'race relations', a theory that was (at least as far as they were concerned) superior. But the ideas of 'race' and 'race relations' had no specifically Marxist content. Cox, in the manner of mainstream sociological thinking, noted and then passed by the uncertainties about the biological meaning of 'race', and defined 'race' as 'any group of people that is generally believed to be, and generally accepted as, a race in any given area of ethnic competition' (1970: 319). What distinguished a group as a 'race' was their real or imputed physical characteristics (1970: 402), and hence he defined 'race relations' as 'behaviour which develops among peoples who are aware of each other's actual or imputed physical differences' (1970: 320).

The process by which these significations were established and reproduced did not capture Cox's interest and, consequently, he accepted the existence of 'races' as distinctive, immutable collectivities. This verged on reification when he argued that it was impossible for human beings to establish 'new races' and that an individual becomes a member of a 'race' by birth in the course of inheriting certain inalienable physical characteristics (1970: 423). Thus, although he claimed that 'races' were social, and therefore human, constructions, once created they were attributed with the character of permanence: they became 'things in themselves', discrete social collectivities whose presence had to be related to other social collectivities. The problem then became one of locating 'races' within Marxist analysis, which attributes primacy to class and class relations.

In order to assess Cox's attempt to do this, another conceptual matter requires attention. In the light of the centrality of the concept of racism to much contemporary Marxist writing, it is intriguing that Cox explicitly rejected its use. He noted that the concept had been used, by Ruth Benedict, to refer to a 'philosophy of racial antipathy' (1970: 321, 480), and he repudiated this on the grounds that it tended to lead to the study of the origin and development of specific ideas. Although Cox did not use this terminology, he was in fact rejecting idealism. Cox sought alternatively to develop a materialist analysis that identified the class interests and exploitative practices which gave rise to what he preferred to describe as 'race prejudice', a notion that predated the creation of the concept of racism.

In the manner of the mechanistic and economistic Marxism that had not been challenged from within the Marxist tradition in the late 1940s, a now familiar argument resulted from this materialism. Cox proposed that, historically, 'race prejudice' was a recent phenomenon, and that its origin lay in the development of capitalism. He claimed that 'race relations' arose from the proletarianisation of labour power in the Caribbean, 'race prejudice' being the rationalisation developed by the bourgeoisie for its inhuman and degrading treatment of the work force. Thus, 'race prejudice' was defined as 'a social attitude propagated ... by an exploiting class for the purpose of stigmatising some group as inferior so that the exploitation of either the group itself or its resources or both may be justified' (1970: 393). It therefore facilitated a process of labour exploitation, and hence arose after that system of exploitation had been established (1970: 532).

But exploitation and proletarianisation are, within the framework of Marxist theory, universal capitalist processes. Because 'race relations' are not deemed to have arisen from the process of proletarianisation within, for example, Europe, it follows that it is necessary to identify what distinguishes the exploitation and proletarianisation that give rise to 'race relations' in the Caribbean. 'Race relations', Cox argued, arose when the bourgeoisie successfully proletarianised 'a whole people' (i.e. a 'race'). This happened in the Caribbean and the USA but not in Europe, where only a section of 'white people' (i.e. part of the 'white race') were proletarianised (1970: 344). For Cox, this did not alter the *essential* identity of the two processes: in both instances, a group of people was subordinated to a bourgeoisie whose primary interest was the exploitation of the former's labour power. Hence, for Cox, 'racial antagonism' was in essence class conflict (or political-class conflict as he conceptualised class struggle) because the latter arose from the exploitation of labour power (1970: 333, 453, 536). It follows that 'race relations' and 'race prejudice' arose from the historically specific processes of colonialism and imperialism that accompanied the development of capitalism as a world economic system (1970: 483).

Cox theorised 'race relations' as, simultaneously, a specific form of group relations and a variant of class relations. Their specific character arose from the imputed existence of 'races' as collectivities distinguished by real or alleged physical differences. Much of Cox's attention was focused upon 'races' distinguished by skin colour, and he referred to 'whites' and 'Negroes' as distinct 'races'. In this respect, his theoretical approach remained wholly within an emergent academic tradition which had incorporated common-sense understandings and definitions about 'race' into scientific analysis in the course of breaking with nineteenth-century biological and anthropological analysis. The work of Park, Warner, Dollard and Myrdal, about which Cox was so critical, was characterised by what was at the time a radical view that 'race relations' were social relations between collectivities which defined themselves as 'races', rather than biologically determined relations between biologically distinct and discrete 'races' (Banton 1987: 86–93, 99–110). These writers established 'race relations' as a particular sociological specialisation or field of study and Cox sustained and reinforced this paradigm by seeking and claiming to offer a Marxist theory of 'race relations'.

It is easy to criticise Cox's analysis for being functionalist and economistic (Miles 1980, 1982: 81–7, George 1984: 139–47). Here I identify an additional difficulty with Cox's analysis, the significance of which will be discussed further later in the chapter. We have seen that Cox argued that 'race prejudice' was a rationalisation of proletarian-isation in the Caribbean. Cox did not elaborate on this interpretation, but it is not consistent with the Marxist conception of capitalism as a mode of production (although it is consistent with Wallerstein's (1979) 'world systems' analysis of capitalism).

If capitalism is understood as a mode of generalised commodity production in which the ownership and control of the means of production are held in the hands of the bourgeoisie, to which the working class is thereby forced to sell its labour power in return for a wage with which it can then purchase the means of subsistence in the form of commodities, the concept of proletarianisation refers to the social process by which a section of the population is transformed into sellers of labour power. Historically, this has entailed the divorce of a section of the population from the means of production in order that it should have no choice but to transform its labour power into a commodity which is exchanged within a labour market.

But this is not what happened during the colonisation of the Caribbean in the seventeenth century (Miles 1987a: 73–93). In order to establish commodity production, those who gained control over much of the land (by a combination of force and the establishment of private property rights) brought first European and then African migrants to the region and created indentured and, subsequently, slave relations of production. Under these relations, the labourer did not commodify labour power but was forced to provide labour power to the person who either purchased by contract the right to utilise that labour power or purchased the individual as a chattel. There was no labour market where the buyers and sellers of labour power met to realise their material interests. Rather, labour power was exploited and a surplus realised by means of unfree relations of production. What distinguished the establishment of agricultural commodity production in the Caribbean, and in several other parts of the world, was the *absence* of proletarianisation.

It has been noted many times that Marx's theoretical and historical analysis of the development of the capitalist mode of production, by virtue of being confined to the example of England and more generally to Europe, is of little value to an analysis of the historical development of the forces and relations of production outside Europe (e.g. Robinson 1983). With certain exceptions, much of the theoretical and historical work intended to 'rescue' Marxist analysis from this lacuna was undertaken only after the 1960s. Consequently, when Cox was formulating his Marxist theory of 'race relations', he was doing so in a Eurocentric vacuum. Few attempts had been made within the Marxist tradition at that time to analyse systematically the activities of merchant and finance capital outside Europe.

Hence, we may regard his creation of a Marxist theory of 'race relations' as a refraction of the then contemporary silence within Marxist theory about the formation of unfree relations of production in the colonial context. In an attempt to comprehend and explain that context, Cox identified 'race relations' as the unique characteristic of the process of colonisation, a process which in all other respects had a universal, capitalistic character. Hence, Cox focused on the signification of phenotypical difference which was used subsequently by the colonising class to frame the expropriation of labour power, and so elevated the ideological notion of 'race' to the status of a theoretical concept within Marxist theory.

While Cox's theory is rarely the starting point for Marxist analyses of racism (cf. Solomos 1986: 87–8), his theoretical project, the construction of a Marxist theory of 'race relations', has since been pursued by Marxist writers in the United States and elsewhere. For example, in the mid-1980s, Szymanski bemoaned the fact that the Marxist theory of 'race relations' was in a 'deplorable state'. He claimed that no systematic Marxist theory had been created, and in order to fill this gap, he sought to 'outline a Marxist understanding of race and racism by using some of the ideas of Louis Althusser' (1985: 106). While Cox's work was ignored, Szymanski retained the idea of 'race' as an analytical category. It was, along with racism, represented as something that Marxism should theorise: 'Race and racism . . . should be understood as relationships or "structures" ' (1985: 108). What distinguishes 'race' as a structure or relationship from all others was not explained, although Szymanski claimed that 'biological races' are 'imaginary representations in the Althusserian sense' and that 'race' is socially constructed by the mode of production (1985: 108).

Szymanski shared with Cox a simplistic materialism and a theoretical project, namely the construction of a Marxist theory of 'race' that is both parallel with and distinct from liberal and conservative theories. It occurred to neither that, by positing 'race' as the subject of a theory (whether it be Marxist or non-Marxist), it is accorded uncritically with a reality *sui generis* which is unwarranted. Some recent British radical writing reproduces the problem, although all variants (e.g. Solomos 1986, Gilroy 1987) reject the economism that shaped Cox's work. The Marxist perspective that I have proposed insists on the deconstruction of the idea of 'race' as the basis for analysing the significance of racism within the development of the capitalist world economic system and has its origin, in part, in the political economy of labour migration. However, at least in its early version, the political economy of labour migration was also characterised by economism and an uncritical utilisation of the idea of 'race'.

THE CHALLENGE OF MIGRATION THEORY

The post-1945 migrations from the Caribbean and the Indian subcontinent brought to Britain men and women in search of a wage who were understood by state officials and large sections of the British population to be members of distinct 'races'. Rather than signify them as British subjects, which they were, they were designated as 'coloured' and 'colonial' people whose presence would change the 'racial character' of the British population (e.g. Carter *et al.* 1987: 335, also Joshi and Carter 1984). In the light of the fact that sections of the British ruling class commonly justified colonialism as an attempt to 'civilise inferior races' and sought special methods of administration and economic compulsion to achieve this (e.g. Lugard 1929), this is unsurprising. However, there was little political or academic interest in this migration until the hostile, and largely racist, reaction to the migration found a place on the domestic political agenda (Miles 1984b).

Up until 1958, 'race relations' were, in common-sense terms, a colonial 'problem': the racist attacks on British subjects of Caribbean origin in that year in England were interpreted by the state as evidence that the problem of 'race relations' had been transferred to the 'Mother Country'. When British academics began to take an interest in these domestic developments, they drew upon concepts, theories and political strategies derived from the United States and South Africa (Rich 1986a: 191–200), all of which had 'race relations' as the object of analysis. Most of these academics were anthropologists by training and liberal in political perspective (e.g. Banton 1967).

The first major challenge from within the Marxist tradition to this 'race relations' paradigm came with the work of Castles and Kosack published in the early 1970s (1972, 1973, cf. Bolaria and Li 1985). They demonstrated the parallels between the determinants and consequences of migration to Britain and of migration to other nation states in north-west Europe. Thereby, they deflected the institutionalised comparison between Britain and the United States and South Africa (evident, for example, in the early writing of Banton (1967) and Rex (1970)), arguing that it was more useful to analyse comparatively the British experience of post-1945 migration in the context of the reconstruction of capitalism throughout Europe.

Castles and Kosack opened their seminal work by rejecting the dominant sociological paradigm of 'race relations'. They argued that all contemporary capitalist societies contain a distinct stratum of people who occupy the worst jobs and live in inferior housing, and that in many of these societies this stratum is composed of immigrants or the descendants of immigrants. This immigration was explained as a consequence of uneven capitalist development on a world scale and immigrant workers were identified as having a specific socio-economic function found in all capitalist societies, namely to fill undesirable jobs vacated by the indigenous working class in the course of the periodic reorganisation of production. This stratum of immigrant workers thereby came to constitute a 'lower stratum' of the working class, which was thereby fragmented. Hence, for Castles and Kosack, the analytical focus was not 'race' or 'race relations', but the interconnections between capital accumulation, migration and class formation (1973: 1–13).

But in proposing this paradigm shift, Castles and Kosack did not reject 'race' as an analytical concept. Rather, they subordinated it to a political economy of labour migration and class relations: that is, they retained the category of 'race' in order to deny its explanatory significance. When referring to the total number of eight million immigrants in western Europe, Castles and Kosack claimed that 'At the most two million of them can be considered as being racially distinct from the indigenous population' (1973: 2). In other words, because only a minority of the immigrants occupying this subordinate proletarian position were members of a 'race' distinct from that of the majority, neither 'race' nor racism could be the factor which determined occupation of this structural site in class relations (1973: 2). Rather, their social position was determined by the 'normal' working of the capitalist mode of production. The fact that Castles and Kosack used the idea of 'race' as a classificatory concept in this way without explanation or definition testifies to its unproblematic status amongst Marxist writers during the 1970s.

This political economy of migration paradigm has been embraced by Sivanandan (1982, 1990), who also criticised academic 'race relations' analysis and sought an alternative perspective on the British situation. Sivanandan reproduced several of the central themes in the work of Castles and Kosack (1973), and of Nikolinakos (1975). He referred specifically to the importance of a reserve army of labour (or an underclass) to sustain capitalist expansion and to divide the working class, and to the 'cheapness' of a migrant labour system wherein the costs of the production and reproduction of labour power are met within the social formation from which the migrant originates and to which he or she is returned (Sivanandan 1982: 105–6, 1990: 153–60, 189–91).

Sivanandan's initial focus was not so much upon western European capitalism in general as on British capitalism in particular. For example, he devoted considerable attention to the state immigration controls of the 1960s which transformed British subjects from the Commonwealth into aliens who could enter Britain only on a temporary basis with a work permit (Sivanandan, 1982: 108–11; 1983: 2–3). But his analysis of the British situation was effected by a set of general Marxist categories and via an analysis of capitalism as a world system, categories and a perspective which equally structure his more recent interest in Europe (1990: 153–60). Formally, there is little that is new in this aspect of Sivanandan's work. This is confirmed by his critique of the recent neo-Marxist analysis of Thatcherism which is signalled by the notion of 'New Times', a critique which reaffirms the importance of the funda-mental struggle between capital and labour (1990: 19–59). What does distinguish Sivanandan's work, making his voice and contribution distinctive, is the central place that the idea of 'race' occupies in his analysis: for example, the journal that he edits is called *Race and Class*, a title that places the idea of 'race' on an analytical level equivalent to class.

Sivanandan's use of the idea of 'race' is usually subordinated to the concept of racism. Put another way, his focus on 'black struggle' highlights the resistance of some British citizens of Asian and Caribbean origin to the racism, particularly institutionalised racism, that structures their lives: in the course of analysing the nature and effects of racism, Sivanandan employs the idea of 'race'. For example, Sivanandan claims that the migrant labour system 'prevents . . . the horizontal conflict of classes through the vertical integration of race – and, in the process, exploits both race and class at once' (1982: 104). Elsewhere, he refers to hierarchies of 'race' within the working class (1982: 113) and to the significance of learning about 'other races, about other people's cultures'

(1983: 5). In these formulations 'race' is attributed with an independent reality, equivalent to class as well as to sex, as in the argument that 'racism is not . . . a white problem, but a problem of an exploitative white power structure; power is not something white people are born into, but that which they derive from their position in a complex race/sex/class hierarchy' (1985: 27). More recently, in an interview, he has commented concerning the journal that he edits: 'Yet *Race and Class* never subsumes race under class. It looks at race in terms of class, while at the same time bringing to an understanding of the class struggle the racial dimension' (1990: 14).

What Sivanandan means by his use of the idea of 'race' is rarely clearly stated: it usually functions to mark a symbolic site for the organisation of autonomous political resistance to capitalism, imperialism and racism, and, for this very reason, clarification of its meaning is unnecessary for him. But, in one of his less commonly cited papers in which he analyses South Africa as an exceptional capitalist formation, he does address (and reject) the argument that the use of the idea of 'race' implies a legitimation of racist classifications of the human species (1982: 161–71). He defends the common-sense definition of 'race' as a reference to a group of persons who share the same descent or origin, adding that group differences (presumably phenotypical differences) are 'an observable fact' (1982: 163). Thus, Sivanandan uses the idea of 'race' to refer to distinct, biologically defined groups of people. As a result, 'race' is as much a reality as class, both concepts referring to some quality that all people possess. Sivanandan observes, for example that 'Each man was locked into his class and his race, with the whites on top and the blacks below' (1982: 166), and that 'The settlers . . . were (and are) a slender minority, distinguished by race and colour' (1982: 168).

For Sivanandan, 'racial groups' therefore have a reality *sui generis*, a reality which parallels but also mediates class: hence, South Africa is exceptional only because 'race is class and class race – and the race struggle is the class struggle' (1982: 170). Yet, it is not the supposed reality of racial difference that matters theoretically or politically, but rather the use made of that difference by the 'race' (as mediated by class) that possesses the greatest amount of power. In other words, what matters most is the 'racist ideology that grades these differences in a hierarchy of power – in order to rationalise and justify exploitation' (1982: 163). For Sivanandan, the primary object of political struggle is the racism that legitimates capitalist exploitation and, hence, he observes that racism cannot be abolished by rejecting the idea of 'race' (1982: 162). However, it does not follow from this that the critique of the idea of 'race' is not an important moment in the struggle against racism.

The shift in Marxist theory away from the construction of a Marxist theory of 'race relations' towards an analysis of the expression and consequences of racism within the framework of a political economy of migration represented a major theoretical break. It permits an analysis of the expression and consequences of racism within the framework of the dynamic process of capital accumulation, and situates the analysis of racism at the centre of Marxist theory (e.g. Miles 1982, 1986). But, for the Marxist writers mentioned to this point (see also Wolpe 1980, 1986, Wallerstein 1988), this was accomplished in the absence of any critical evaluation of 'race' and 'race relations' as analytical concepts. Rather than sweep the theoretical shelf clean, these writers retained certain core ideas of the 'race relations' paradigm and repackaged them with the central Marxist concepts of class, capital accumulation, reserve army of labour, etc. For Castles and Kosack, and for Sivanandan, the idea of 'race' has been retained in a form which suggests that the human population is composed of a number of biological 'races'.

MARXIST THEORIES OF POLITICAL AND IDEOLOGICAL CRISIS

The development of a political economy of migration has been largely ignored by another strand of Marxist theory which has been concerned almost exclusively with the political and ideological crisis of British capitalism. This concern results from a preoccupation with the rejection of economism and an adoption of a field of analysis usually described as cultural studies. Given its concern with the social construction of meaning, one might expect that a cultural studies perspective, especially one that is allied with Marxism, would regard the critical evaluation of the idea of 'race' as a central and urgent task. Surprisingly, this has not been so.

The important work of Stuart Hall is central to this strand of Marxist theory. Hall's focus has been upon the role of the British state in reconstructing British society in the face of a series of political and ideological conflicts which have occurred in a conjuncture dominated by the declining profitability of British capital. Hall has devoted some attention to the role of the expression of racism in the resulting organic crisis of British capitalism and the rise of the authoritarian state (e.g. Hall et al. 1978, Hall 1978, 1980). While his observations have been theoretically grounded and influential, they are fragmented and have not been accompanied by a rigorous theoretical examination of the concepts employed.

Elsewhere, I have suggested that, in the absence of such theoretical work, Hall represents 'race' as an independent force in itself (Miles, 1982: 176–7). Here, I cite another example: in a much celebrated paper, Hall argues that 'At the economic level, it is clear that race must be given its distinctive and "relatively autonomous" effectivity, as a distinctive feature' (1980: 339). This reification of 'race' is reproduced in the equally well-known work of the 'Race and Politics Group' of the Centre for Contemporary Cultural Studies (CCCS), of which Hall was previously the Director. Hall's previously cited assertion was subsequently echoed approvingly in the work of the CCCS group (1982: 11, my emphasis):

> Although . . . we see race as a means through which other relations are secured or experienced, this does not mean that we view it as operating merely as a mechanism to express essentially non-racial contradictions and struggles in racial terms. These expressive aspects must be recognised, but *race must also be approached in its autonomous effectivity.*

In both these formulations, 'race' is represented as a determinant force, something which has real effects and consequences (although for the 'Race and Politics Group' these effects are absolutely rather than relatively autonomous). But what 'race' is, what the character of this 'feature' is, is never defined. We are left to search for the clues which identify the meaning that lies behind the silence.

Hall refers to 'different racial and ethnic groups' (1980: 339), suggesting that he employs 'race' to identify groups differentiated by biological characteristics (see also 1980: 342). If this is his meaning, it parallels Sivanandan's usage. But this does not help us comprehend the claim that 'race' is a reality which has relatively autonomous effects within social relations. Without additional clarification, the claim remains vacuous and each new, approving citation only reinforces its unintelligibility.

Similarly, the meaning attributed to the idea of 'race' in the work of the CCCS 'Race and Politics Group' (1982) is unclear and problematic (see Miles 1984a). One of the members of this group, Paul Gilroy, has subsequently responded to this critique, and to the broader argument upon which the critique was based (Miles 1982), as a prelude to an important analysis of the historical and contemporary expression of racisms, and their articulation with nationalism in Britain. Given that Gilroy states his agreement with my critique of 'race relations sociology' (1987: 40n), one expects him to reject the use of 'race' as an analytical concept in his more recent work. But this is not so. Moreover, the manner in which the idea of 'race' is theorised and celebrated in this recent text is characterised by a number of contradictions (Miles 1988b).

Gilroy begins by claiming that the idea of 'race' has a descriptive value (1987: 149) *and* that it is an analytical concept (1987: 247): ' "Race" must be retained as an analytical category not because it corresponds to any biological or epistemological absolutes, but because it refers investigation to the power that collective identities acquire by means of their roots in tradition.' But if there is a reason to attribute the idea of 'race' with analytical status, *that is if one represents it as a concept which can be employed to explain social processes*, it must refer to a real, identifiable phenomenon which can have (autonomous) effects on those processes. Yet, if this is so, it is not clear why ambiguity should be expressed about the concept by the (inconsistent) use of inverted commas around it. Is Gilroy wishing to signal that there is something essentially problematic about the use of the term (which is the justification for my consistent use of inverted commas)? Or is the occasional absence of inverted commas an indication of some real (but unexplained) difference in the usage and meaning of the term?

If 'race' is an analytical category that identifies a material object, what are its features? Gilroy offers several definitions. 'Race' is variously described as an effect of discourse (1987: 14), a political category that can accommodate different meanings (1987: 38, 39), and a relational concept (1987: 229). These descriptions are confusing. If 'race' is an effect of discourse, or a political category, or a relational concept, how is it distinguished from the other effects of discourse or other political categories or other relational concepts? These descriptions by themselves do not refer to any specifically identifiable phenomenon: they do not provide identifying criteria.

Elsewhere, 'race' is represented both as a thing in itself when Gilroy refers to the 'transformation of phenotypical variation into concrete systems of differentiation based on "race" and colour', as well as a social collectivity when he refers to 'racial groups' (1987: 18), when he defines 'race formation' as the 'manner in which "races" become organised in politics' (1987: 38), and when he claims that 'Races are political collectivities not ahistorical essences' (1987: 149). The former implicitly refers to what he subsequently identifies as an ahistorical essence because it has a biological character (although the distinction between 'race' and skin colour adds to the confusion), while the latter identifies a specific form of social collectivity – but we are not told how this differs from any other social collectivity (for example, classes). Hence, within Gilroy's text, 'races' are represented as really existing collectivities, although there is an ambiguity over whether these collectivities are biologically constituted or are the product of the articulation of racism and the expression of resistance by those thereby excluded and exploited. Ironically, his complaint that the Scarman Report fails to define what is meant by the reference to the Brixton riots as 'racial' (1987: 106) refracts precisely the same ambiguity in his own text.

This ambiguity is further expressed in the contradiction between the representation of 'race' as a particular type of social group and the argument that 'race' has never been anything other than an idea, a social representation of the Other as a distinct sort of human being. The latter is expressed in the claims that ' "Race" has to be socially and politically constructed' (1987: 38) and that 'race' is only a device for the categorisation of human beings (1987: 218). These assertions parallel my own arguments (1982, 1984a) and hence I can agree with his claim that 'the attempt to make "race" always already a meaningful factor, in other words to racialise social and political phenomena, may be itself identified as part of the "race" problem' (Gilroy 1987: 116).

But Gilroy resists accepting the logical conclusion of this observation. The definition of a 'race' problem is synonymous with the racialisation of social relations, and this process of attributing meaning to real or invented somatic (and cultural) variation can only be analysed and deconstructed consistently by eliminating all conceptions of 'race' as a thing in itself, with the power to have effects. This does not require denying that the idea of 'race' is a constituent element of everyday common sense: the issue is whether or not such usage is transferred into the conceptual language that is used to comprehend and explain that common sense. I see no reason to do this. There are no 'races' and therefore no 'race relations'. There is only a belief that there are such things, a belief which is used by some social groups to construct an Other (and therefore the Self) in thought as a prelude to exclusion and domination, and by other social groups to define Self (and so to construct an Other) as a means of resisting that exclusion. Hence, if it is used at all, the idea of 'race' should be used only to refer descriptively to such uses of the idea of 'race'.

A comment is also required on Gilroy's apparent rejection of Marxism. Throughout 'There Ain't No Black in the Union Jack' (1987), he allies himself with those who argue that a Marxist analysis of capitalism based on the historical instance of nineteenth-century Europe is inappropriate in the late twentieth century. This argument takes a number of (not always consistent) forms, but usually includes the assertions that the number of people involved directly in industrial production in advanced 'capitalist' social formations is declining and that, as a result, the industrial proletariat can no longer be the leading and progressive political force that it was in the past.

Echoing writers such as Gorz and Touraine, Gilroy claims that the leading forces of resistance in the contemporary western world are social movements based around 'race', gender, demands for nuclear disarmament, etc., all of which are conceived as being disconnected from production relations. Consequently, 'if these struggles . . . are to be called class struggles, then class analysis must itself be thoroughly overhauled. I am not sure whether the labour involved in doing this makes it either a possible or a desirable task' (Gilroy 1987: 245). Class struggle, for Gilroy, has been transcended by 'the forms of white racism and black resistance' which he describes as 'the most volatile political forces in Britain today' (1987: 247).

If, in Gilroy's view, class theory cannot be overhauled, he has dispensed with a theory of class struggle in favour of what is sometimes called 'race' struggle. Here, Gilroy seems to identify with the 'Black radical tradition' as Robinson (1983) describes it, a tradition which rejects Marxism as an adequate theory of revolution for 'black people' (1983: 1–6) and which is terminating the 'experimentation with Western political inventories of change, specifically nationalism and class struggle' (1983: 451). This is confirmed by Gilroy's approval (1987: 38) of the work of Omi and Winant, which rejects class analysis on the grounds that it neglects 'the specificity of race as an autonomous field of social conflict' (Omi and Winant 1986: 52).

Others have responded in different ways to this critique of Marxist class analysis (e.g. Hyman 1983, Wood 1986, Balibar 1988d, Sivanandan 1990: 19–59, 169–95). It is more relevant to note here that Gilroy's theoretical approach to the analysis of 'white racism and black resistance' is very different from that used by Sivanandan. The latter's critique of the theory of 'New Times' associated with the writing of Stuart Hall and others states an allegiance to those key concepts of Marxism which Gilroy has rejected. Thus, while both Sivanandan and Gilroy distance themselves from what they see as Eurocentric Marxism (partly because of its 'inability' as they see it to deal with 'race'), Sivanandan reclaims Marxism in order to contextualise 'race' relative to class while Gilroy rejects Marxism in order to establish the absolute autonomy of 'race' apart from class. This important difference reminds us that neither Marxism nor the 'black radical tradition' is monolithic, but rather both refer to many diverse and, indeed, contradictory strands.

In sum, the work of Hall and the CCCS collective exhibits an untheorised incorporation and reification of the idea of 'race'. Indeed, they elevate the idea to a central analytical position in their respective analyses of the political and ideological crisis of British capitalism. At the same time, their adherence to some version of dialectical and materialist analysis leads them in an antithetical direction, one that if pursued to its logical conclusion would result in a rejection of the use of the idea of 'race' as an analytical concept. For example, Hall has argued (1980: 338): 'The question is not whether men-in-general make perceptual distinctions between groups with different racial or ethnic characteristics, but rather, what are the specific conditions which make this form of distinction socially pertinent, historically active.' Here Hall recognises that it is not biological characteristics (real or imagined) in themselves which have determinate effects. Rather, in certain historical conjunctures and under specific material conditions, human beings attribute certain biological characteristics with meaning in order to differentiate, to exclude and to dominate: reproducing the idea of 'race', they create a racialised Other and simultaneously they racialise themselves. Yet Hall's recognition of this remains tainted by the way in which he reifies 'race' when he refers to 'groups with different racial . . . characteristics' as if these were natural facts. Nevertheless, he does highlight the significance of the social process by which the idea of 'race' is ideologically constructed and so, in contrast to the political economy of migration, this strand of Marxist analysis hints at the possibility of a deconstruction of 'race' as an analytical concept.

'RACE' AS AN IDEOLOGICAL CONSTRUCTION

Certain currents in the French materialist tradition offer a more reflexive and critical approach to the use of the idea of 'race' as an analytical concept, reaching conclusions which parallel my own (Miles 1982, 1984a, Miles and Phizacklea 1984: 1–19) and which are emergent within some critical, if not Marxist, writing in the USA (e.g. Fields 1982, 1990, Goldberg 1990b). The work of Colette Guillaumin is the most important in this context (e.g. 1972, 1980, 1988).

She has argued that use of the idea of 'race' necessarily suggests that certain social relationships are natural and therefore inevitable. Social relations described as 'racial' are represented as somatically determined and therefore outside historical, social determination. Consequently, the idea of 'race' is transformed into an active subject, a biological reality which determines historical processes. This amounts to a process of reification, as a result of which that which should be explained becomes an explanation of social relations. Guillaumin writes (1980: 39):

> Whatever the theoretical foundations underlying the various interpretations of 'racial' relations, the very use of such a distinction tends to imply the acceptance of some essential difference between type of social relation, some, somewhere, being specifically racial. Merely to adopt the expression implies the belief that races are 'real' or concretely apprehensible, or at the best that the idea of race is uncritically accepted; moreover, it implies that races play a role in the social process not merely as an ideological form, but as an immediate factor acting as both determining cause and concrete means.

Guillaumin concludes (1980: 39, see also 1988: 26):

> the fact that such relationships are thought of as racial by those concerned (and sometimes this is as true of the oppressed as of the oppressors) is a social fact, and it ought to be examined as carefully and sceptically as any other explanation offered by a society of its own mechanisms. Such explanations can only refer to a particular time and place.

The analytical task is therefore to explain why certain relationships are interpreted as determined by or expressive of 'race', rather than to accept without criticism and comment that they are and to freeze and legitimate that representation in the idea of 'race relations' as social relations between 'races'. Hence, any analytical use of the idea of 'race' disguises the fact that it is an idea created by human beings in certain historical and material conditions, and used to represent and structure the world in certain ways, under certain historical conditions and for certain political interests. The idea of 'race' is therefore *essentially* ideological (Guillaumin 1980: 59).

These arguments do not deny that there is considerable somatic variation between individual human beings. But the signification of phenotypical features in order to classify human beings into groups simultaneously designated as *natural* is not a universal feature of social relations. In Europe, it began in the eighteenth century: for the idea of naturalness is even more 'modern' than the idea of 'race' (Guillaumin 1988). Certain somatic features (some real and some imagined) were socially signified as natural marks of difference (e.g. skin colour), a difference that became known as a difference of 'race'. Moreover, these marks, conceived as natural, were then thought to explain the already existing social position of the collectivity thereby designated by the mark (cf. Fields 1990: 106). This social process of signification was (and remains) an important ideological moment in a process of domination. The idea of 'race' thereby came to express *nature*, something given and immutable, with the result that what was in fact the consequence of social relations became understood as *natural*: and so 'race' was thought of as a determinate force, requiring social relations of domination to be organised in a specific form, thereby obscuring their human construction. By utilising the idea of 'race' as an analytical concept, social scientists deny the historicity of this social process, freezing it with the idea that the naturalness of somatic difference ineluctably constitutes eternal human collectivities.

These arguments have been rarely addressed directly by Marxist writers, many of whom continue to defend the retention of 'race' as an analytical concept. Anthias (1990), for example, argues not only that 'race' should be retained as an analytical concept but also that its relationship to class should be specified. Anthias advocates retention of the idea of 'race' as an analytical concept to denote 'a particular way in which communal or collective differences come to be constructed and understood', one that refers to 'immutable fixed biologically or physiognomically based difference' (1990: 22). If this is all the meaning that the idea of 'race' embodies in being transformed into a concept, then this is precisely the meaning that is denoted by the concept of racialisation (Miles 1982: 120, 150, 1989a: 74–7). In other words, the *social process* that Anthias refers to with the idea of 'race' is better denoted by the concept of racialisation.

But why does she ignore this concept in order to retain the idea of 'race' as an analytical concept? It is because she has chosen arbitrarily the class/'race' articulation as the starting point for her analysis (1990: 19): having made such a choice, she is required to theorise the idea of 'race' into an analytical concept in order to sustain the paradigm which constitutes her point of departure. Thus, rather than *first* reflect critically on the historical evolution of the idea of 'race', and on the implications of its attributed meaning through time, in order to *second* reach a conclusion about the validity of transforming it into an analytical concept, Anthias precludes the very possibility of such an epistemological evaluation by electing without any critical reflection to employ the idea of 'race' as a concept positioned relative to class. As a result, while acknowledging the 'mythological representations that surround it' (1990: 23) and while agreeing with me that the concept of racism should be separated from the idea of 'race' (1990: 22–4), she invests those very same mythological representations with an analytical status by treating the idea of 'race' as a scientific concept with an object in the real world. This is expressed in her various references to 'race formation', 'race processes', to the distinct ontological status of 'race', to 'race phenomena' and to 'racially organised communities' (Anthias 1990: 20, 21, 35).

So, the case against the incorporation of the idea of 'race' into Marxist theory (and indeed into sociological theory) as an analytical concept can be summarised as follows (see also Miles 1982, cf. Goldberg 1990b). First, all theoretical work is an integral part of the social world. We live in a world in which the nineteenth-century biological conception of 'race', although discredited scientifically, remains an important presence in 'common sense': large numbers of people continue to believe, and to act as if they believe, that the world's population is divided into a number of discrete, biologically distinguishable groups, i.e. 'races' (cf. Fields 1990: 95–101). Although this conception (especially in its explicitly racist incarnation) is rejected by most sociologists and Marxists, their conceptions and theories of 'race' and 'race relations', where they resonate in the wider structure of social relations, fail to challenge common sense. Indeed, by failing to explain consistently and explicitly their sociological conception of 'race' as a social construction, they implicitly (and often explicitly) endorse common sense (Rozat and Bartra 1980: 302, Smith 1989: 3, 11), and hence sustain an ideology which Barzun called a 'Modern Superstition' (1938) and which Montagu described as 'Man's [sic] Most Dangerous Myth' (1974).

A recent example of such an endorsement of the commonsense idea of 'race' is found in an argument which is intended to explicate 'the salience of race as a *social construct*': Smith (whose work, while not falling formally within the Marxist tradition, is nevertheless influenced by writing that is) suggests that the analysis of the salience of 'race' (1989: 3) 'should centre not on what race explains about society, but rather on the questions of who, why and with what effect social significance is attached to racial attributes that are constructed in particular political and socio-economic contexts'. Here, the reference to 'racial attributes' resonates with all those 'mythological representations' of the nineteenth-century idea of 'race' as a biological type of human being characterised by certain somatic attributes. While there are all the usual sociological qualifiers (in the form of references to social processes of signification and construction), Smith's reference to 'racial attributes' as the *object* of the ascription of meaning implies that there is some biological 'reality' underlying the somatic features thereby signified: an attribute denotes the existence of some other thing which, given the description 'racial', can only mean that that thing is a 'race'. This is an example of the way in which the idea of 'race' as a natural division lives on, is reconstituted and renewed, by a critical sociological analysis which seeks to deny such a 'reality' by reprocessing the idea of 'race' as an analytical concept.

This is also illustrated by a paper in a collection of essays intended to demonstrate recent advances in the critical analysis of racism (Goldberg 1990a). Christian (1990) offers a radical analysis of Afro-American women's literature which prioritises as the conceptual framework 'the intersection of . . . race, class, and gender' (1990: 135). The novel that is the central focus of her analysis is described as 'an exploration of the ways in which race affects the relations among women', and its author is considered to have demonstrated 'not only that race, class, and gender intersect but that they are never pure, exclusive categories. None of these categories exist on their own. Rather, there are men or women of one class or another, of one race or another' (1990: 136, 143).

Thus, second, the reification of 'race' as an active subject, and 'race relations' as a distinct variety of social relations, represents somatic differentiation as an active determinant of social processes and structures. It follows that 'the ideological notion of "race" does not have the rigour of an objective scientific definition, despite all later attempts to rationalise it' (Lecourt 1980: 282). Its use obscures the active construction of the social world by those people who articulate racism and by those who engage in exclusionary practices consistent with racism. Our object of analysis, the active determinant of exclusion and disadvantage, is therefore not physical difference in itself, but the attribution of significance to certain patterns of, or the imagined assertion of, difference and the use of that process of signification to structure social relationships. The use of 'race' (and 'race relations') as analytical concepts disguises the social construction of difference, presenting it as somehow inherent in the empirical reality of observable or imagined biological difference.

Third, the incorporation of ideological conceptions into Marxist and sociological theory has structured historical and empirical investigation in a manner which leads to comparative analyses of limited theoretical and political (including policy) relevance. By defining 'race' and 'race relations' as the subject of study, comparative attention is directed to those other social formations where identical social definitions prevail, usually South Africa and the USA. In other words, comparative analysis is determined by certain common ideological features (i.e. by phenomenal forms), rather than by a historical materialist analysis of the reproduction of the capitalist mode of production (i.e. by essential relations). Yet, considered in terms of the historical dynamic of capitalist development, these two social formations (by virtue of their colonial origin and historical dependence on unfree labour) have little in common with post-1945 economic and political developments in Britain, despite sharing a common ideological definition of 'race' as a social problem (but see Small (1991a) for an important alternative analysis).

Attention has thereby been distracted from the other social formations of north-west Europe where the interdependence of capital accumulation and labour migration has resulted, since 1945, in the permanent settlement of populations which are often culturally distinct from the indigenous populations. It is only in Britain that the political definition of this settlement as problematic has been defined as a matter of 'race': elsewhere it has been defined as a 'minority problem' or 'immigrant problem', for example. But these ideological variations are grounded in a common economic and political process, leaving one to pose the question 'Why?'. This question can only be investigated by first deconstructing 'race' as an analytical concept, for only then does investigation come to focus upon the political and ideological processes by which the idea of 'race' has been utilised to comprehend this process of migration and settlement.

CONCLUSION

In so far as Marxism asserts that all social relationships are socially constructed and reproduced in specific historical circumstances, and that those relationships are therefore in principle alterable by human agency, then it should not have space for an ideological notion that implies, and often explicitly asserts, the opposite. The task is therefore not to create a Marxist theory of 'race' which is more valid than conservative or liberal theories, but to deconstruct 'race', and to detach it from the concept of racism. By deconstructing the idea of 'race', the effects of the process of racialisation and of the expression of racism within the development of the capitalist world economic system are more clearly exposed (Miles 1982, 1987a, 1989a, Miles and Phizacklea 1984: 4–19) because the role of human signification and exclusionary practices is prioritised. And where racialisation and racism structure aspects of the reproduction of the capitalist mode of production or any other mode of production, then that mode appears in another of its historically specific forms.

This can be illustrated by returning to consider the argument that 'race relations' arose from the proletarianisation of labour in the Caribbean. I have already argued that there was no proletarianisation of labour in this region during the seventeenth and eighteenth centuries because slave rather than wage relations of production predominated after an initial period during which indentured labour was prevalent. In a context where unfree relations of production were widespread, the initial enslavement of Africans was not in itself remarkable. It was only after Africans were enslaved that African people were represented in negative terms as an Other and that certain of their phenotypical characteristics were signified as expressive of their being a different (and inferior) type of human being. This racialisation of a population that was confined to the provision of labour power under slave relations of production was intensified with the emergence of the idea of 'race' and its utilisation to dichotomise the owners of the means of production and the suppliers of labour power as being naturally different 'types' of human being.

Similar processes of racialisation and a similar expression of racism occurred elsewhere in the world (and not only outside Europe) in the eighteenth and nineteenth centuries as colonial settlement was followed by the expansion of commodity production. As in the case of the Caribbean, these instances were usually accompanied by the forced migration of a group of people who were destined to provide labour power under relations of direct politico-legal compulsion. I have argued elsewhere (1987a: 186–95) that in all these instances of unfree relations of production, through a process of racialisation, racism became an ideological relation of production: that is to say, the ideology of racism constructed the Other as a specific and inferior category of being particularly suited to providing labour power within unfree relations of production. Racialisation and racism were thereby ideological forces which, in conjunction with economic and political relations of domination, located certain populations in specific class positions and therefore structured the exploitation of labour power in a particular ideological manner.

It is important to stress the historical dialectic of these instances. On the one hand, racialisation and racism structured production relations in a historically specific, ideological manner. They therefore had real, independent effects. Thus, those people who provided labour power under slavery, indenture and various forms of contract were encapsulated in economic relations of unfreedom and ideological relations of exclusion from humanity. Each dimension articulated with the other to constitute a particular totality of class, and thereby distinguished those so constituted not only from the dominant class that monopolised the means of production but also from those constituted in waged relations of production elsewhere in the world. On the other hand, the construction of unfree relations of production possessed a universal dimension in so far as they necessitated processes of economic, political and ideological subordination and in so far as they were moments in the emergence of a world capitalist economic system, embodying an articulation of different modes of production.

The same concepts of racialisation, racism and exclusion can be utilised in relation to migration from the 'periphery' to the 'centre' of the capitalist world economic system since 1945. This migration, determined by the capital accumulation process (Miles 1986), resulted in the placing of a large proportion of migrants in vacant positions in the working class. However, for many of these migrants, their entry and residence were determined by a contract system which restricted their ability to commodify their labour power, placing them in a specific politico-legal position within the working class (Miles 1987a: 143–67). But all have also been signified as either biologically or culturally distinct, or both. Where they have been racialised, where racism has been expressed and where exclusionary practices have occurred, migrants and their children have been often (although not exclusively) confined to certain economic positions within the working class, occupying semi- and unskilled, manual jobs. More recently, with the crisis of capital accumulation and the restructuring of capital, racism and exclusionary practices have served to exclude a proportion of migrants and their children completely from the labour market, locating or relocating them within the relative surplus population.

In these instances, racialisation, the expression of racism and exclusionary practices effect the reproduction of the capitalist mode of production, situating people in specific economic positions within wage labour or excluding them from the labour force, and thereby constituting the relative surplus population. But they do so in a particular ideological manner. These processes therefore create not only particular fractions of classes (and the relative surplus population is as much a distinct and necessary class position within the capitalist mode of production as the proletariat), but also resistance which has as its objective the elimination of racism and exclusion. And that resistance has often (although not exclusively) utilised the idea of 'race' as an ideological focus for political organisation and struggle, thereby establishing a dialectical process of racialisation and overdetermining the fractionalisation at the level of economic relations (e.g. Miles 1987b).

These processes can all be analysed within the framework of Marxist theory without recourse to the transformation of the idea of 'race' into an analytical concept. Using the concepts of racialisation, racism and exclusionary practice to identify specific means of effecting the reproduction of the capitalist mode of production, one is able to stress consistently and rigorously the role of human agency, albeit always constrained by particular historical and material circumstances, in these processes, as well as to recognise the specificity of particular forms of oppression.

Chapter 2

Nationalism and racism: antithesis and articulation

It is sometimes said that butlers only truly exist in England. Other countries, whatever title is used, have only manservants. I tend to believe this is true. Continentals are unable to be butlers because they are as a breed incapable of the emotional restraint which only the English race is capable of. Continentals – and by and large the Celts, as you will no doubt agree – are as a rule unable to control themselves in moments of strong emotion, and are thus unable to maintain a professional demeanour other than in the least challenging of situations.

(Ishiguro 1990: 43)

INTRODUCTION

More than a decade ago, Tom Nairn claimed provocatively that the theorisation of nationalism was one of the greatest failures of Marxism (1981: 329). It is not clear whether this charge, or world events themselves, were responsible for the subsequent flurry of theoretical writing on nationalism by writers who identify themselves in one way or another with the Marxist tradition (e.g. Anderson 1983, Blaut 1987, Hobsbawm 1990, Nimni 1991).

Fortunately, most of these writers have avoided attempting to rectify this failure by seeking to imagine, on the basis of the scattered fragments and claims throughout the 'collected works', what Marx would have said if he had lived longer. While there is some value in identifying and reflecting on the nature of Marx's theory of nationalism (Haupt *et al.* 1974, Cummins 1980, Connor 1984, Blaut 1987, Nimni 1991), such as it was (although to call it a theory is perhaps to exaggerate the significance of the fragments), its problems and contradictions, along with the political transformation of the world capitalist system in the past century, limit its utility in the light of contemporary realities. The theorising of the past decade (both Marxist and non-Marxist) has been especially concerned with the current significance of nationalism, but has also sought to trace its origins in the interstices of the historical development of capitalism or, in the case of the influential writing of Gellner (1983), in the transition from agrarian to industrial society.

The publication of these texts has been paralleled by an increasing interest in the nature and origin of nationalism on the part of writers concerned with the expression of contemporary racisms in Europe (e.g. Gilroy 1987, Balibar and Wallerstein 1991). In various ways, these writers have argued that the expression of contemporary racisms derives in part from the renewal and revision of nationalism which, in turn, is shaped by the consequences of decolonisation and of the internationalisation of capitalist production since the end of the Second World War. These arguments have led to discussion about the nature of the articulation of racism and nationalism expressed in the state's attempt in western Europe to reconstruct hegemony at a time of social dis- and reorganisation of capitalist social formations.

Most of the recent Marxist attempts to construct a theory of nationalism refer to its articulation with racism, although only Anderson evaluates this articulation in any detail (1983: 141–54). However, Nairn, in the course of his pioneering contribution to the analysis of English nationalism (see also Wright 1985, Colls and Dodd 1986, Newman 1987), offers a number of theses about the interrelated influence and role of racism which warrant consideration (Nairn 1981: 273–8, 294). Although it is doubtful whether either Anderson or Nairn would claim to have provided a systematic analysis of the articulation of nationalism and racism, each advances a number of theoretical and historical generalisations.

Anderson argues that nationalism and racism are antithetic ideologies (1983: 136): 'The fact of the matter is that nationalism thinks in terms of historical destinies, while racism dreams of eternal contaminations, transmitted from the origins of time through an endless sequence of loathsome copulations: outside history.' Furthermore, he rejects Nairn's view that racism derives from nationalism (Nairn 1981: 337). But Nairn fails to offer a coherent justification for this assertion, and most of his comments on the relationship between racism and nationalism focus on a single historical example, that is the role of racism in the expression of English nationalism since 1945. Nairn's analysis of this role concentrates primarily on the ideology articulated by, and the political impact of, a single politician (Enoch Powell). He maintains that racism has only a limited potential for political mobilisation under the banner of a right-wing nationalism in England (1981: 276), and that the resort to racism in England results from the absence of the main mobilising myth of nationalism, an idea of 'the people' as an active political subject (1981: 294–5, for a critique see Newman 1987). In other words, the expression of racism is a secondary *substitute* for the absence of a coherent, modern and bourgeois English nationalism.

In advancing these claims, Nairn and Anderson pay only cursory attention to the nature and history of racism. This contrasts with their considerably more detailed and analytically sophisticated consideration of the nature and history of nationalism. Partly for this reason, their comments on the interrelationship between nationalism and racism, despite their innovatory character, are problematic. While there are important differences in the nature and reproduction of the ideologies of racism and nationalism, their interrelationship is not as fixed as Anderson and Nairn, in their different ways, suggest. *Contra* Anderson, I shall argue that nationalism and racism are not necessarily distinct and antithetical ideologies, while *contra* Nairn, I shall argue that racism does not derive from nationalism as if it were some secondary, dependent and derivative ideological form.

In the light of these arguments, I shall evaluate the influential claim that a 'new racism' has been invented (Barker 1981). Barker's argument, while advanced within the Marxist tradition, was not intended to correct the historical failure identified by Nairn concerning nationalism. Barker is silent about nationalism: hence, he makes no attempt to consider the extent to which the 'new racism' has drawn upon, or is expressive of, nationalism. In other words, he ignores the possibility of an articulation of nationalism and racism, largely because he has inflated the scope of the concept of racism so that it incorporates nationalism.

These arguments are supported by a more limited range of historical and empirical material than that employed by Anderson. But my disagreement is with one facet of his argument and I am in broad agreement with his central thesis. My method is closer to Nairn, who makes a number of theoretical claims about the nature and origin of nationalism which are sustained primarily by a detailed analysis of the example of the United Kingdom. The empirical/historical content of this chapter is largely limited to the UK, although the context is broadened in order to take account of the influence of British colonialism.

This empirical focus on the UK requires a preliminary comment. As elsewhere, the process of nation-state formation in the UK incorporated at different times emergent or extant states and culturally differentiated populations. The mode of incorporation left intact an institutional basis for the reproduction of quasi-national political identities, particularly in Scotland. There is therefore a sense in which the UK remains a multinational state. Consequently, it is necessary to remain aware of the significance of distinctions between these separate national political units and national identities (for example, between England and Scotland, and between English and Scottish national (political) identities). At the same time, the UK constitutes a single legal-constitutional unit, although with England as its core, a situation that sustains a more fluid English/British identity within England. This elasticity does not occur in Scotland and Wales, where a sharper distinction with England tends to be drawn, a distinction that creates a greater ambiguity about Britishness (e.g. Miles 1987c). I shall comment briefly on the significance of this for the articulation of nationalism and racism.

THE PROCESS OF INCLUSION AND EXCLUSION

The ideas of 'race' and 'nation' are categories of simultaneous inclusion and exclusion. They identify socially constructed boundaries which separate the world's population into discrete groups which are commonly (although not exclusively) alleged to be naturally distinct. Considered abstractly, the criteria signified in the process of categorisation and division are discrete. Concerning the idea of 'race', the object of signification is biological: commonly, it is a phenotypical feature (e.g. skin colour, hair type, shape of the head), but genetic and other less immediately visible biological phenomena (e.g. blood) are also signified. In the case of the idea of 'nation', the criterion is usually cultural in character (e.g. language, 'way of life'). In practice, it is often difficult to sustain this distinction because 'cultural' characteristics can be represented as 'natural' and therefore biological endowments (e.g. Taguieff 1990: Chapters 1 and 3).

In both cases, the signified criteria may be invented or imagined. But they can also be real in the sense that the signified characteristics are empirically verifiable: it is indeed the case that some people have a pinkish/white skin or speak a language that is described as German. The facts of difference may not necessarily be in dispute although the definition of naturalness is problematic, especially where it is alleged that those possessing the characteristics form a naturally constituted group. Herein lies a process of reification because (as discussed in Chapter 1) the criteria of inclusion and exclusion are interpreted as the determinants or signs of the groups' difference, rather than the act of signification which attributes meaning to the differentiating feature and the subsequent inclusionary and exclusionary practices that place members of the groups in different structural locations.

Such an argument emphasises the role of ideological construction, a theme that has been prominent in the analysis of the idea of 'nation' and of nationalism for some time (e.g. Kohn 1945, Anderson 1983: 14–16). This emphasis is less consistently evident in the case of the idea of 'race' (but see Chapter 1 and Miles 1982, 1989a). That both ideas or categories are socially constructed and reproduced can be illustrated by extending the relevance of Anderson's conception of the 'nation' as a specific form of *imagined community* (1983: 15–16) to comprehend the way in which the idea of 'race' serves as a socially constructed category of inclusion and exclusion. Within Anderson's theoretical framework, this is a valid extension of his analysis because he argues that most communities are imagined, and that the most important criterion by which to distinguish between imagined communities is the style of their imagination (1983: 6).

Like 'nations', 'races' (in the sense popularised by nineteenth-century European science) are imagined in the dual sense that they have no real biological foundation and that all those included by the signification can never know each other. Moreover, they are commonly imagined as communities in the sense that the population (*qua* 'race') is thought to be bound together by a common feeling of fellowship: possession of the signified phenotypical characteristics (e.g. skin colour) is interpreted as a sign that the persons share some fundamental essence that constitutes an unalienable bond between them. Hence, 'races' are also imagined as limited in the sense that, once the boundary is marked by the phenotypical characteristic, it defines the presence of other 'races'. Utilising Anderson's formal definition of 'nation' as a type of imagined community, the only criterion which does not apply in the case of the idea of 'race' is that of sovereignty.

Hence, formally, the ideas of 'nation' *and* 'race' both have the potential to become the defining criterion of particular imagined communities. In the case of the idea of 'race', this is well illustrated by the recent writing of Omi and Winant (1986: 61–8) and Gilroy (1987: 38–40), who employ the concept of 'racial formation' to refer to the process by which various social forces shape and reshape the meaning and boundaries of racialised categories. For example, those excluded by racism may use the idea of 'race' to define the focus and parameters of strategies of resistance to exclusion. Thus, these people having been excluded as an inferior 'race', the meanings are inverted in order to construct a positive identity and to define the population that becomes a political subject in the name of the idea of 'race', conceived as an imagined community of resistance.

But this does not exhaust the comparison of the ideas of 'race' and 'nation'. They also define populations in a way which includes a range of social differentiation within the resulting imagined communities. Viewed from the perspective of Marxist theory, these are supraclass categories because, collectively, those people signified and categorised by skin colour or language, etc., usually occupy a range of different structural locations in the relations of production. Moreover, each can be used to make an ideological appeal to an imagined commonality in order to create a sense of community which overrides the conflicting interests arising from the social relations of production.

Furthermore, both categories are simultaneously inclusive and exclusive. In a process of differentiation by (for example) skin colour, the identification of Us as 'white' is an inclusive process which is paralleled by the exclusion from the imagined community of 'whiteness' of all those who lack this characteristic. In other words, by defining Us as white, an Other is synchronically defined as those who lack that particular quality: beyond the boundary of 'whiteness' there exist Others who share the quality of being 'non-white'. The same consequence results where the process of differentiation functions in reverse, that is, by an initial act of exclusion rather than inclusion. If the Other is initially differentiated as 'black', this signification is an implicit creation of a boundary beyond which We are situated because We lack that characteristic and possess some other (e.g. 'whiteness').

At a more general level of abstraction, the signification of a population as a 'race' (or a 'nation') by reference to a real or imagined characteristic X is to signify simultaneously the existence of other 'races' (or 'nations') which are identifiable by the absence of X (and the presence of Y, Z . . .). Thus, where *ego* identifies *alter* as a member of a particular 'race' (or 'nation'), *ego* is also engaged in a process of self-identification as a member of another 'race' (or 'nation'). Similarly, the idea of 'race' may be employed by *ego* as a mode of self-identification, one that also creates other 'races' beyond 'one's own'. Any act of differentiation and categorisation using the ideas of 'race' and 'nation' is a synchronous act of inclusion and exclusion, whether or not *ego* or *alter* are signified explicitly as possessing or lacking the criterion in question. This applies equally to the use of the general categories of 'race' and 'nation' as well as to the signification of specific characteristics in order to differentiate between alleged 'races' and 'nations'.

When distinguishing racism from nationalism, Anderson assumes (mistakenly) that the category of 'race' is always used as a method of negatively evaluated exclusion and that the category of 'nation' always functions as a positively evaluated category of inclusion. In reality, as we shall see below, the 'race' category can also be used as a positively evaluated means of inclusion, as a means of self-identification, which synchronically excludes. Moreover, use of the idea of 'race' for the purpose of self-identification and differentiation can function to define the parameters of a 'nation'. In other words, the ideas of 'race' and 'nation' can be overlapping categories, each functioning to define the parameters of the other.

RACISM AND NATIONALISM: FINDING THE COMMON GROUND

The ideas of 'race' and 'nation' have each been placed at the centre of formally distinct theoretical formations which seek to explain social and historical variation and to characterise that differentiation as *natural*. The creation in western Europe of '-isms' around these two criteria of social classification occurred at the same time. During the late eighteenth and the nineteenth centuries, the idea of 'race' was appropriated by an ever-increasing number of biologists and anthropologists who were enquiring into the significance of human physiological variation. Many of them became obsessed with the classification of the human species into discrete groups by reference to one or more phenotypical characteristic (Stepan 1982, Gould 1984). Banton described the consequence of their endeavours as the 'doctrine of racial typology' (1977: 47) while Comas referred to it as 'scientific racism' (1961: 303).

Scientific racism claimed, first, that the human species could be divided into a number of discrete biological types which determined the endowment and behaviour of individuals, and which therefore explained the cultural variation of the human species. It followed that conflict between individuals and groups was the consequence of their biological constitution. Second, it was argued that the 'races' of which the world's human population was composed could be ordered hierarchically: certain 'races' were destined for biological and cultural superiority over the other, inferior 'races'.

These arguments gained considerable credibility. In part, this was because they were advanced by people who practised as scientists in a period when science was, for the first time, widely regarded as proficient in revealing the truth about the world (Stepan 1982: xv). Equally, if not more, significant, these arguments were used to interpret political and economic conflicts in various parts of the world where, for example, the British state, merchants and capitalists had economic and political interests (Curtin 1965: 383, Biddiss 1979: 11–31). Scientific racism could therefore explain and legitimate the dominant role of British capitalism within the emergent world economic system.

It follows that one of the more general characteristics of racism is that it is an ideology which signifies some real or alleged biological characteristic as a criterion of other group membership and which also attributes that group with other, negatively evaluated characteristics. The racialised Other is additionally conceived as a biologically self-reproducing population through historical time (Miles 1989a: 78–9). But (and this is a point that has remained suppressed in my earlier writing) the racialisation of the Other as a naturally inferior group can equally well be effected by the identification of a collective We as a naturally constituted population characterised by a set of positively evaluated characteristics. This is because the imagined community of 'race' is always a limited community beyond which other, racialised imagined communities are considered to exist. *Both* processes of signification and representation constitute analytically distinct moments of racism. Racist ideologies are therefore relational: they imagine and construct the existence of a multiplicity of racialised populations whose attributed and differentially evaluated characteristics refract and so define each other, often (but not exclusively) in binary, hierarchical oppositions.

The idea of 'nation' was theorised concurrently with the theorisation of 'race' (Kohn 1945: 3, cf. Hobsbawm 1990):

> Nationalism as we understand it is not older than the second half of the eighteenth century. Its first great manifestation was the French Revolution, which gave the new movement an increased dynamic force. Nationalism had become manifest, however, at the end of the eighteenth century almost simultaneously in a number of widely separated European countries.

The object of this signification and theorisation was also the world's population, which was divided into discrete units. It was argued that the human species was naturally divided into 'nations', each of which had a distinctive and unique character and mode of expression. 'Nations' were eternal and had destinies which they were impelled to realise. And each of these naturally constituted populations was bound to a defined territory where it had the right to live and to organise its own affairs without the interference of other 'nations'.

Thus, the boundary of the 'nation' was also the boundary of a self-contained political system (Gellner 1983: 1). Occupation of a territory and the organisation of some form of political representation, so the theory of nationalism continued, would ensure the full realisation of the 'nation's' specific qualities. Smith claims (1983: 23, see also 1991: 73–4):

> Fundamentally, nationalism fuses three ideals: collective self-determination of the people, the expression of national character and individuality, and finally the vertical division of the world into unique nations each contributing its special genius to the common fund of humanity.

The ideology of nationalism therefore specifies an ideal political organisation of the world into nation states, founded on the principle of popular sovereignty. In the context of its formation, nationalism was therefore a revolutionary doctrine because it sought to overturn monarchy and aristocratic government by an appeal to the popular will of 'the people' who *were* the 'nation' (Hobsbawm 1990: 18–20).

In this sense, unlike the theorisation of 'race', the theorisation of 'nation' led to a specific political project. For much of the nineteenth century, nationalism was synonymous with a struggle for political sovereignty within defined spatial boundaries and for some form of representative government, although the franchise was usually limited to, at best, just half of the adult population (i.e. men). Nationalist theory, therefore, identified particular objectives which had specific political consequences for the formation and organisation of the nation state. By way of contrast, there was no single political strategy that emerged from the general theory of biological, hierarchical differentiation expressed in the idea of 'race'. This was not only because there was little agreement about the boundaries between the supposed 'races', but also because scientific racism did not posit a single, coherent political object.

The theorisation of 'race' and 'nation' took place at a time of 'internal' European political and economic reorganisation and 'external' colonial expansion, in the course of which the range of human cultural and physiological variation became more widely known to a larger number of people. The extension of capitalist relations of production increased the circulation of commodities and of people, and this increasing mobility, migration and social interaction provided part of the foundation upon which the ideologies of racism and nationalism were constructed. The increasing profusion of physiological and cultural variation, as recognised in western Europe, became the object of intellectual curiosity and, thereby, of the theoretical practice of scientists and philosophers. But it also became the focus of political attention and action as populations within and beyond Europe were nationalised and racialised by the state, which was seeking to achieve broader objectives (see Chapter 3). The mental production of scientists and philosophers therefore had a specific utility for those who had more practical and immediate concerns and interests in the promotion of capitalism within emergent national boundaries.

Nationalism and racism nevertheless occupied a common terrain in so far as both posited a *natural* division of the world's population into discrete categories. Furthermore, these apparently distinct categories could be interrelated so that they overlapped or became synonymous. This potential was grounded in the very nature of scientific racism, which asserted a deterministic link between biology and cultural variation and expression. Because 'nations' were identified as naturally occurring groups identifiable by cultural *differentiae*, it was logically possible to assert that these symbols of 'nation' were themselves grounded in 'race', that 'blood or race is the basis of nationality, and that it exists externally and carries with it an unchangeable inheritance' (Kohn 1945: 13). A racialised nationalism could then conceive of certain 'nations' as eternally contaminated, and therefore outside history (cf. Anderson 1983: 136).

And, indeed, such arguments became increasingly common during the nineteenth century as the 'nation' was imagined less as a 'people' bound together by a common interest in the overthrow of political domination by an absolute monarch or an autocratic landed aristocracy (or both), and more as a population defined primarily by a certain language, set of customs and discrete historical origin (Hobsbawm 1990: 19–22). In such circumstances, the 'nation' was increasingly constructed in opposition to 'foreigners', both inside and beyond the territory claimed by the 'nation' as its ancestral 'home'. The early revolutionary content of nationalism was further weakened by the appropriation of this culturalist identification of the 'nation' in the last quarter of the nineteenth century by right-wing political forces (Hobsbawm 1990: 102–8). Given, too, the naturalising component of both nationalism and racism, 'races' and 'nations' became virtually synonymous in the thoughts of many intellectuals, politicians and 'men of practical affairs'.

One example of such meshing is found in the writing of Robert Knox, who was one of the most influential European advocates of racism during the middle of the nineteenth century (Banton 1987: 54–9, also Stepan 1982). He was concerned primarily with the extent to which *intra-European* conflicts were grounded in 'race' (Biddiss 1972: 572), the significance of which is discussed in Chapter 3. In his key work, Knox claimed in the opening pages: 'The fact, the simple fact, remains just as it was: men are of different races. Now, the object of these lectures is to show that in human history race is everything' (1850: 2). Consequently, for Knox: 'The results of the physical and mental qualities of a race are naturally manifested in its civilisation, for every race has its form of civilisation' (1850: 56).

Knox's determinism was absolute. He claimed that each 'race' struggled to form its own laws, literature and language in accordance with its biological characteristics. And because these cultural phenomena were biologically determined, they could not be socially transmitted (1850: 6). By implication, each 'race' needed to reside in a limited territory where its distinctive capacity for 'civilisation' could be realised. For Knox, 'race' and 'nation' were therefore interrelated, even synonymous. This is evident in Knox's concern about the 'multiracial' character of Britain (1850: 378):

> The really momentous question for England, as a *nation*, is the presence of three sections of the Celtic race still on her soil; the Caledonian, or Gael; the Symbri, or Welsh; and the Irish, or Erse; and how to dispose of them.

In Knox's racist theory of history, the all-determining character of 'race' shaped all aspects of cultural expression and capacity, with the result that the category of 'nation' dissolved into that of 'race': the interdependence of the categories was hierarchical, and biology dominated (cf. Banton 1987: 57). A disciple of Knox, Kelburne King, developed this articulation in an essay titled 'An Inquiry into the Causes which have led to the Rise and Fall of Nations' which was published in 1876 (reprinted in Biddiss 1979: 173–86). The object of historical analysis was presented as a changing sequence of dominant 'nations', the process and pattern of change being explained as a function of 'race'. Distinguishing between pure and mixed 'races', King interpreted European history as a continuous sequence of the 'rise and fall of nations' in which 'race' was the determining force.

Similar arguments were formulated by others elsewhere in Europe. In France, Gobineau also argued that 'race' was the absolute determinant of historical development (cited in Biddiss 1970: 41, see also Todorov 1989: 153–64):

> I was gradually penetrated by the conviction that the racial question

overshadows all other problems of history, that it holds the key to them all, and that the inequality of the races from whose fusion a people is formed is enough to explain the whole course of its destiny.

Consequently, the rise and fall of 'nations' was, for Gobineau, the result of degeneration. A 'nation' degenerated when (cited in Biddiss 1970: 59):

the people has no longer the same intrinsic value as it had before, because it has no longer the same blood in its veins, continual adulterations having gradually affected the quality of that blood. In other words, though the nation bears the name given by its founders, the name no longer connotes the same race.

Writers such as Gobineau and Knox represent a particular strand of nineteenth-century historical writing within Europe. Not all nationalist and racist theories took such a deterministic form (Todorov 1989), and, moreover, their arguments were challenged by others who rejected to varying degrees biologically deterministic theories of social history. Nevertheless, their historical interpretation demonstrates that the categories of 'race' and 'nation' are not necessarily antipathetic but can be ordered in a hierarchical interdependence in which 'race' determines 'nation'. In these analyses, the two ideas function jointly as categories of inclusion/exclusion. I shall illustrate this shortly by reference to a tradition of English historical writing which employed the idea of 'race' to explain the origin of the English 'nation'.

Of course, the categories of 'race' and 'nation' predate the construction of the ideologies of racism and nationalism, and each has its own history of shifting meanings. By itself, this does not obviate the argument that racism can be an integral element of nationalism: the purported existence of a hierarchical division of the world's population into 'races' advanced by scientific racism often served as the initial differentiation, upon which claims about the political self-determination of naturally divided populations were erected. This is evident in certain fascist ideologies (e.g. Nolte 1965: 277–86, Hayes 1973: 20–30).

Nevertheless, in the light of recent arguments which conflate the ideologies of racism and nationalism (arguments which will be discussed further below), it is necessary to clarify the divergences between the two ideologies in order to sustain the formal distinction between them. There are two aspects to the formal analytical distinction proposed here. First, there is no necessary reason why any particular 'nation' should be naturalised and identified by 'race'. 'Nations' can be identified by (sometimes naturalised) cultural criteria as well as by a constituency of common political interest, with cultural criteria subordinated or even ignored. Second, nationalism is an ideology which has an explicit political objective as a constituent defining element, that is, the formation of a supraclass political unit within which there is collective mass political organisation and representation. The political principles of nationalism may not be democratic but they have always been populist (Nairn 1981: 41). No similar political objective constitutes a defining feature of the ideology of racism.

RACISM AND NATIONALISM IN ENGLISH HISTORY

While the ideology of nationalism was created in the late eighteenth century, interest in tracing the supposed origin and character of the people that constituted a 'nation' preceded the French and Industrial Revolutions that so decisively shaped the conjuncture in which nationalism emerged. Thus, while nationalism is certainly a *modern* phenomenon, the formation of the original 'historic nation states' of Europe, usually under the control of absolute monarchies (Nairn 1981: 107), was facilitated by the creation of myths of origin and character by the dominant class (cf. Smith 1991).

In other words, some European nation states were created in the absence of nationalism, but nevertheless with the assistance of legitimating ideologies of origin and difference. For some four centuries, the idea of 'race' has been prominent in English historical and political writing whenever an assessment of the origin and characteristics of the English as a people and of the English nation has been made (Banton 1977: 16–26). By the mid-seventeenth century, there was (MacDougall 1982: 49) 'the first comprehensive presentation in English of a theory of national origin based on the belief in the racial superiority of the German people, a theme repeated a thousand times in succeeding centuries'.

This myth of origin was shaped by two political events. The first was the English Reformation. In order to sustain their challenge to a church based in Rome, the defenders and ideologists of the Reformation identified the existence of, and their interests with, an autonomous Christian church in Saxon England. Second, the English Civil War was waged over the power of Parliament. Those opposed to the monarchy claimed that Parliament was an institution of great antiquity, with origins in the German democratic tradition, from which the Saxons were considered to have originated (Banton 1977: 16–18, MacDougall 1982: 31–2, 56–62, Newman 1987: 189–91). Hence, in mid-seventeenth-century England, the ideas of the existence of an Anglo-Saxon church and

Parliament, and of an original Anglo-Saxon 'race' suppressed and oppressed by a foreign 'race' since the Norman invasion in 1066, legitimated political revolution. The result was a conception of Englishness which was associated with a supposedly inherent capacity for freedom (a capacity materialised in the antiquity of Parliament). This image of racialised national origin and character has since been utilised in different conjunctures by the state as an element of its hegemonic strategy (e.g. Colls 1986: 30–1, Colley 1989: 173–5) and by radical political movements seeking to legitimate their challenge to the ruling class (Newman 1987: 159–225).

The idea of 'race' employed in these seventeenth-century discourses referred to descent or lineage rather than to the existence of discrete biological categories of people ranked in a fixed hierarchy (Banton 1977: 18–25). Nevertheless, the idea of lineage suggested the inheritance of characteristics and traditions through time and therefore a certain kind of fixity that was natural and eternal: it is but a short step from the idea of inheritance then to utilise notions such as 'breeding' and 'blood' to sustain a conception of inviolable difference expressed through history. The result closely approximates that created by the racialised typologies of scientific racism. Such a conception was expressed in the profusion of handbills, broadsheets and songsheets that were distributed widely in England in 1803 after the passing of the Militia Service Bill in the context of the outbreak of war between Britain and France: English blood provided the metaphor that linked past with present in an unbroken chain, creating a superlative stereotype of the English, against which an image of the French 'character' was invented in binary opposition. Thus, manifesting this 'character', the French were, *inter alia*, mad, monsters, beasts, criminals and savages, and were thought to be especially susceptible to a perverted sexuality (Cottrell 1989: 260–9, see also Newman 1987: 228–33). In the course of the struggle for world economic and political domination in the nineteenth century between European states and bourgeoisies, nationalism and racism were often entangled in this way.

Moreover, given the interconnection between the idea of an Anglo-Saxon 'race' (an idea that less consistently sustains an imagination of Britain as a nation, because of the presence of supposedly Celtic 'races', but ideological consistency is also subordinate to ideological effectivity) and a sense of historically transmitted Englishness, the subsequent shift towards the idea of 'race' as a fixed biological category ensured that the Englishness came to be viewed in fixed terms by the nineteenth century. Thereafter, a proportion of the English population regarded themselves as a discrete biological 'race' whose superiority allegedly originated in their German origins, in the inherent courage and desire for freedom on the part of the Saxons, in the inherent superiority of their language and institutions (especially Parliament) and in a natural ability for science and reason (MacDougall 1982: 94, Hayes 1973: 33). The idea of the existence of the English as a superior 'race' was an inclusive categorisation which necessarily had exclusive implications, especially where social relations were established with populations who were not so fortunately endowed by 'nature'. The colonial project, established by the activities of English merchant capital in the late sixteenth and seventeenth centuries, provided one such context, while competitive commodity production within Europe provided another. Concerning the former (MacDougall 1982: 129–30):

> On balance, the myth of Anglo-Saxonism served England's national purposes well. Belief in their racial supremacy encouraged visionary Englishmen to look beyond their shores to other continents and proceed to build a great world empire to support a vibrant domestic society.

While this conclusion conflates a complex process into a simplistic, one-way determination, the construction of a sense of Englishness upon the idea of 'race' was developed not only in relation to political conflicts within Europe, but also in relation to external economic and political interests beyond Europe. This construction had a long genesis which can be traced at least as far back as the early written records of English explorers who established contact with Africans from the mid-seventeenth century. This contact led to a reconsideration of a number of important ideological assumptions about a range of issues ranging from the validity of biblical explanation to the criteria for beauty (Walvin 1973: 21–2, Jordan 1974: 3–25). Subsequent relations with African and other populations were increasingly shaped by economic considerations in the light of the expanding activity of merchant capital. And the idea of 'race' had an increasing utility in explaining the nature of those populations and the subordinate economic position to which they were assigned as a source of unfree labour. I have analysed elsewhere the complex interaction between this economic dimension and the political and ideological relations in the generation and reproduction of racism in England (Miles 1982: 95–120, 1987c).

Here, the most significant point is that this racism locked together in a symbolic embrace a number of populations with very different historical origins: seen with English eyes, the English 'race' and the various colonised 'races' mirrored the qualities of each other in an interdependent hierarchy. Structured by the discourse of 'race', the superiority of one was refracted by the inferiority of the other. By the middle of the nineteenth century, the idea of 'race' was central to a world view, articulated and reproduced by the English bourgeoisie and sections of the working class, which served as a category of synchronic inclusion and exclusion. This ideological construction had a phenomenal adequacy because there was a real difference in productive relations and material wealth between England and much of the rest of the world at this time (Curtin 1965: 293–4). This material difference warranted explanation, and racism provided one.

However, this material and political superiority was not as 'eternal' as some versions of nationalism professed. By the end of the nineteenth century, British economic and political domination within the world capitalist system was under threat from a number of sources within Europe and beyond. The age of imperialism exposed the extent to which other European nation states and other territorially based capitalisms, not to mention competing colonising forces (such as the Boers in South Africa), were in a position to challenge British domination. It was during the last quarter of the nineteenth century that a new, right-wing English patriotism, which was simultaneously royalist and racist, was created against this background of changing international relations (Summers 1981: 73–4, Cunningham 1989: 77–8). Both the Boer War and the growing economic and military power of the recently unified German nation became potent symbols of the potential for national decline and for the loss of empire, and therefore also the point of departure for a discourse of national regeneration as part of a strategy intended to neutralise such threats (Summers 1989: 241). While this confirms the importance of the colonial Empire as a material base for the reproduction of racialised conceptions of Self and Other, it also demonstrates that the self-identity of the British nation as expressive of a distinct 'race' was intimately connected with changing circumstances *within* Europe: the whole world was racialised, including Europe, in an attempt to comprehend the rise of competing European capitalisms, each embodied in a separate national shell, and each seeking its 'destiny' on the world stage (see Chapters 3 and 5).

What is significant about the many strands that ran through the debate within Britain at this time was the way in which the idea of 'race' underpinned the idea of the English or British nation that was in need of resuscitation: 'race' was employed centrally as a category of inclusion, as a means of sustaining a positive self-identification (cf. Barkan 1992:

15–65). For example, with the vocal support of a number of pressure groups (Summers 1981), militarism was part of the state's solution: it was argued that the defence of the nation's interests required a fit and virile national army. The Director-General of the Army Medical Service told the Inter-Departmental Committee on Physical Deterioration in 1903 that 'Were all classes of the community able to provide their offspring with ample food and air space, a healthy race would be produced, and the proper material to fill the ranks of the Army would probably soon be obtained' (Summers 1989: 242). Implicit in such schemes was an inclusive (supraclass), racialised concept of nation, albeit one which implicitly conceded that superiority was not assumed 'naturally' (for the quality of the 'race' had declined) but could nevertheless be restored.

By such means, the regeneration of the 'imperial race' became a practical priority for the British state. Joseph Chamberlain was one prominent member of the ruling class who employed the discourse of 'race' and blood to characterise Anglo-Saxons as 'born to govern' and as the leading force in world history. Hence, for Chamberlain, the future of the 'Anglo-Saxon race' was inseparable from the maintenance of Empire because it was, by definition, an 'imperial race' (Mock 1981: 193–4). And the prime responsibility for producing this 'imperial race' fell to women, who were cast in the role of breeders of men. For example, within the eugenics movement, there was concern about the 'new women' who were thought less fit 'to become the mothers of a stronger and more virile race, able to keep Britain in its present proud position among the nations of the world', as one doctor expressed it in 1911 (cited in Davin 1989: 212). Motherhood therefore had to be taught so that women would fulfil their primary, 'natural' purpose, the preservation and improvement of the 'English race'.

Preservation and improvement of the 'race' was thought to be only one part of the task if national superiority was to be assured on a world scale. The age of imperialism had witnessed a scramble for new colonial settlements by the leading European nation states and this had promoted fears that sparsely settled British colonies might be overrun by other European 'races' with pretensions to imperial pre-eminence. It was suggested in 1905 that the maintenance of the Empire 'would be best based upon the power of a white population proportionate in numbers, vigour and cohesion to the vast territories which the British democracies in the Mother Country and the Colonies control' (cited in Davin 1989: 204). Given the high rate of child mortality and a falling birth rate, this solution again placed women as the bearers of children in the front line of the defence of the 'imperial race' that comprised the English or British nation.

But for the Fabian, Sydney Webb, and for many others, reproducing the 'race' was also a domestic necessity. In 1907, Webb advocated an increase in the British population and expressed concern that the supposedly fitter and more virile sections were limiting the size of their families. He believed there was a danger that, if the less desirable elements of the British population continued to 'breed' at their current rate, there would be an overall deterioration of the English 'race' and the numbers would be made up by 'freely-breeding alien immigrants' (cited in Davin 1989: 214). Thus, Webb added his voice to a broader strand of concern that the national interest was threatened by a quantitative and qualitative decline in the English or British 'race'. The ideas of 'race' and 'nation' were effectively synonymous in this early twentieth-century debate about the identity and future of the English or the British in world history. This was typical of a trend evident in many nation states in western Europe (Hobsbawm 1990: 108, Barkan 1992: 17).

The historical evidence surveyed here suggests that a conception of Englishness has been defined and developed since at least the mid-seventeenth century in order to construct a self-identity as well as to identify and exclude various Others. This specific instance of the imagination of nation has employed the idea of 'race', although the precise meaning of the idea has changed through time. But, irrespective of this changing meaning, the idea of 'race' has not been derivative or secondary, but an integral construct defining both the form and content of the attributed and real differentiation. This ideological project was grounded simultaneously in real political struggles which were central to the successful emergence of capitalism in England, and in the emerging pre-eminence of English merchant and industrial capital within the growing world economy.

There are reasons to agree with Nairn's claim that English nationalism is unusual because it was constructed in the absence of a need to mobilise a working class to force through a bourgeois revolution to establish the political preconditions for capitalist development. Thus (Nairn 1981: 43): 'The result was a particularly powerful inter-class nationalism – a sense of underlying insular identity and common fate, which both recognised and yet easily transcended marked class and regional divisions.' But, from the seventeenth century, that sense of 'insular identity and common fate' was additionally cemented by the idea of 'race' and, during the period of world dominance of English industrial capital, by the ideology of scientific racism. Indeed, it is because 'stale, romantic, middle-class nationalism has survived on the surrogates of imperialism and foreign war for nearly a century' (Nairn 1981: 273) that racism occupies such a central fissure in the edifice of Englishness: colonialism, imperialism, militarism and foreign war (including wars within Europe) have been widely explained and legitimated by the idea of the inevitable biological struggle for survival between discrete and hierarchical 'races'. The idea of the English or British as an 'imperial race' was especially effective in the context of this history.

Hence, racism is not a new, centrally defining element of an English nationalism undergoing transformation to fit new economic and political circumstances in the late twentieth-century (Nairn 1981: 79–80, 294), but is, rather, a long-established core element of English (and British) nationalism which has been reinterpreted and reconstructed in order to make it appropriate and meaningful in the post-colonial world. The definition of England in this nationalism is one in which 'to be English is to be against necessary outsiders, a member of an occult secret society diffused throughout the merely legal collectivity of liberal democracy' (Wright 1985: 125). But in the context of the declining fortunes of English capitalism, it has been brought forward to play a new role in a partially reconstituted form in order to identify a 'new' outsider who has allegedly slipped in through the back door, illicitly and with the connivance of various 'traitors'.

RACISM AND NATIONALISM IN CONTEMPORARY ENGLAND

Since the early twentieth century, there have been major changes in the political and economic context within which the ideas of 'race' and 'nation' articulate and are made to do their work. Colonial empires that were once legitimated by racism have broken up. The nineteenth-century doctrine of scientific racism has been widely discredited (although not eliminated) by the consequences of the rise of fascism in Germany (Barkan 1992). These and other changes make the explicit expression of nineteenth-century forms of racism in the formal political arena difficult. This applies just as much to other European social formations as to England (see, for example, Taguieff 1990, Balibar and Wallerstein 1991). A number of writers have commented on this (e.g. Hall 1978, Seidal 1986). And Barker claimed in the early 1980s to have identified a 'new racism' which has superseded the 'old racism' (understood to refer to the scientific racism of the nineteenth century).

This supposedly novel ideological constellation dispenses with the notion of the world's population being divided into 'races' in a hierarchy of superiority and inferiority, and claims instead that it is natural for individuals to wish to form exclusive groups. Barker identifies the core of this 'new racism' as follows (1981: 21):

> It is a theory of human nature. Human nature is such that it is natural to form a bounded community, a nation, aware of its differences from other nations. They are not better or worse. But feelings of antagonism will be aroused if outsiders are admitted. And there grows up a special form of connection between a nation and the place it lives.

Barker's argument has been influential amongst writers in the Marxist tradition, and his conceptualisation of racism has been incorporated uncritically into a number of accounts of the current ideological and political crisis of British capitalism (e.g. CCCS 1982). While Barker's thesis highlights certain central features of the changing conjuncture, it is not without its difficulties. My reservations about Barker's thesis (see also Miles 1992) precede a discussion of the more recent articulation of racism and nationalism in England.

The notion of a 'new racism' presupposes an analysis of an 'old racism': what are the characteristics of the 'old racism' that have been (supposedly) discarded because they are not appropriate to the 'New Times'? Barker is silent about the nature and origin of this 'old racism'. Indeed, he seems to deny the existence of what might first be thought to be the 'old racism' when he claims, without adducing any evidence, that it is 'a myth about the past that racism has generally been of the superiority/inferiority kind' (1981: 4). In the light of the vast quantity of historical evidence to which so many people have contributed (e.g. Montagu 1964, Gossett 1965, Stepan 1982, Gould 1984), one is tempted to conclude that this constitutes a rewriting of history which abolishes a whole chapter of European thought (not to mention racism in Europe). With this claim, Barker dispenses with over two hundred years or more of racist theorising without as much as a single citation to supporting evidence. And in the absence of a characterisation of the 'old racism', we have no adequate measure of what it is that is new about the 'new racism'. Indeed, if there never was an 'old racism', Barker's 'new racism' cannot be new.

Furthermore, Barker's concept of racism is vague. It is poor philosophical logic to deny the validity of other definitions of racism while retaining the term as a key analytical category in the absence of a clear alternative explanation of what the concept refers to. The closest that Barker comes to providing an analytical content for his concept is in a claim that an assertion about the naturalness of xenophobia is a form of racism because 'it sees as biological, or pseudo-biological, groupings that are the result of social and historical processes' (1981: 4). For Barker, therefore, a racist assertion appears to be one which incorrectly identifies any socio-historically constituted group as the product of biological determination. This is an extremely broad definition which, for example, offers no means of differentiating racism from either nationalism or sexism. Moreover, we are not offered any account of how or why this conceptualisation relates to or improves on other accounts.

Finally, the empirical object of Barker's analysis is confined to the texts and speeches of leading members and supporters of the Conservative Party in Britain. This is a rather limited terrain upon which to erect a theory about the emergence of a 'new racism'. It is a myopic conceptualisation because it leaves out of account a considerable range of ideological production. For example, analysis of National Front propaganda and other related literature published during the 1960s and 1970s demonstrates that the scientific racism of the nineteenth and early twentieth centuries has remained central to the activities of neo-fascist political organisations (Billig 1978: 138–52). Moreover, members of neo-fascist organisations express a crude scientific racism which forms one of the linchpins of their political ideology (Billig 1978: 261–83): this 'old racism' therefore has a contemporary expression. Barker also ignores the imagery of the English working class, where more 'classical' forms of racist expression abound (e.g. Dummett 1973, Phizacklea and Miles 1979, 1980).

Moreover, the significance of the political discourse of the leadership of the Conservative Party lies not only in its content but also in its object. The Party's new leadership of the 1970s and the 1980s was engaged in a political mobilisation in a context where an 'old racism' was a significant ideological force but where there were strong pressures against its explicit reproduction within the formal political arena. The emergent right-wing leadership sought to legitimate and incorporate the racism which had been used to build political support for the National Front during the 1970s, but it was necessary to do so in a way which did not entail the articulation of the explicitly racist constructs voiced in the bus queue and the workplace (Reeves 1983: 172–203). Barker identified as the 'new racism' that part of the official discourse with which this was achieved, but he largely ignored the wider everyday discourses which created the possibility of such an incorporation.

An important dimension of the post-1945 period has been the way in which successive British governments have responded to political agitation to impose immigration controls on the entry of those who used to be called 'coloured' Commonwealth citizens (Miles and Phizacklea 1984). The political discourse employed has been overtly and covertly racist, although within the formal political arena, references to inherent biological inferiority to legitimate the demand for such exclusion have been rare. Rather, the migrants have been simultaneously racialised and signified as the cause of economic and social problems for 'our own people' (Miles 1984b, 1988a). Equally to the point, the actual legislation passed by successive governments draws in effect a distinction based on phenotypical difference as a basis for removing the right of entry and settlement of people who were previously entitled to do so. This entailed an institutionalisation of racism in the practice of the British state, and legitimated common-sense racism. Moreover, by removing the right of entry to, and settlement in, the United Kingdom from certain categories of British subject, the state established new (racist) criteria by which to determine membership of the 'imagined community' of nation.

How, then, can one classify the dominant political discourse of the Conservative Party from the mid-1970s to the late 1980s? Barker describes that discourse as one which refers to 'human nature' to explain why people constitute 'nations' within a defined territory, within which a common way of life and a sense of national consciousness can be maintained. Furthermore, it is equally 'human nature' that members of this 'imagined community' should seek to exclude those with a different way of life and, therefore, with a 'natural home' elsewhere. This is an argument which, in part, closely resembles some of the classic claims of nineteenth-century nationalism. To redefine this nationalist argument simply as a 'new racism' requires a conceptual shift which results in a dissolution of any formal distinction between nationalism and racism. Indeed, Barker's analysis is completely silent about the nature and origin of nationalism.

The centrality of nationalism to the Conservative Party's creation of a populist unity (Hall 1983) was revealed in the political discourse of the Prime Minister during and after the Falklands War. During this short phase of political history, the 'surrogates of imperialism and war' (Nairn 1981: 273) were shown to have a continuing capacity to redefine and reinvigorate a sense of Englishness or Britishness. Indeed, the suggestion that another war could reinvigorate this defining characteristic of English/British nationalism was proven to be highly prophetic (Nairn 1981: 274). The Prime Minister argued in July 1982 after the defeat of 'the Argies' by 'our boys' (cited in Barnett 1982: 150):

When we started out, there were the waverers and the fainthearts, the people who thought that Britain could no longer seize the initiative for herself . . . that Britain was no longer the nation that had built an Empire and ruled a quarter of the world. Well they were wrong. The lesson of the Falklands is that this nation still has those sterling qualities which shine through our history.

For Margaret Thatcher, the task was to sustain and redirect this positive sense of national identity, attained through military conflict, to reorganise civil society and correct economic decline. In other words, this was a speech which explicitly connected the contemporary with the past in order to identify a future project for an entity whose social identity was reconstructed as a result of an external threat. The burning hulk of the *Sir Galahad* was used to illuminate and simultaneously reconstruct the boundary of the imagined community of the English or British. 'Great power' nationalism flickered into life once more as some of 'our boys' participated in the ultimate sacrifice at the altar of nationalism.

But if nationalism more accurately describes a part of the political discourse of the Conservative Party analysed by Barker, what of racism? It has been argued that English nationalism is particularly dependent on and constructed by an idea of 'race', with the result that English nationalism encapsulates racism. In other words, racism is the lining of the cloak of nationalism which surrounds and helps define the boundaries of England as an imagined community. The *obscured centrality* of the idea of 'race' was revealed in the course of the emergency debate in the House of Commons on 3 April 1982 on the Falklands crisis. Margaret Thatcher drew upon the idea of 'race' in an attempt to sustain a sense of 'nation' (cited in Barnett 1982: 30):

The people of the Falkland Islands, like the people of the United Kingdom, are an island race. Their way of life is British; their allegiance is to the Crown. They are few in number but they have the right to live in peace, to choose their way of life, and to determine their own allegiance. Their way of life is British; their allegiance is to the Crown.

And others heard and legitimated this stretching of the boundary of the imagined community of the British nation to include the people of the Falkland Islands. An editorial in *The Times* two days later included the claim (cited in Barnett 1982: 97): 'We are an island race, and the focus of attack is one of our islands, inhabited by islanders.'

Thus, the idea of 'race' continues to articulate with the idea of 'nation' in order to define Englishness or Britishness. The echo of racism that arises from this articulation is evident in Thatcher's positive reference to Britain's history as an imperial power in the aforementioned speech: while the idea of the British as an 'imperial race' is no longer appropriate, the history of imperialism remains central to at least right-wing definitions of the British character. As Rushdie (1982) pointed out, British people of Caribbean and Asian origin are unlikely to have such a positive view of those 'sterling qualities' of the English or British which the Empire was reputed to have revealed. Thus, the imagined community 'revealed' by the Falklands War was one which excluded ideologically those who had not been earlier excluded physically because they arrived before the passage of racist immigration laws. Indeed, Margaret Thatcher had herself defined this Caribbean and Asian presence as a threat to Englishness or Britishness. In 1978, she had suggested (cited in Miles and Phizacklea 1984: 5):

> And, you know, the British character has done so much for democracy, for law, and done so much throughout the world, that if there is a fear that it might be swamped, people are going to react and be rather hostile to those coming in.

The Conservative government reinforced this notion of Englishness or Britishness, which is shaped by the idea of 'race', in its British Nationality Act, 1981. The Act brought nationality law into line with the racist categories constructed in earlier immigration law and immigration rules (Dixon 1983: 173):

> The crucial irony of the 1981 Act is that it is designed to define a sense of belonging and nationhood which is itself a manifestation of the sense of racial superiority created along with the Empire, while simultaneously it cuts the ties of citizenship established in the same historical process. The ideology of Empire is reconstructed: while Thatcherism rejects the essential expansionism of Empire in favour of 'isolationism', its supremacism, chauvinism and racism are preserved.

Thus, the ideas of 'race' and 'nation', as in a kaleidoscope, merge into one another in varying patterns, each simultaneously highlighting and obscuring the other.

The ideological articulation is neither a simple, mechanical reproduction of long-established ideas and images, nor homogeneous. Both nationalism and racism require a conscious and continuous reconstruction, in the course of which 'old' ideas are invested with 'new' meanings. 'History' has to be renegotiated and resignified in order to (re)create a sense of the past appropriate to the particular conjuncture and the political project for the future. Traditions are invented to create a sense of historical continuity (Hobsbawm 1983: 2). This requires that events and material artefacts from the past are selected for attention and made relevant to the imagined present and future. In the case of English nationalism, the events selected include those which evince a sense of external threat over which 'the English people' triumph, especially events concerning war and imperialism (Wright 1985: 84, 179–80). The continually reconstructed sense of the English past, in which 'race' is an ever present reification, signifies the English 'nation' (and therefore the idea of 'race') as an ever present collective subject, defining the criteria of inclusion around the ability to sustain pride in bloodshed and colonial exploitation. But, in order that these reconstructions resonate, they must articulate with contemporary experience.

The centrality of racism to English nationalism is revealed once this is understood. The post-1945 Caribbean and Asian presence in Britain has been signified as a previously external threat that is now 'within', so that the 'old order' is threatened by its presence. As a result, because 'our' collective existence is supposedly challenged, resistance (even a new war) must be organised. The prominent and desirable features of 'our' culture' are spotlighted and reified by the assertion that they are in danger of being negated by the consequences of the presence of an Other: what was once conceived of as eternal is resignified as transitory. As Wright puts it, 'objects take on the aspect of heritage as they are endangered and the basic terms of their existence come into question' (1985: 95), and this applies equally to cultural forms such as marriage norms which are supposed to be 'threatened' by 'their alien ways' (that is, the 'arranged marriage' system).

A testimony to the historical specificity of this articulation in the case of England is found by considering the example of Scotland. Here, nationalism has a specific historical and cultural content and became an influential political force during the 1960s and 1970s. Its articulation with racism is therefore, in part, also specific to the particular historical circumstances of Scotland. Individual Scots and Scottish companies were prominent in British colonial history (e.g. Smailes 1981, Cain 1986, Calder 1986) and there is evidence to suggest that this involvement in Empire played a part in sustaining the reproduction of racism in Scotland. But if this is so, it is paradoxical that the post-1945 Asian migrants to Scotland have not been the object of a systematic and hostile political agitation as happened in England (although this is not to deny that racist images of these migrants are commonly expressed in everyday life in Scotland).

Part of the explanation for this lies in the fact that the particular political compromise embodied in the Act of Union of 1707 between England and Scotland ensured the reproduction of a distinct proto-state apparatus and national identity. In this context, political nationalism in Scotland during the twentieth century has tended to focus on the perceived economic and political disadvantages of the Union. Nationalism in Scotland during the 1960s and 1970s therefore identified an external cause of economic disadvantage/decline, without reference to 'race', while in England the idea of 'race' was employed to identify an internal cause of crisis, the presence of a 'coloured' population which was not 'truly' British. Thus, in Scotland, the 'national question' has partially displaced (although not eliminated) the influence of racism in constructing the political agenda in this period, suggesting that racism is not as central to nationalism as in England (see Miles and Dunlop 1986, 1987, Miles and Muirhead 1986, Miles 1987c).

CONCLUSION

The interrelationship between the ideologies of racism and nationalism is not, by definition, one of polar opposition. They have a common historical origin and formal characteristics which simultaneously overlap and contrast. Both claim the existence of a natural division of the world's population into discrete groups which exist independently of class relations, although in the case of nationalism a culturalist definition of the boundary of the nation can be subordinated to a political definition. But the ideology of nationalism, unlike that of racism, specifies a particular political objective (national self-determination) and therefore a blueprint for political organisation on a world scale.

It may be true, as Anderson observes (1983: 129), that the cultural products of nationalism are often evaluated in positive emotional terms while those of racism are associated with negative emotions. There are times when a love/hate dichotomy does seem to mirror precisely a dichotomy between nationalism and racism. But such a simple dichotomy ignores much that requires explanation. The dialectic of inclusion and exclusion that is integral to the formation of imagined communities around the ideas of 'nation' and 'race' produces more complex patterns of identification and organisation than Anderson recognises: the idea of 'race' can be employed to sustain a positive evaluation of a supraclass population. The self-identification of the English as a 'race' has a long history, in the course of which the notion of the English as an 'imperial race' marked one particular moment. In this moment, 'love of nation' entailed a 'love of race'.

Additionally, certain forms of fascist ideology which incorporate a racist theory of history have advanced a nationalist project which utilises an idea of 'race' to project a positive 'historical destiny' as well as 'eternal contaminations'. This was clear in the case of German fascism, where a theory of 'race' was used first to define the criterion of positive inclusion. The imagined community of the German 'nation' was therefore identified by a positively evaluated signification of supposed 'racial' characteristics (Hayes 1973: 20–1, 37). In this instance, the idea of 'race' was not only an 'eternal contamination' grounded in negative emotion but was also used to generate a positive sense of a German 'nation'. However, this boundary of inclusion was synchronically a boundary of exclusion which identified an Other who did not and could not belong to the imagined community and which prepared for its physical extermination (Fleming 1986). Indeed, the 'race' category and the ideology of racism can be ideal vehicles for positive assertions about historical destiny because they are often grounded in arguments about alleged biological determinism: nothing sustains an idea of historical certainty better than a reference to biology.

Thus, while there is a place for theoretical reflection (e.g. Balibar 1988c), an assessment of the interrelation between racism and nationalism is also dependent upon the historical analysis of specific examples of articulation. The example I have pursued demonstrates that the parameters of an imagined community of nation can be specified and legitimated by racism. In other words, the ideologies of racism and nationalism can be interdependent and overlapping, the idea of 'race' serving as a criterion of simultaneous inclusion and exclusion so that the boundary of the imagined 'nation' is equally a boundary of 'race'. In the case of English nationalism, given its historical genesis, this means that racism is one of its core components.

Chapter 3

The civilisation and racialisation of the interior

European expansion overseas, therefore, set the stage for racist dogmas and gave violent early expression to racial antipathies without propounding racism as a philosophy. Racism did not get its currency in modern thought until it was applied to conflicts within Europe – first to class conflicts and then to national.

(Benedict 1983: 111)

Discontented native in the colonies, labour agitator in the mills, were the same serpent in alternate disguises. Much of the talk about the barbarism or darkness of the outer world, which it was Europe's mission to rout, was a transmuted fear of the masses at home. Equally, sympathy with the lower orders at home, or curiosity about them, might find expression in association of ideas between them and the benighted heathen far away.

(Kiernan 1972: 330)

INTRODUCTION

This chapter discusses the evolution of the theoretical debate in Britain about the changing meaning of the *concept* of racism. It deals only secondarily with the history of racist ideologies. While the anatomy of that history has been surveyed in some detail (e.g. Poliakov 1974, Mosse 1978, Geiss 1988), what is considered relevant to examine in such histories depends upon what is thought to warrant description as an instance of racism. I have made other contributions to the debate about the scope of the concept of racism (1982, 1989a, 1989b, 1991a) and this chapter reconsiders certain of the problems that are central to the ongoing discussion. It proposes that a definition of the concept of racism should take account of the racialisation of the *interior* of Europe as well as the *exterior* (see also Miles 1992), and that an explanation for the expression of racism should be grounded in an account of the evolution of class domination and the formation and reproduction of the nation state.

THE IDEA OF 'RACE' AND THE CONCEPT OF RACISM

In the English language, the word *racism* is now used widely in public and political debate. This gives the impression that it is a universal, or at least a long-established, concept. In fact, it is a recent creation. The word did not exist during the eighteenth and nineteenth centuries, the period during which the ideology that we call racism was systematised in European thought. As noted in Chapter 1, it was first used in the English language in the 1930s: it was translated into English from German where it appeared somewhat earlier, in parallel with its first use in French (Taguieff 1987: 122–38).

During the late 1930s and early 1940s, stimulated by events in Germany, a number of European scientists and intellectuals refuted the validity of the scientific idea of 'race' (e.g. Huxley and Haddon 1935, Barzun 1938, Hirschfeld 1938, Benedict 1983, Montagu 1979). While these writers did not agree on the scientific validity of the idea of 'race', they were all critical of the way in which it had been utilised to inferiorise the Jews and other minorities in Germany. The appearance of the concept of racism at this time therefore represented an important political and ideological rupture in European history: it signified a rejection of a central strand of German fascism and, as a result, racism named a specific discourse which was considered to be abhorrent. In this context, Ruth Benedict defined racism in 1942 as 'the dogma that one ethnic group is condemned by nature to congenital inferiority and another group is destined to congenital superiority' (1983: 97). This summarised the content of the three propositions that Barzun had identified earlier as the essence of 'race-thinking' (1938: 18–21). The substance of this definition was repeated and augmented by Michael Banton in the late 1960s (1970: 18), although he subsequently rejected the concept of racism in favour of that of 'racial typology' (1987: ix, but see Banton 1992).

The creation of the concept of racism refracted an imprint of the circumstances within which it was conceived. Benedict's definition accentuated the notion of biological inferiority which had been central to 'race' theory in Europe since the eighteenth century. Banton's augmented conception defined the concept of racism more precisely to refer to an ideology that posits the existence of 'races' as discrete and permanent biological divisions of the human species which can be ranked hierarchically. Thus, employing this definition, in order to talk of racism one must demonstrate that the idea of 'race' constitutes a central organising ideological theme in a discourse which takes the form of a logically organised structure of assertions.

Some fifty years after Benedict's book was published, two analytical problems arise from such a definition. First, given that the concept has a specific historical origin, its meaning refracting key features of that period, can it have any analytical value when considering different conjunctures? For example, does the concept have an object in an earlier era when the notion of 'race', in so far as it existed, did not have the same connotations of biological inferiority? Furthermore, there is a long history to the construction and reproduction in Europe of negatively evaluated images of Muslims, Africans and Jews (Said 1985, for a summary see Miles 1989a: 11–40). While these populations were not originally conceptualised as 'races', European images implicitly or explicitly ranked these Others as inferior to those who made the evaluation. Moreover, before the early seventeenth century as well as thereafter, signified differences were often explained in biblical terms, while skin colour was interpreted as a sign of difference in a context where the 'black/white dichotomy' was overlain with parallel negative and positive evaluations. Can we describe these images and discourses as racism in the absence of an explicit notion of 'race' and of an assertion of natural and permanent inferiority?

A similar problem arises for the period since 1945. In so far as the 'final solution' was 'legitimated' by a theory of biological inferiority, then the notion of 'race' is inevitably impregnated with the smoke of the crematoria where so many human bodies were disposed of. In much of the post-Holocaust world, what amounted to a taboo on the official use of the notion of 'race' was reinforced by the activities of UNESCO which were intended to discredit the notion of 'race' as defined by nineteenth-century science. During the 1950s and 1960s, UNESCO assembled on four separate occasions a group of scientists who were asked to summarise the scientific evidence concerning the nature of 'race' (Montagu 1972). The result was a demonstration that the barbarism of the 'final solution' rested on 'a scientifically untenable premise' (Montagu 1972: x).

The effect has been uneven. In certain European countries (notably Germany, the Netherlands and France), the negative connotations of the notion of 'race' have helped to ensure that it has largely disappeared from official political and much everyday discourse. Explicit references to human differentiation in terms of a fixed biological ranking, and sustained by assertions of congenital inferiority, are equally rare (although belief in the existence of 'races' remains widespread). While such notions are still central to the ideology and political propaganda of neo-fascist and extreme right-wing political organisations and movements (e.g. Anne Frank Stichting 1985), they cannot be used easily or effectively to mobilise opinion and political support within the official, 'respectable' political arena.

The British situation is different in so far as the notion of 'race' is not only widely used in political and public discourse but has also been attributed with a formal legal status (for example, with the formation of the Race Relations Board in 1965). This latter use results from legislation which has made discrimination on the basis of 'race' a legal offence. It has also been legitimated by the social sciences, and specifically by those academics and researchers who have identified 'race relations' as an object of theory and of empirical study (e.g. Rex 1970) (for a critique of 'race relations' sociology, see Miles 1980, 1982, 1984, 1988b; cf. Guillaumin 1980). But these uses of the notion of 'race' occur in a context where there are strong sanctions against assertions which suggest that racialised groups are biologically inferior. As elsewhere in Europe, an explicit discourse of biological inferiority and of a hierarchy of 'races' is largely confined to neo-fascist and extreme right-wing political organisations and movements (e.g. Billig 1978) and to the private arenas of everyday life.

Throughout Europe, racism has become a category of abuse, a means of declaring one's political opponent an immoral and unworthy person. A majority of people in western Europe seek to avoid being so labelled and they adjust their discourse and actions accordingly (van Dijk 1987). Thus, in the post-Holocaust world, the concept of racism as defined by Benedict rarely seems to have a subject in the wider world beyond the fascist fringe. Applying such a definition in a rigorous fashion, one would conclude that racism emerged as an influential ideology in Europe in the eighteenth century, flowered in the nineteenth and early twentieth centuries, and withered and died rather quickly in a few years after 1945. An advocate of this view would not deny that, in the periods before and after this era of racism, there were negative discourses about non-Europeans. He or she would claim only that these were not racist discourses. What remains to be explored is the possibility that the meanings embodied in the idea of 'race' have been transferred to other notions and discourses (Guillaumin 1972).

There is a second analytical problem arising from Benedict's definition. Much popular discourse about the Other consists of a formally incoherent combination of allusions, representations and allegedly factual claims, the meaning of which is derived from the unstated assumptions shared by those who participate in the discourse. Such discourses do not take the form of a logically constructed hierarchy of assertions and certainly cannot be described as scientific (cf. Todorov 1989: 113–19). In relation to Benedict's definition, they cannot be classified as instances of a doctrine, at least not in so far as this carries the meaning of an ordered sequence of logical assertions. But does this mean that racism only appears in the form of systematically ordered, written texts, texts which purport to be a contribution to scientific debate, or prepared political speeches which identify a particular population as a biologically inferior Other?

RE-DEFINING THE CONCEPT OF RACISM

So, is the original definition of racism that arose from the conjuncture of the 1930s adequate for the contemporary period? In the last two decades, some British theorists and researchers have addressed this question. John Rex's work constitutes one of the most important sociological attempts to deal with the analytical problems previously mentioned (1970, 1986). Rex was a member of one of the UNESCO committees of experts and he participated in the discussions about the concept of racism that took place in 1967. His own writing on the concept of racism echoes some of the arguments set out in the subsequent UNESCO statement which proposed a revision of the definition offered by Benedict in 1942. The importance of Rex's intervention in the late 1960s and early 1970s lies in that, in the light of the changing forms of discourse within the formal political arena, he redefined the concept and concluded that racism remained a significant political force within Britain. Rex argued that biological arguments have functional substitutes and that (1970: 159)

> the common element in all these theories is that they see the connection between membership of a particular group and of the genetically related sub-groups (i.e. families and lineages) of which that group is compounded and the possession of evaluated qualities as completely deterministic.

The question has also been addressed from within the Marxist tradition, a tradition invigorated by the theoretical rupture with Stalinism and economism. I have discussed the work of Martin Barker in Chapter 2 and I shall refer to my contribution later in this chapter (e.g. Miles 1982,

1987c, 1989a, 1989b, 1991a). One of the more important theoretical innovations arising from this tradition is the idea that the concept of racism refers to an ideology which is flexible and plastic, one which appears in different forms in disparate historical conjunctures, and which has various populations as its object, rather than as a single ideology with a fixed set of attributes. Stuart Hall, for example, has warned against 'extrapolating a common and universal structure to racism, which remains essentially the same, outside of its specific historical location' (1980: 337), and prefers to speak about 'historically-specific racisms' (1980: 336, see also Goldberg 1990a). More recently, Cohen referred to 'anti-Semitism and colour prejudice' as 'distinctive modalities of racism, with their own histories and structures of meaning' (1988: 15).

This theme was developed by a research collective which worked under Hall's direction in the late 1970s. The collective also argued that racism contains contradictory themes and ideas and is constantly in flux (CCCS 1982: 9–11). Furthermore, they suggested that the racism expressed in contemporary Britain has deep historical roots: ideas and arguments derived from colonial history are continually reworked as a result of contemporary endogenous political and economic forces, with the result that old ideas are given new meanings by being combined with novel themes and images (1982: 11–12, 48, 66, 68, 70, 74).

RESERVATIONS AND LIMITATIONS

These theoretical innovations are important: yet while they solve certain difficulties, they also reproduce old problems and create some new ones (Miles 1987d, 1989a, 1990a). First, those writers who have argued that the concept of racism should not refer to a single, static set of images and beliefs have avoided formulating a definition of racism (e.g. Hall 1980, CCCS 1982, Cohen 1988). These writers fail to specify what it is that the historically specific racisms have in common in order to warrant description as instances of racism. Concerning the work of Hall and the CCCS collective, this is partly because they have not undertaken a comparative analysis of contemporary racisms. Indeed, often implicit in their writing is the assumption that the only contemporary form of racism in Britain is that which has people of Caribbean and South Asian origin as its object. Even if this were the case during the 1970s (and I doubt that it was), it is not true for the late 1980s, a period which has witnessed the growth of an increasingly explicit racism against Jews (e.g., *The Independent*, 27 November 1990). The expression of anti-Irish racism is even more consistently ignored.

This is not the case with Phil Cohen's work. By intending to document the historical evolution of different forms of racism in English history, Cohen's analysis constitutes an important innovation. Yet, in asserting that 'colour prejudice' and 'anti-Semitism' are different forms of racism (1988: 15) in the absence of a definition of racism, we cannot know what they share in common in order to warrant description as instances of the same genus of ideological phenomenon. While there is a definition of racism implicit in Cohen's account of the evolution of English racism, the reader is left to draw this out, thereby creating the space for ambiguity and even contradiction where different readings of the text are possible.

In this respect, Barker's contribution (1981) is superior in so far as he attempts to identify what it is that different forms of racism have in common. But, and this is my second reservation, Barker's definition of racism is so broad that it has little discriminatory power. As I have suggested in Chapter 2, there are many discourses which (mistakenly) reinterpret socially constructed groups as the product of biology. Discourses about nation, especially nationalist discourses, commonly conceive of different nations as biologically or naturally constituted and, as a result, they would be classified as instances of racism according to Barker's definition. There are good reasons to object to the elimination of the distinction between racism and nationalism, with the result that Barker's redefinition of racism requires revision. I have argued elsewhere (1992) that Taguieff's analytical distinction between a *racisme inégalitariste* and a *racisme différentialiste* (1987: 321–3) better expresses Barker's chronological distinction.

Third, in so far as the recent British discussion about the nature of racism has tended to assume that its nature and origin are to be explained largely or exclusively in relation to the colonial project (e.g. Fryer 1984: 133–84, cf. UNESCO 1980), that discussion is limited in its relevance to other contexts, including earlier periods of British history (Miles 1991b) and other European nation states (Miles 1989a: 111–21). This colonial paradigm became hegemonic during the late 1960s and the 1970s. It was shaped by Marxist theory and by anti-colonial struggles in the periphery of the capitalist world economy, as well as by political ideologies of 'black liberation' which originated in colonial situations and in the United States.

Broadly, the argument is that racism is the product of British colonialism, an argument that, as we have seen in Chapter 1, was central to the work of Oliver Cox. Since the use of racism to legitimate slave labour, notions of African and Indian inferiority have been reproduced in the colonial and domestic contexts for three centuries or more as a justification for colonial exploitation. Consequently, when the colonised (or ex-colonised) subject migrated to the 'Mother Country', colonial discourses (in which the idea of 'race' is central) have been used to comprehend this presence. Hence, contemporary British racism is explained as a reworking of longer-established images and stereotypes which extend the long history of the subordination of 'black' people. For some writers (e.g. Essed 1991), discourses which attribute 'black' people collectively with a set of negative attributes become defined exclusively as racism: by definition, racism becomes a 'white' ideology which has only 'black people' as its object. A corollary of this argument is the claim that the inevitable visibility of skin colour ensures the reproduction of racism in a post-colonial world where 'white people' associate 'blackness' with inferiority.

There is no doubt that the history of colonialism, and specifically the reproduction of a colonial imagery of biological inferiority, is an important determinant of the contemporary expression of racism in a number of European countries. Elsewhere, I have argued that colonial history is an important determinant of contemporary British racism (1982). However, if it is assumed or argued that the colonial paradigm of racism constitutes a universal explanation for the nature and origin of racism, there are reasons to be more critical of its explanatory power.

It reifies skin colour as an active determinant of social relations. The visibility of somatic characteristics is not inherent in the characteristics themselves, but arises from a process of signification by which meaning is attributed to certain of them. In other words, visibility is socially constructed in a wider set of structural constraints, within a set of relations of domination. Many physical characteristics (both real and imagined) have been and continue to be signified as a mark of nature and of 'race' (cf. Guillaumin 1988). Moreover, cultural characteristics have also been, and continue to be, signified to the same end. The reification of skin colour therefore mistakenly privileges one specific instance of signification and ignores the historical and contemporary evidence which shows that other populations (Jews, Irish people, etc.) have been signified as distinct and inferior 'races' without reference to skin colour (Miles 1982, 1991b).

Moreover, it restricts analysis of the nature and determinants of racism to a debate about the effects of colonial exploitation. In the light of the origin of the concept of racism, and of the manner in which the idea of 'race' has been utilised elsewhere in Europe to inferiorise and exclude Jews (to cite just one example), this is a problematic conception. The economic and social positions of Jews in nineteenth- and twentieth-century Europe cannot be understood as a situation, or a product, of colonialism. Hence, this paradigm is unable to explain those conjunctures in which the racialised and excluded population has not been colonised.

Analysis of such contexts requires consideration of the articulation between racism and nationalism within Europe. Not all European nation states have a significant colonial history, while, concerning those that do, colonial history does not neutralise the influence of other determinants of the expression of racism. Consequently, the colonial paradigm is partial in its explanatory power because, as I shall show shortly, it fails to comprehend the way in which the discourse of 'race' has been an integral component of nationalist discourses and of ruling-class conceptions of subordinate classes within Europe. On a more contemporary note, it is also unable to analyse the intensification of anti-Jewish racism in eastern and central Europe that has developed following the collapse of communist governments (e.g. Ascherson 1990).

EXPLAINING RACISM: THE SIGNIFICANCE OF THE INTERIOR

In a recent book which defends the continued use of racism as an analytical concept (1989a, 1991a), I commence with a descriptive history of European representations of Others resident beyond Europe. This point of departure implies that an explanation for the origin and reproduction of racism within Europe is to be found through an examination of the signification of populations outside the emergent political/territorial (later, national) boundaries of Europe, in the places that are 'not-Europe'. This assumption has an affinity with the colonial paradigm discussed in the preceding section. Both perspectives locate the primary dynamic for the development of racist discourses in the identification within an emergent national 'community' of an Other that is to be found *outside* either the boundary of Europe or a specific European national boundary. These analyses therefore subordinate or ignore the way in which the idea of 'race' has been historically central to internal processes of subordination and domination, to ideological processes which have as their object populations resident *within* emergent nation states in Europe. In other words, it was not only the European *exterior* that was racialised by certain classes of Europeans: there was also a racialisation of the *interior* of Europe.

An analysis of the latter does not deny the influence of the colonial project upon the emergence and reproduction of racism, either in the past or contemporarily. Rather, it demonstrates that the emergence and reproduction of different modalities of racism do not have a single determinant. Otherness is not a singular quality assigned to one group: it is a dialectically plural attribute. There has always been a multiplicity of Others, with the quality being attributed to different subjects in different contexts, often with the result that the same population has functioned as Other and Us at different historical moments. Consequently, there is constant interplay in the identification of the symbols of Otherness as they are applied conjuncturally to different populations: the idea of 'race' has been employed to signify not only populations colonised in Africa and elsewhere but also populations subject to the power of the nationalised ruling classes within Europe.

In other words, if we are to take seriously the idea that there are historically specific racisms, it is necessary to undertake a wide-ranging but historically specific analysis of different conjunctures. In carrying out that analysis, we should take account of the historical affinity between processes in the interior of, and exterior to, Europe. This is because we need a theoretical basis independent of colonialism to explain non-colonial racisms; moreover, colonial racism may not necessarily have an exclusively colonial origin.

This affinity between racisms of the interior and of the exterior can be demonstrated by reference to the ideology of the civilising mission. A central theme of colonial racism during the nineteenth century was the claim that colonisation had as one of its objectives the *civilisation* of 'backward' or 'childish races' (e.g. Fryer 1984: 184–5). European merchants and planters, along with their political and ideological agents (including the administrators and missionaries), deployed this discourse to explain why the labour power of the colonised was exploited through relations of direct domination. They argued that the civilisation of the colonial 'races' was to be achieved by, in some combination, conversion to Christianity, the provision of elementary education (to teach 'good manners' and to ensure at least some degree of literacy, if only to read the Bible) and the organisation of labour in order to ensure commodity production: hence, forced labour was legitimated on the grounds that it instilled discipline, order and respect in a 'race' that was 'barbarous' and 'savage'. In such instances, colonial exploitation was achieved, *inter alia*, by means of a civilising process which entailed an inferiorisation of the colonial subject and practices of cultural imperialism.

The civilisation project preceded European colonialism and commenced *within* Europe: thereafter, it was pursued simultaneously within and beyond Europe. By investigating this history, one can identify the different forms that the project has taken and the different populations which have been its subject. But in each instance, the civilisation project has been initiated by a class, or a fraction of a class, in order to establish and to legitimate a social hierarchy, and therefore a set of relations of domination. The first social collectivity to 'benefit' from the process of civilisation was the European feudal ruling class which, self-consciously, civilised itself.

In France, notions of *politesse* and *civilité* were used by the feudal aristocracy to contrast the refinement of their behaviour with that of the 'inferior' people whom they ruled. Hence, they expressed (Elias 1978: 39)

> the self-image of the European upper class in relation to others whom its members considered simpler or more primitive, and at the same time to characterise the specific kind of behaviour through which this upper class felt itself different to all simpler and more primitive people.

This 'specific kind of behaviour' entailed a wide-ranging transformation of everyday actions and speech, with a particular emphasis upon the control of bodily functions: the outcome was to 'make all bodily functions more intimate, to enclose them in particular enclaves, to put them "behind closed doors" ' (Elias 1978: 189).

The process having been initiated within the feudal ruling class in the sixteenth century, if not earlier, the emergent bourgeois class in different European nation states subsequently appropriated it (Elias 1978: 49, 100–1). Indeed, the bourgeoisie became its leading exponent once it had displaced the aristocracy as the ruling class. By the early nineteenth century, the bourgeoisie, conscious of its material achievements and more firmly in political control in at least certain parts of Europe, began to assert that its values and manners were more a matter of *inheritance* than a social construction. In these circumstances the notion of civilisation (Elias 1978: 50)

> serves at least those nations which have become colonial conquerors, and therefore a kind of upper class to large sections of the non-European world, as a justification of their rule, to the same degree that earlier the ancestors of the concept of civilisation, *politesse* and *civilité*, had served the courtly-aristocratic upper class as a justification of theirs.

This civilising mission was not a cause of colonialism. But as a multifaceted process, it originated in the development of processes of social differentiation and legitimation initiated by the ruling class within feudal Europe and, thereafter, it came to link the interior and the exterior of the European world as it became increasingly structured by capitalist relations of production and by the bourgeoisie.

In the course of the evolution of the capitalist mode of production within Europe, two other collectivities became the object of this ideological project as it was embraced by the rising bourgeoisie: these were the soon to be proletarianised peasantry, and the proletariat itself. The process of proletarianisation had ideological dimensions, while the proletariat itself was a potential (and often a real) threat to the survival of the ruling class, necessitating strategies of ideological subordination as well as direct force. Both instances demonstrate that the task of civilisation from above, a task in which the state was heavily involved alongside the emergent bourgeoisie, did not only have externally colonised subjects as its object. The dominant class and the state were also confronted with the task of civilising other categories of inferior Other, other 'savages', living within the boundary of the nation state (Elias 1978: 104). And here too the civilisation project was dependent upon a preceding signification of these interior Others as inferior Others.

This is revealed through the study of the articulation of the evolution of the nation and the expansion of the capitalist mode of production in Europe in the nineteenth century. The late eighteenth and the nineteenth centuries were the era of 'nation making' in Europe, of *nationalisation* (cf. Balibar 1988a: 122–6, Noiriel 1991: 84–93), in the course of which, *inter alia*, peasant producers were 'freed' and inserted into the capitalist mode of production in a number of ways (the most dramatic of which took the form of depriving them of their means of production in order to create an urbanised factory proletariat). This was not an exclusively economic process: integral to it were the ideological and political processes of nationalisation and civilisation, both of which were bound up with the creation of national systems of education by the state.

One of the better-documented examples concerns France. During the second half of the nineteenth century, the peasantry, especially in the south and west of France, was signified by intellectuals, politicians and officials in Paris as living 'like savages'. Their material conditions of existence were interpreted as a symbol of their 'inner nature'. This uncivilised condition was understood to signify that they had not been *assimilated* into the French way of life (Weber 1977: 3–22). Compared with the remainder of the French population, peasants were therefore often thought to be a different type of human being, to be a different 'race'.

During the nineteenth century, the French peasant lived an isolated life with few or no relations with others beyond a radius of a fifteen or twenty kilometres, and was largely economically self-sufficient, although extremely poor. Following the French Revolution, the view from Paris (or rather from the Parisian apartments of the bourgeoisie and state functionaries) was that a way had to be found to *assimilate* this savage and alien 'race'. That is, the French peasant had to be simultaneously civilised and nationalised, which meant that he or she had to subordinate himself or herself to what was then a revolutionary idea of the French nation. When measured against the material and political conditions of the preceding feudal social order, this entailed a certain kind of liberation, although it was a liberation with strict limits.

It encompassed not only the introduction of, *inter alia*, the commodity form, market relations, machinofacture and the development of mechanical transport systems, but also the introduction of an education system that would, where necessary, force children to stop speaking their imputed inferior 'mother tongue' and become literate in French, and much more. If the state ruled through the medium of the French language, then those subject to that rule had to become literate in French in order to comprehend what they were required to be and to do (Weber 1977: 72). Nationalisation was therefore as much an ideological as a material process: the racialised peasant had to learn to imagine the nation, and to come to believe that he and she belonged to it. In so doing, the cultural life of the peasant was transformed, a transformation that was understood ideologically in Paris as civilisation. Cultural forms, such as the French language, identified by the dominant class and the state as a symbol of the nation, became a means of domination over the peasantry, but also potentially a means by which they might subsequently achieve their own liberation.

This process was not confined to France: it occurred throughout Europe (Connor 1990), but in different forms and with different determinants. A second example can be drawn from Scottish history. Following the suppression of the Jacobite revolt in 1745, the British state sought to pacify and civilise the population of the Highlands of Scotland by the introduction of the Protestant religion, the creation of a sense of loyalty to the King and the imposition of the principle of 'industry', the latter in the form of a value and a material force (Womack 1989: 5). During the second half of the eighteenth century, the subject of this strategy, the Highlanders, were signified as a culturally alien Other, whose distinctive dress, language, manner and mode of material subsistence were interpreted as marks of the membership of a distinct and inferior 'race'. Specifically, they were seen as 'uncouth savages', as 'barbarians', as a 'race' that was spatially and culturally beyond the boundary of civilisation: violence and a capacity for warfare were thought to be inherent characteristics of the Highlander and of the social relations of Highland life (Womack 1989: 27, 38).

One instance of this signification of barbarity was apparent in the Scottish Exhibition of National History, Art and Industry which was staged in Glasgow in 1891. As part of the 'amusement' section of the Exhibition, a Highland and an African village were 'reconstructed' and inhabited by Africans and Highlanders respectively (Kinchin and Kinchin 1989: 117–23). This was the era when Glasgow functioned self-consciously as the Second City of Empire: thus, those who visited the Exhibition were provided with a dual measure of their advancement, a representation of the savagery and backwardness of the Other who still existed (and so threatened), not only in the Dark Continent but also in the mountains that they could see beyond Loch Lomond.

This 'amusement' embodied a perverse articulation of the racisms of the interior and exterior of Europe. In reality, the supposedly natural capacity of the Scottish Highlander for warfare had been harnessed in the pursuit of British civilisation beyond the shores of Britain by using the Highlands as a reservoir for recruitment to the British armed forces: naturalised barbarity was then transformed into an agency of civilisation when the violence had as its object even more inferior, colonised 'races' beyond the boundary of Europe. A 'representation' of this history at the Scottish Exhibition would presumably have been more difficult to classify as 'amusement'.

The 'savage' peasantry (and its transformation into a nationalised proletariat) was not the only subject for civilisation within Europe. For the dominant class in Paris, there was another 'savage race' resident within the French nation. This threat was perceived in the neighbouring *arrondissements* rather than in distant rural regions, in *les provinces*. For the Parisian bourgeoisie of the early nineteenth century, the working class was commonly viewed as 'savage' and 'barbarian' (Chevalier 1973: 359–61). Proletarians were represented as a distinct physical type, as having a set of somatic characteristics which expressed their supposed physical and moral degeneration (1973: 385). Indeed, sections of the working class were portrayed occasionally as having the features of animals, a representation that symbolised dramatically their alleged subhumanity (1973: 414–15). These representations were commonly considered to be differences of 'race' (Chevalier 1973: 361, 408): French bourgeois thought in the early nineteenth century was influenced by phrenology (Chevalier 1973: 412), a form of scientific investigation that played an important role in the evolution of scientific racism (Gould 1984). In this way, sections of the Parisian working class were racialised and Balibar has described this as an instance of le «racisme de classe» (1988b: 277–80).

In Britain, during the same period, another population of 'urban savages' was identified by intellectuals sympathetic to the state and to the urbanised professional and bourgeois class in a conjuncture where two political issues articulated (Lorimer 1978: 101, 129, 204). First, there was concern about the extension of the franchise to a section of the manual working class. For many within the ruling class, this was a potentially dangerous venture because it was not known whether those to be allowed to participate in the formal political arena of the nation would exercise their new electoral powers 'responsibly'. Second, as in France, there was concern about the existence in the growing industrial cities of the relative surplus population, of a class which included paupers and those in irregular and erratic employment. This was the dangerous class par excellence, a population that was seen to lack a work ethic, to be without morals: in sum, this class was thought to be degenerate, uncivilised and perhaps uncivilisable. As a result of involvement in criminal activity or forms of political protest, or both, it was potentially a source of disorder. The material and cultural gap between this class and the professional and bourgeois classes was thought by some amongst the latter to be so wide as to connote that the former was a different kind of human being, a 'race' apart (Lorimer 1978: 110, 210).

The existence of this dangerous class required explanation, and one was found in the associated ideas of the existence of a natural order and of biological determination (Lorimer 1978: 100). Class position was therefore a product of 'breeding', the consequence of 'something' that was in the blood. For example, in the late nineteenth century, a theory of urban degeneration was widely articulated. One prominent argument claimed that recent migrants into London from adjacent rural areas were biologically superior to the London born, being physically stronger and more intelligent. In the Darwinian struggle for survival, they were better equipped biologically, with the result that, given the intense competition of urban life, the London born were being forced increasingly into idleness and pauperism. The ultimate cause of degeneration was their biological constitution, and not the conditions of urban life themselves. For some writers, the solution was to allow this biologically inferior population to die out (Jones 1976: 129–30, 286–90, 308–10). Not only did these arguments explain the superior position of the 'civilised' professional and bourgeois class relative to the inferior position of the 'urban savages'. They could also be used to explain and justify the intermediate position of the 'respectable' working class, and perhaps even its admission into a fuller participation in the affairs of the nation. There is another pertinent dimension to the racialisation of the interior of Europe. The process of ruling, of reproducing domination, within each nation state was contested, both from within the nation state and from other nation states. Within the nation state, the composition of the European ruling classes was undergoing a metamorphosis as a result of the increasing significance and power of the industrial bourgeoisie, while conflict between merchant and industrial capital located in different nation states was one determinant of political conflict between different nation states. The question of 'Who rules?' was therefore of central political importance, and the resulting struggles were fought out on both the political and the ideological terrain.

The innovative concept and historical analysis of 'codes of breeding' (Cohen 1988: 63–78) testify to this. There were a number of variants of these codes: for example, the *aristocratic* code asserted that, as a result of breeding, the ability and entitlement to govern was the prerogative of the aristocracy. In other words, knowledge of how to govern was 'passed on through the blood'. This naturalisation of domination took on a particular significance in conjunctures where an aristocratic class, materially based in the ownership of land, found its political position challenged by the rise of an urbanised bourgeoisie. One way of defending a position of domination when it is challenged is to resort to the idea that ruling is a natural capacity, and this is well expressed through ideas of breeding and blood.

The utility of the notion of breeding as a category of inclusion and exclusion is evident in its flexibility. Within the English language, the word integrates two formally distinct meanings. On the one hand, it refers to biological reproduction, and so entails a reference to ancestry and descent. On the other, it refers to civility, culture, good manners, refinement. That is, it refers to those things that were the substance and outcome of the process of civilisation (Elias 1978). It is therefore ideologically weighted in such a way that these two meanings articulate and overdetermine each other: to 'have breeding' is, by definition, to belong to a collectivity which, over successive generations, reproduces itself and civilised values and behaviour. In this way, the discourse of civilisation can be grounded in a notion of biological reproduction, for which blood can be a metaphor. Such a discourse can be appropriated and utilised by any group seeking to naturalise its position of domination through a notion of superiority grounded in the positive meaning attached to being civilised.

The boundaries of blood have been drawn and redrawn depending upon conjuncture and interests. Hence, during the nineteenth century, in certain circumstances the English working class, or fractions thereof, were signified by the dominant class as 'a different breed', an uncivilised 'race', but in other circumstances, as a constituent part of the English (or British) 'race', a 'breed' which contains 'in its blood' civilised and democratic values. As we have seen in Chapter 2, here racism and nationalism articulated. The result was a racialised nationalism or a nationalist racism, a mercurial ideological bloc that was manipulated by the ruling class (or rather by different fractions of it) to legitimate the exploitation of inferior 'races' in the colonies, to explain economic and political struggles with other European nation states, and to signify (for example) Irish and Jewish migrants as an undesirable 'racial' presence within Britain.

In the light of this evidence, there is reason to believe that the development of colonial racism in Europe cannot be explained adequately without taking account of the determination and influence of domestic racisms, of racisms of the interior. This is to revive an older argument. The evidence set out above parallels analyses offered in the first critical studies of racism published during the 1930s. These texts (e.g. Barzun 1938, Benedict 1983) retain a continuing significance in so far as their authors sought to identify the structural determinants of racism within Europe.

Barzun (1938) outlined a history of 'race-thinking' in Europe, paying particular attention to France (cf. Todorov 1989). His main focus was the competing claims about divisions of 'race', and the social effects of these supposed divisions, *within* Europe. Barzun identified a number of determinants of the intensification of racism in Europe between 1870 and 1914, including the rise of nationalism, the effects of industrialisation, the emergence of the popular press, and the increase in literacy (Barzun 1938: 183). He also mentioned 'imperialism and prestige-diplomacy' (1938: 183). That the racialisation of the interior of Europe should be regarded as an influential force is highlighted by Barzun's summary of the main lines of debate about 'race' in this same period. Three of the four strands were concerned with conflicting accounts of 'race' typologies within Europe, while the fourth concerned colonialism (1938: 185).

A similar emphasis is evident in Benedict's historical account of the evolution of racism. She argued that European colonialism constituted one arena within which racism was expressed, but she maintained that colonialism did not in itself structure the creation of racism as a coherent philosophy. She asserted that racism emerged in its most systematic form during the nineteenth century in response to *class* and *national* conflicts *within* Europe (1983: 111). In particular, she referred to the significance of aristocratic legitimations of their self-proclaimed 'right to rule', and to the increasing tendency during the late nineteenth and early twentieth centuries to interpret national conflicts in Europe in terms of 'race'. Cohen's recent work (1988) echoes the significance of Benedict's argument.

The importance of these themes have been highlighted more recently by Banton's historical analysis of the changing meanings of the idea of 'race' within Europe (1977, 1987). In the earlier study, he emphasised that the idea of 'race', in the sense of a physical category of human being, was first employed to interpret the evolution of European history before it was used to identify and explain social relations elsewhere in the world, including colonial situations (1977: 18–19). Moreover, he suggested that the use of the idea of 'race' to interpret historical developments in Europe was influenced by contemporary political struggles within Europe.

In conclusion, it is clear that the ruling classes of Europe sought to racialise and civilise populations within as well as beyond Europe. Indeed, the civilisation project has its origin *within* Europe and was subsequently exported to the colonial situation as the sphere of exploitation was extended to include the Americas, Africa and south-east Asia. And, just as racism was an important dimension of the colonial project, so it was integral to legitimations of bourgeois domination and of the creation and extension of capitalist relations of production within Europe during the nineteenth century. While the explanations for these interior and exterior racisms may be historically specific in the first instance, the generality of racism is also a striking feature of the eighteenth and nineteenth centuries. And if racism has been, not an 'abnormal' ideology confined to playing a sordid role outside Europe, but rather an ideology integral to the constitution of nationalised bourgeois social formations within Europe as well as to the constitution of colonial social formations grounded in unfree relations of production, then we may need to recommence the search for a general theory of racism.

ON RACISM AND NATIONALISM: THE SIGNIFICANCE OF THE 'GERMAN CHARACTER'

In the light of the history of the racialisation of the interior of Europe, I move on to consider an aspect of the contemporary situation, the significance of which is highlighted by the concept of *interior racism*. The point of departure is a text which was the focus of controversy in

Britain during 1990, a text that provides a rare glimpse of contemporary ruling class anxiety that parallels earlier instances mentioned elsewhere in this book.

On 24 March 1990, following the collapse of the communist government in the German Democratic Republic, the British Prime Minister and Foreign Secretary met with six 'distinguished authorities' on German history for a confidential discussion about the consequences of the unification of Germany. The Prime Minister's private secretary later drafted a memorandum recording the discussion. Like the meeting, the memorandum was confidential. The latter was later leaked to a national newspaper (*The Independent on Sunday*, 15 July 1990) following an interview given to a weekly journal by the Secretary of State for Trade and Industry, Nicholas Ridley, in which he made a series of allegations about German domination of the European Community. He was forced to resign amidst suggestions that he was expressing views that he shared with Margaret Thatcher (e.g. *The Independent*, 13 July 1990).

The confidential memorandum began by describing 'the Germans themselves':

> Like other nations, they had certain characteristics which you could identify from the past and expect to find in the future. It was easier – and more pertinent to the present discussion – to think of the less happy ones: their insensitivity to the feelings of others (most notable in their behaviour over the Polish border), their obsession with themselves, a strong inclination to self-pity, and a longing to be liked. Some even less flattering attributes were also mentioned as an abiding part of the German character: in alphabetical order, *angst*, aggressiveness, assertiveness, bullying, egotism, inferiority complex, sentimentality. Two further aspects of the German character were cited as reasons for concern about the future. First, a capacity for excess, to overdo things, to kick over the traces. Second, a tendency to over-estimate their own strengths and capabilities.

Whether or not this statement accurately reflected the views of the then Prime Minister, or indeed the views of the 'experts' who were present, is not relevant here. It is sufficient to note that it was drafted by a government official who believed that he was summarising accurately the content of the discussion that took place on 24 March.

How are we to characterise this statement? The fact that it constructs for 'the British' an Other within Europe ('the Germans') is pertinent in the light of the preceding argument about the racialisation of the interior of Europe. Is it therefore an expression of racism? Or, as some commentators proposed at the time, is it an expression of nationalism? Our answer to these questions depends not only on how we interpret the statement, but also on how we define racism. For those whose concept of racism is grounded exclusively in the colonial paradigm, the answer is negative: the discourse does not originate in a colonial history and the population that is the object of the discourse is not 'black'. However, if it is assumed that racism has various historically specific forms, it can be argued that the memorandum expresses another (non-colonial) modality of racism. This returns us to the problem of what it is that different racisms have in common in order to be classified as instances of racism.

Three assertions are made in the memorandum. First, 'the Germans' are described as a nation (and not a 'race'). Second, the distinctive characteristics of German people are signified as fixed and permanent and, therefore, as natural and transhistorical. Third, although there is no explicit assertion of inferiority, the characteristics are negatively evaluated. Using Barker's definition of racism (1981), the memorandum does embody a racist discourse. While notions of 'race' and hierarchy are absent, the memorandum intimates the existence of a collectivity which possesses certain fixed attributes and which exists unchanged through time. This can be understood to mean that the German nation is a natural, pseudo-biological collectivity. Given that the historical evidence is to the contrary (that is, that the German nation is more accurately conceived as the product of a historical process of nationalisation), the memorandum is falsely attributing the existence of this collectivity to a biological, or pseudo-biological, cause.

If Barker's concept of racism is judged problematic for the reasons stated in Chapters 1 and 2, we can consider alternative definitions. Elsewhere (1989a: 73–84), I have suggested that racism is a form of ideological signification which constructs a social collectivity as a discrete and distinct, self-reproducing population by reference to certain (real or imagined) biological characteristics which are purported to be inherent, and which additionally attributes the collectivity with other negatively evaluated (biological and/or cultural) characteristics. Racism, therefore, attributes meaning to the human body, either somatically or genetically, in order to construct an Other which reproduces itself through historical time and space. It should be noted that this definition does not bind the concept of racism to the explicit presence of the idea of 'race'. Neither does it require the notion of hierarchical ranking. Finally, it is a definition which, in the context of European history, includes as instances of racism (see Miles 1989a, 1991b) many of the negative significations of European populations.

Using this definition, it seems that the memorandum does not express a racist discourse. While the collectivity ('the Germans') is identified as a discrete, self-reproducing population, and is considered to possess certain negatively evaluated cultural attributes, it has not been signified by reference to real or imagined biological characteristics (such as, for example, skin colour, facial characteristics, skull shape and capacity). Yet, I have argued above that racist discourses do not necessarily assert explicitly the existence of 'races'. Consequently, we discover an ambiguity in my definition of racism: in the text under discussion, 'the Germans' are nevertheless 'represented as having a natural, unchanging origin and status, and therefore as being inherently different' (Miles 1989a: 79).

The difficulty arises from the fact that, in nationalist discourses, the nation is often represented as a *natural* collectivity, identified by specific permanent cultural characteristics. The memorandum provides a good illustration: attributes such as aggressiveness are identified as 'abiding' components of the 'German character'. Formally, the object created by this discourse, in so far as it is a transhistorical, natural collectivity which is attributed with certain negatively evaluated attributes, is identical to the object created by a racist discourse. But 'the Germans' were not identified using (real or imagined) biological characteristics.

The problem is that both 'cultural' and 'biological' attributes can be signified to suggest the existence of self-reproducing social collectivities which are naturally and therefore permanently distinct. In other words, the ideologies of nationalism and racism both comprise processes of signification which portray discrete social collectivities as naturally constituted. And where 'cultural difference' is represented as natural and immutable, then it has all the qualities signified by the notion of 'biological difference', with the result that the distinction between racism and nationalism seems to have been dissolved.

This appears to leave my concept of racism open to the same objection as that which I have made with respect to Barker's concept. Moreover, it leads to the conclusion that the memorandum on the 'German character' expresses a racist discourse. However, this assumes that the distinction between racism and nationalism is unidimensional. Is it sufficient to argue that the basis for the articulation between racism and nationalism pivots exclusively around the object of signification (i.e. either 'culture' or 'biology') used to distinguish a plurality of 'natural collectivities'? I believe not, for I have emphasised in Chapter 2 that the specificity of nationalism is to be found in the claim that each naturally distinct nation should organise itself politically within a specified territory. This observation requires further discussion.

The claim that each 'naturally distinct' nation has the right of political self-determination constructs an ideological terrain on which all 'recognised' nations are in principle equal. Within the framework of nationalist discourse, while each nation necessarily has a different set of (sometimes fixed) characteristics, and while certain of those characteristics might be signified negatively by members of other nations with the result that they become a mark of difference (if not inferiority), it is a principle that each nation has an equivalent right to existence and self-expression, so long as the territory that it occupies does not overlap with that claimed by another nation. Nationalist discourses therefore differentiate, and differentiation prepares for the possibility of exclusion, but it is an exclusion which accepts the legitimacy of the existence of the nationalised Other within another territory wherein it constitutes a 'sovereign people'. In this way, beliefs about the differences between, and the alleged inferiority of, other nations can coexist with a more abstract ideological construction of the respective social collectivities as homologous.

This is not the case with racism. Racism constructs (real or imagined) difference as natural not only in order to exclude, but additionally, in order to marginalise a social collectivity within a particular constellation of relations of domination. All racisms are instances of the ideological *marginalisation*, within a social formation, of a supposedly distinct social collectivity which is thought to reproduce itself through time and space, and which has been signified as naturally different, usually (but not exclusively) by reference to real or alleged biological characteristics. That is to say, the outcome, and often the intention, of racist discourses is to deny to a racialised collectivity certain rights and resources, or sometimes all rights and resources (including the right to human life), which others within the same social formation possess. And, by virtue of the difference alleged, this exclusion does not admit to the possibility of an equality of being at another level. The moment of discourse is the moment of ideological marginalisation, which precedes exclusion in material practice (and/or which is inscribed in material practices of exclusion).

Racism is therefore not only a discourse which creates the Other in a particular ideological form (i.e. usually, but not necessarily exclusively, by reference to real or alleged biological characteristics but *always* by reference to 'nature'). It is also a discourse of marginalisation which is integral to a process of domination: and those who articulate racism always necessarily situate themselves within relations of domination. For this reason, the official memorandum cited above does not embody a substantively racist discourse, even if there is the formal appearance of racism. While 'the Germans' are constructed as a negatively evaluated 'natural collectivity', they are not inferiorised as a prelude to the denial of rights and resources, not least because the British state does not occupy a structural position which would permit it to dominate the 'German people'. The memorandum embodies a substantively nationalist discourse: 'the Germans' are recognised as another 'nation' with independent interests which nevertheless conflict with those of 'the British'. The negative attributes accorded to 'the Germans' simultaneously justify 'British interests' as legitimate and explain the 'unacceptable' behaviour of the German state but they do not inferiorise in order to marginalise.

As a result of this elaboration of the definition of racism, one can see more clearly how certain modalities of racism can play a central role in the instigation and/or reproduction of a structure of domination *within* a social formation, a social formation which may or may not be colonised. There are two interlinked dimensions to this. First, the construction of naturalised difference through racism sanctions an inequality of practice: the racialised Other is denied various kinds of resource which, in a situation of scarcity, are allocated to those considered to belong. Examples include the denial of the right to possess and sell one's labour power as a commodity, the denial of the right to vote and to belong to political parties, and the denial of access to certain occupations or to certain state-distributed resources (education, housing, hospital treatment). The marginalised collectivity may be the peasantry or fractions of the working class, as well as particular cultural minority groups, whether or not of recent migrant origin.

Second, the construction of naturalised difference creates, in turn, a naturalised hierarchy of acceptability and belonging within a social formation. In a context of scarcity and class differentiation, this facilitates the ideological identification of certain social strata within the subordinate classes (which are defined as belonging and therefore as having a natural right of access to scarce rights and resources) with the institutions responsible for the organisation of production and distribution of material resources and political rights (i.e. with capitalists and the institutions of the local and the national state). In this way, racism can map the boundary of the nation, and can help to forge a notion of national unity *contra* the racialised and marginalised collectivities. This hegemonic project must, however, always have contradictory consequences, not least because of the continuity of political and economic inequality between the classes who imagine themselves as homologous.

CONCLUSION

Elsewhere, I have suggested that it is necessary to examine the articulation of racism and nationalism in nineteenth-century Europe in order to explain the racialisation of a non-colonial Other that took place in that historical period (1989a: 111–21). But the theoretical significance of this evidence was not elaborated. This can now be done in the light of the preceding discussion. The implication of the evidence presented here is that, when accounting for the origin and reproduction of the various modalities of racism within Europe, more emphasis needs to be placed upon the interrelationship between class formation and reproduction, and nation-state formation and reproduction, *within* Europe. This is not to deny the significance of colonialism, but rather to contextualise colonialism within the historical development of the capitalist mode of production.

Concerning class formation and reproduction within European nation states, the bourgeoisie has always sought to legitimate its position of domination over other classes. For example, during the early nineteenth century, an ideology of 'breeding' justified political and economic privilege by representing class differences in terms of somatic or genetic characteristics. For a certain period, this *«racisme de classe»* justified the exclusion of the peasantry and working class from full or equal participation in the political system. Later in the nineteenth century, the nation was constructed and reproduced, was imagined in some way as a homogeneous collectivity with common interests. In this process of nationalisation, the dominant class sought to represent certain of its characteristics as collective characteristics of the nation. One means of constructing a basis for the membership of the nation has been to measure 'belonging' by reference to 'breeding' and the somatic or genetic form, the body. This entailed defining 'We' the nation, in relation to an Other which was found within and/or outside the territorial boundary of the nation.

The history of Europe is therefore bound up with the history of racism on a number of different levels. For more than two centuries, racialisation has been an important dimension of class relations and class struggle within *and* beyond Europe. In the course of the struggle to sustain domination, Europeans in different class positions have racialised each other, as well as inward migrants and those populations that they colonised beyond Europe. During the twentieth century, there have been further examples of the racialisation of the interior of European nation states (as in the case of the Jews), as well as a racialisation of larger-scale inward migrations, including colonial and non-colonial migrations, since 1945. Consequently, historically, racism has had as its object populations occupying different class positions and having different economic and cultural origins.

When we consider the nature and parameters of racism within contemporary Europe, the 'dead weight' of history is a more considerable burden than is often recognised. A recent discussion of the creation of the 'Other' within Europe (Gundara 1990) illustrates this limitation. The main emphasis is upon the historical conflicts between Christendom and Islam and various dimensions of colonialism, and there is only a passing reference to anti-semitism, and no reference at all to other subjects of the racialisation of the interior of Europe, examples of which have been discussed above. The implication of this chapter is that racism is more deeply threaded through the historical evolution of capitalism because it has played a central role in the constitution of relations of domination *within*, as well as *beyond*, Europe.

Part II

Migration theory and history

Chapter 4

Theorising migration: possibilities and problems

The Irish famine of 1846 killed more than 1,000,000 people, but it killed poor devils only. It did not do the slightest damage to the wealth of the country. The exodus of the next twenty years, an exodus which still continues to increase, did not, as for instance the Thirty Years' War did, decimate the means of production along with the human beings. The Irish genius discovered an altogether new way of spiriting a poor people thousands of miles away from the scene of its misery. The exiles transplanted to the United States send sums of money home every year as travelling expenses for those left behind. Every troop that emigrates one year draws another after it the next. Thus, instead of costing Ireland anything, emigration forms one of the most lucrative branches of its export trade.

(Marx, 1976: 861–2)

INTRODUCTION

In 1969, Cambridge University Press published a collection of essays on migration edited by John Jackson. Viewed retrospectively, this seems to have marked simultaneously the birth, and the passing away of, a British sociology of migration. A more recent book by the same author (Jackson 1986) carries the same title as the earlier work and, in the light of its brevity and the absence of a supporting British literature, it appears more as an epitaph than a rebirth for a British sociology of migration. There have been attempts to enact a resurrection (or perhaps a virgin birth) at or beyond the periphery of the discipline of sociology. For example, Castles and Kosack (1973) established the importance of a political economy of migration for an understanding of, not only post-1945 colonial migration to Britain, but also the patterns of migration into western Europe from the late 1950s until the early 1970s. This analysis was subsequently updated and extended by Castles *et al.* a decade later (1984). And Annie Phizacklea and I, working within the same theoretical tradition, have set out in various contexts a case for a systematic analysis of migration (e.g. Phizacklea and Miles 1980, Miles 1982, 1987a, Phizacklea 1983). More recently, Cohen (1987) has contributed to this tradition with a theoretical and historical overview of international migration in the context of the debate about the changing nature of the international division of labour.

But, in the main, responsibility for the development in Britain of a theoretical and empirical analysis of migration within the evolution of capitalist societies has been claimed by academic disciplines other than sociology. Geographers have made a substantial, although largely descriptive, contribution. Peach's account of Caribbean migration to Britain (1968) remains the most widely cited British text on the subject and, with colleagues, he has contributed more recently to the analysis of migration from the Indian subcontinent (Clarke *et al.* 1990, see also Robinson 1986). Salt has written extensively on post-war migration into western Europe (Salt and Clout 1976) and on the international migration of professional, managerial and technical labour (1984, 1988). And Ogden and White, who have individually contributed to the European migration literature (e.g. in Glebe and O'Loughlin 1987), have jointly edited a series of essays on migration within and into France (Ogden and White 1989).

British social historians have also made a notable contribution. Colin Holmes has written widely on the history of migration to Britain (e.g. 1978, 1988, 1991), while James Walvin has summarised the available historical evidence in an accessible form (1984). Pooley and Whyte (1991) have edited a collection of essays which provide a more specialised insight into the recent work of social historians interested in reconstructing the social history of migration. One should also mention here the widely cited work of Fryer (1984), Ramdin (1987) and Visram (1986), although they have been concerned to document the presence in Britain of the colonised populations of the Caribbean and the Indian subcontinent. However, important though all this historical work is, it is again largely descriptive and contains few theoretical insights on the determinants and significance of migration.

The other academic discipline in Britain to have made a contribution to the study of migration is anthropology. Watson's well-known book, *Between Two Cultures* (1977), is generally considered to be an anthropological account of the main ethnic communities resident in Britain, but it can also be read as a study of post-1945 migration to Britain which utilises the notion of chain migration as the central explanatory concept. The ethnographic tradition, which is central to much social anthropology, encourages an explanatory account of migration which is grounded in social networks, and so the concept of chain migration has been routinely employed in anthropological analyses of the Caribbean and south Asian presence in Britain since 1945 (for an interesting analysis which extends beyond the study of social networks, see Ballard 1990). A more recent book by Alison Shaw, which describes the evolution and character of the Pakistani community in Oxford, stands (and falls) in this same tradition in that it draws upon the same conceptual framework to explain migration from Pakistan (Shaw 1988: 22–5). However, Shaw has only a passing interest in migration, having set herself the primary objective of dismantling some of the stereotypes held in Britain about people of Pakistani origin.

While migration research is being conducted within these academic disciplinary boundaries, its continuing marginality in Britain is further indicated by the absence of a British-based academic journal devoted specifically to migration (although *Immigrants and Minorities* does provide a forum for historical research on migration). This contrasts with the USA and the rest of Europe. The *International Migration Review*, published in New York, is one of the leading international journals while *International Migration*, *Revue Européenne des Migrations Internationales* and *Migration* (published respectively in Geneva, Poitiers and Berlin) provide a European focus for research and discussion (although there is some British participation in the editing of two of these journals).

In part, the absence of a sociology of migration reflects inadvertently a hegemonic assumption that Britain has evolved as a nation state in the absence of any large-scale, inward migration of people. There is considerable political investment in the convictions that Britain is a culturally homogeneous society whose island status has protected it from 'invasions' of various kinds over many centuries, and that its future is dependent upon the maintenance of vigilance at the borders in order to guarantee this homogeneity in the future. Seen from this perspective, post-1945 migration from the Caribbean and south Asia to Britain is an aberration. As a result, some right-wing politicians have concluded that this migration was the outcome of the deceit of an earlier generation of politicians who refused to consult the British people about their wishes. If they had done so, and acted upon the British people's 'good sense', so the argument continues, this migration would have been terminated at an early stage and the 'racial composition' of the British nation would not have been changed.

The ideological character of these claims is easily revealed. While in comparison to settler capitalist nation states such as the United States, Canada and Australia, inward migration to Britain has not been such a major source of economic and demographic growth and has usually been exceeded by emigration, the historical writing previously referred to shows that there have been a number of numerically and culturally significant migrations to Britain over the past two centuries. Moreover, until recently, the majority of these migrations originated from Europe: the post-1945 migration from colonies and ex-colonies in the Caribbean and the Indian subcontinent is anomalous only in this more specific sense.

Even if it is conceded that the scale of inward migration to Britain is comparatively limited (in comparison with nation states such as the United States or Australia, as well as France, cf. Noiriel 1988), the same cannot be said for emigration from Britain. The history of British colonialism is not only a history of exploitation by means of unfree labour, military domination and administrative regulation, but also a history of emigration to, and settlement in, North America, Africa and Australasia. The settler colonies (Denoon 1983) were developed to a large extent as a result of 'voluntary' and state-organised emigration of both the surplus population created in Britain by those multiple processes which accompanied the creation of industrial and urban capitalism, and a section of the urbanised proletariat (e.g. Carrothers 1929, Malchow 1979, Smith 1981, Baines 1985).

The scale of this emigration was considerable, especially during the nineteenth century. For both the seventeenth and eighteenth centuries, net emigration from Britain was in the region of 0.5 million persons (Baines 1985: 56–8). After 1815, the number of emigrants rose dramatically. For example, between 1861 and 1900, some 4.25 million people left English and Welsh ports for a non-European destination and, while about half probably returned at a later date, this means that more than 2 million people emigrated permanently from England and Wales during this period (Baines 1985: 279). Emigration from Scotland and Ireland was proportionately greater than from England and Wales, although the absolute numbers were smaller (Baines 1985: 10). This large-scale emigration from Britain was part of a wider movement of population out of Europe to 'New Worlds' during the nineteenth century (Baines 1985: 8–44, 1991), a process that continued on a large scale until the middle of the twentieth century.

There is another reason for the absence of a British sociology of migration. It is also due to the dominant position of the 'race relations' paradigm within British sociology. Those working in the framework of this paradigm have produced a discrete interpretation of colonial migration and its consequences by means of a critical analysis of the discourse and policy advanced by the state, but they have rarely sought to recontextualise this migration systematically by analysing it within the wider framework of British migration history. Their concern has been primarily with the consequences of settlement, and specifically with the expression of racism and processes of exclusion, rather than with a comprehensive and contextualised analysis of the determinants and process of migration. To varying degrees, the implicit and explicit models and theories that they have used to account for and explain these consequences reify the idea of 'race' as an analytical concept.

The reference point of their analysis has been the United States and South Africa. In both countries, the colonial enterprise and the use of forms of unfree labour have been interpreted through the medium of the discourse of 'race', from which theories of 'race relations' have been derived. These notions of 'race' and 'race relations' were imported into British academic discourse, by writers influenced by the Weberian as well as the Marxist tradition, to interpret the consequences of post-1945 migrations from British colonies and ex-colonies. As a result, other post-war migrations (not to mention migrations before the Second World War) to Britain have been ignored because they are not conceived to have led to the creation of 'race relations' situations.

THE SIGNIFICANCE OF A SOCIOLOGY OF MIGRATION

The publication in the late 1980s of a number of books on various aspects of migration (e.g. Appleyard 1988a, 1989, Bramwell 1988, Holmes 1988, Sassen 1988, Stahl 1988, Ogden and White 1989, Layton-Henry 1990b) provides an opportunity to consider what might be gained from a systematic analysis of migration. Drawing illustrative material from these recent publications, there are at least two reasons for prioritising a theoretical and empirical analysis of migration.

First, given that the sociology of 'race relations' has implicitly accepted the ideological assumption that equates 'immigrant' with 'coloured person', a challenge to the 'race relations' paradigm pre-supposes a systematic analysis of migration to Britain. This would show not only a continuous history of immigration, but also that, for much of the past two centuries, the majority of migrants to Britain have originated from elsewhere in Europe rather than from colonies and ex-colonies. What is needed is a series of empirical studies of the many 'hidden' or only partially exposed European migrations to Britain, including those from Ireland, Germany, Italy, Hungary and Cyprus.

Recent work on the history of refugee migrations has made an important contribution to this recovery. For example, an edited collection of essays on refugee migrations (Bramwell 1988) reports evidence concerning German, Jewish and Polish migration to Britain which adds usefully to our knowledge. Other research on the arrival and settlement of refugees during and after the Second World War has broadened and deepened our understanding of this important transitional period (e.g. Kay and Miles 1988, 1992, Sword *et al.* 1989). And social historians have recently completed important studies of the Irish, German and Italian presence in Britain (e.g. Swift and Gilley 1985, 1989, Sponza 1988, Colpi 1991, Panayi 1991). But a great deal of historical work remains to be done.

Second, the process of migration is integral to the transition from feudalism to capitalism and to the development of the capitalist mode of production. In other words, migration is a constitutive force within and of capitalist societies, and any analysis which portrays the main dynamics of the evolution of such societies must therefore specify its significance. There are two dimensions worthy of comment here. First, the commodification of labour power is central to the nature and processes of the capitalist mode of production: with the dissolution of relations of personal and/or legal dependence (that is, with the abolition of relations of direct domination over labour), individuals come to possess their labour power as private property and become formally 'free' to migrate to find a buyer for it. Wage labour, when compared to serfdom and slave labour, therefore represents an important transition in the sphere of individual autonomy, although it is an autonomy circumscribed by the new relations of production. The sale of labour power is itself dependent upon the concentration and centralisation of capital, with the result that the temporal duration and spatial location of production, and therefore labour demand, are variable rather than fixed. Consequently, migration is a structural feature of the capitalist mode of production in that those who subsist by means of the sale of their labour power are induced to move from one spatial location to another in response to the ever changing demands of capital for labour.

In abstract, this economic determination of migration functions equally within and across national boundaries although, as we shall see shortly, the state is a mediating institution, especially in the case of international migration. Thus, migrations such as those from rural to urbanising areas within emergent nation states during the early stages of industrialisation in eighteenth- and nineteenth-century western Europe, or those from Mediterranean nation states to north-west European nation states in the 1960s and early 1970s, can to a large extent be explained as the consequence of the diverse processes which sustain the accumulation of capital.

There are a number of examples in the recently published literature. For instance, the interdependence of a great deal of 'internal' and 'international' migration in Africa during the twentieth century has been determined by the demand for labour as a result of investment in mining and agricultural production and the introduction of capitalist relations of production in these economic sectors (Adepoju 1988: 37–8). French migration history (Ogden and White 1989) similarly highlights this interdependence in the evolution of capitalism in France. From the mid-nineteenth century, the urban *départements* gained population consistently at the expense of the rural *départements*, and the rate of population mobility increased continuously during the second half of that century. But, in comparison with the rest of western Europe, this migration proceeded at a slower rate, with the result that a much larger proportion of the French population remained engaged in agricultural production and continued to live in rural areas after the Second World War (White 1989, see also Noiriel 1990). In other words, production relations in the agricultural periphery were not transformed sufficiently to generate a relatively surplus population on the same scale as elsewhere in western Europe.

Historically, the transition from independent peasant production to wage labour has taken several decades, passing through different phases and often entailing, at least temporarily, the reproduction of non-capitalist modes of production. In certain regions of France, internal migration often began as a seasonal migration of, as yet, undispossessed male peasant producers seeking a cash supplement to the means of subsistence independently produced by themselves, or of agricultural male labourers seeking to establish themselves as peasant farmers by earning sufficient money to purchase land (Hanagan 1989). In the Massif Central, it was the temporary migration of young women to rurally based silk factories that helped to sustain rural, agricultural production until the early twentieth century (Ogden 1989a). In other words, temporary proletarianisation was integral to a strategy of sustaining peasant agricultural production in the face of the encroachment of capitalist forces and relations of production, an encroachment that threatened total and permanent proletarianisation. Recent work by British social historians (Pooley and Whyte 1991) opens up the possibility of a more detailed comparative analysis of the complexity of the transition from feudalism to capitalism and of the mediating role of migration in Britain and France.

For example, unlike in Britain, the relationship between proletarianisation and urbanisation, mediated by migration, occurred in France
in the context of a slow rate of 'natural' population increase. As a result,
since the late nineteenth century, internal rural/urban migration has been
accompanied by a substantial (in comparison with Britain) migration into
France from adjacent European nation states and North African colonies
(Ogden 1989a, Noiriel 1990: 119–23). As a measure of this, there were
over a million foreign nationals living in France in 1881, around 2.7
million in 1931, and 1.7 million in 1946. Hence, large-scale international
labour migrations into western Europe are not exclusively a post-1945
phenomenon, as historians have recently emphasised (Noiriel 1984,
1988, Ogden 1991, Singer-Kérel 1991).

The second aspect of the interrelationship between capitalist
development and migration concerns the rise of the nation state as a
political unit. Both Marx and Weber emphasised that the social and
economic conditions necessary for the emergence of the capitalist mode
of production included the prior formation of a strong state capable of
exercising political domination within a bounded territory. And, as the
nation state became the spatial and political unit within which emergent
capitalist classes prospered, then the expansion of the capitalist mode of
production became synonymous with the spatial division of the world
into nation states. This has had contradictory implications: it has
constituted both a stimulus and an obstacle to migration. In other words,
it is possible to explore certain of the contradictions of capitalist
development through an analysis of migration.

On the one hand, the reproduction of the nation as an imagined
community is effected by a policing by the state of its spatial and cultural
boundary in order to determine who belongs and who does not. A
consequence can be the expulsion or flight of individuals and populations
deemed by the state not to belong to the nation. Moreover, political
conflict within the nation state may result in the expulsion or exodus of
the defeated protagonists. The formation and reproduction of the nation
state is therefore often secured at the cost of stimulating emigration. The
significance of these *refugee* migrations will be considered further below.

On the other hand, the construction and policing of national
boundaries within the advanced capitalist world now constitutes a barrier
to the spatial movement of people: as a result of the creation of the legal
category of nationality and (since the late nineteenth century) of
immigration laws, the individual is formally free to migrate only within
the nation state to which he or she 'belongs'. Since 1945, in an attempt to
mediate the resulting contradictions, certain groups of states have created

supranational economic and political units within which their citizens can move without significant restriction (as for example in the case of the European Community), but the right to do so is nevertheless mediated by citizenship of a single nation state which is party to such an agreement (see Chapter 8). This mediating role of the nation and of the state is too often ignored or underemphasised in analyses of labour migrations.

A large proportion of post-1945 labour migration into western Europe was either initiated or sanctioned by the state, which sought to enforce a rotation of individual workers in order to prevent permanent settlement (e.g. Castles *et al.* 1984, Schierup 1990). For reasons that are now well understood (Miles 1986), this strategy failed. Consequently, there is increasing interest in, and concern about, the political status within western Europe of the many millions of migrants and their European-born children who are not nationals of those nation states where the principle of *jus sanguinis* is used to determine nationality (Hammar 1990, Layton-Henry 1990b). In so far as national status determines the exercise of political rights (such as the right to vote), these migrant workers and their children occupy a secondary political status within western Europe. In sum, the state has permitted (often with reluctance) the permanent settlement of a large proportion of the population of migrant origin but continues to deny this same population the full rights of citizenship.

Analyses of post-1945 migration flows into western Europe which concentrate exclusively on their economic character and determination, as if the interests of capital are unidimensional and all-powerful, unmediated by political relations, are not easily able to account for this outcome (Miles and Satzewich 1990, Satzewich 1991). This is not to deny that the principal determinant of many of these migrations has been a labour shortage which has been resolved through the medium of migration. But references to the existence of a labour shortage which is resolved by migration from elsewhere in the world assume that labour markets are politically circumscribed. The terms of the discussion presume the existence of the political institutions of the nation and of the state and so the significance of these political institutions in the determination of international migration flows needs to be rescued from the shadows. In other words, analysis of *international* migration presupposes an examination of the mediating role of the nation as a spatial-political unit and of the state as an institutional complex: because the latter possesses political sovereignty within a territorial boundary, it has the power to determine both entry into and membership of that unit (cf. Zolberg 1981).

Since the late eighteenth century, 'membership' of the nation in

Europe has been concretised in the interrelated notions of nationality and citizenship. The former refers to the legal status of 'belonging' to a nation. During the twentieth century, this status has taken on a material form in the right to be issued by the state with a passport which permits the individual to travel to another nation state but also, and equally importantly, to return to 'his' or 'her' nation state: indeed, it is because the passport usually constitutes proof of the possibility of the latter that its holder is permitted to enter temporarily the territory of another state. Generally, each instance of this legal status of nationality is mutually exclusive: by virtue of belonging to one nation, the individual cannot belong to another (dual nationality is permitted by certain states, but it continues to be regarded as an exceptional condition). The notion of citizenship refers to the social and political rights and obligations that are granted by the state to those members of the nation that it considers are warranted. Historically, these have been gained largely as a result of political struggle by those excluded from political participation, as the history of the widening of the franchise demonstrates.

In a world that has been divided territorially and politically into nation states, each with a discrete nationality and citizenship, the spatial mobility of human beings is therefore politically constrained because their 'right to belong', and their civil rights and obligations are formally valid only within a particular nation state. Spatial movement across national boundaries is therefore conditional upon the granting of both the right of exit from one national territory and the granting of the right of entry into another. In both instances, it is the state that possesses the requisite powers.

Certain of the consequences of these political parameters of international labour migration into western Europe since 1945 have led to a widening debate about their adequacy and legitimacy. As a result, the nature of nationality and citizenship within the European Community will certainly be central to political and academic debate throughout the 1990s and beyond (Layton-Henry 1990a, Balibar 1992, Silverman 1992). Some writers have suggested that this debate originates in the transformation of several of the member nation states of the European Community into multinational and multicultural societies as a result of migration. Consequently, so the argument continues, the idea of the nation as a culturally homogeneous political unit and the nineteenth-century conception of citizenship have now been transformed by events and are in need of revision (Layton-Henry 1990b: 186). The implication is that this (undefined) condition of multiculturalism is historically novel. But is 'multiculturalism' a new feature of western European nation states? I do not believe that it is, for the following reasons.

First, the process of nationalisation (understood to mean, *inter alia*, the creation, amongst those people defined by the state as constituting the nation, of the imagination of the existence of cultural and often 'racial' homogeneity) has always been partial and incomplete. This is demonstrated by the continued existence of spatially discrete cultural variation within each nation state. One simple example of this is the continuing variation in the use of language and/or dialect within almost all western European nation states (including Britain). Moreover, Britain is not the only western European country wherein political movements for national independence continue to have the potential to bring about a political reconstruction of the nation state: in Italy, Spain and France, the idea that there is a culturally, politically and economically homogeneous nation is contested by a variety of political forces (Foster 1980, Coakley 1992, Woods 1992). Nationalisation is therefore an ongoing rather than a completed process, something that has to be constantly struggled for by the state independently of the consequences of immigration.

Second, there have been antecedent migrations into the nation states of western Europe which have resulted in the permanent settlement of populations which were once identified as culturally and 'racially' distinct. In earlier periods, these migrant populations were signified as a challenge to the then prevailing imagined cultural and 'racial' homogeneity of the nation. In the case of Britain, the Irish, east European Jews, Germans and Poles have all been signified in this way at different times (see Chapters 5 and 6). In France, this happened to Polish, Czech and Iberian immigrants, amongst others (e.g. Noiriel 1984). Historical research shows that the negative ideological response to migration often has common themes, from which one can conclude that it is partly independent of the migrant population and of the conjuncture in which it occurs. The claim that the nation state has recently taken on a multicultural character therefore conceals the cultural transformations initiated by earlier migrations, transformations that are now ignored politically in the quest to create a contemporary sense of cultural homogeneity that has to be defended in relation to some new 'invasion'. The previously excluded become included in the context of the signification of a new 'intruder', and the continuing cultural variation is overlooked in the course of reconstructing the nation as culturally homogeneous *contra* another Other.

Third, the nation state is a political 'community' structurally divided by class. These classes are organised (and partly subdivided) not only economically but also culturally. The notion of the nation state as a culturally homogeneous 'community' therefore suppresses the significance of class-based cultural heterogeneity. In contemporary capitalism, this suppression has special ideological significance because those subordinate classes now considered to be part of the imagined community of the nation were previously excluded from the rights of citizenship. It needs to be remembered that at the beginning of the nineteenth century the struggle for political representation and participation was being conducted by another population permanently settled within the national boundary of European nation states, the 'indigenous' working class, sections of which were regarded by the ruling class as a 'race apart', as in need of 'civilisation' (see Chapter 3).

The significance of a theory of migration is, then, that it gives analytical prominence to central economic and political dimensions of the historical evolution of capitalist societies. Hence, migration is worthy of study not only in and for itself, but also because it refracts a broader set of economic and political processes which are constitutive of past and present social formations dominated by the capitalist mode of production. In sum, the process of migration is so inscribed in the central defining characteristics of the capitalist mode of production that an analysis of those characteristics would be incomplete in the absence of a theory of migration.

THE SIGNIFICANCE AND THE LIMITS OF THE ECONOMIC

There is no doubt that the ever changing demand for labour arising from the capital accumulation process is a major precondition of migration within and into capitalist nation states. It follows that much migration within the capitalist world economy can be designated as labour migration. There is considerable evidence in recent publications to illustrate such a conclusion. It has already been argued that recent work on France (Ogden and White 1989) demonstrates the importance of economic factors in the determination of both internal and international migration flows since the nineteenth century. Several other examples are documented in two wide-ranging overviews of world migration (Appleyard 1988a, Stahl 1988). A book by Sassen (1988) offers a more theoretically grounded analysis of the interplay between recent trends in capital accumulation and international labour migration in the contemporary world economy.

But there is a danger in generalising from this evidence in such a way as to limit the notion of migrant so that it refers exclusively to people who move within and across national frontiers in response to the demands of capital (e.g. Papademetriou 1988). In such analyses, the migrant worker is often stereotyped as a person migrating from the 'Third World' to the 'First World' who has a peasant background and who constitutes a culturally distinct (and sometimes inferior) Other. This stereotype has been encouraged by Marxist analyses of twentieth-century migrant labour flows within South Africa and western Europe (e.g. Meillassoux 1981).

There are good reasons to question this stereotype: it is not that such migrations are of no significance but rather that they are not the only form of migration. For example, the scale of contemporary refugee migrations within Africa and south-east Asia is increasingly well documented (see Appleyard 1988a, Stahl 1988). Events in south America and the Middle East have also created large numbers of refugees (Zolberg *et al.* 1989). Estimates of the numbers of people involved can only loosely approximate the reality, but there is no doubt that there are now many millions of refugees in the world as the end of the twentieth century approaches. However, this contemporary refugee crisis is not unique, except perhaps in terms of its scale: the period immediately after the end of the Second World War was also characterised by a major refugee crisis (Bramwell 1988), although it was largely confined to Europe.

Following the defeat of fascism in Germany and Italy, there was considerable economic and political chaos throughout Europe. One measure of this confusion was the displacement or expulsion of many millions of people from their homes and countries of origin. As national boundaries were redrawn, and as the political composition of governments and nation states were transformed, large numbers of people concluded that there was no 'home' for them to return to. Some 14 million Germans were expelled from eastern German provinces and Czechoslovakia after the war. And there were other population transfers within central and eastern Europe, including the forced resettlement of 2.1 million Poles in western Poland (de Zayas 1988: 23, 27). Between 1.5 and 2.0 million people, mainly from eastern Europe, refused to be repatriated from the western-controlled zones of Europe (Boshyk 1988: 199).

The category of refugee is not universal: an international legal definition of refugee emerged only after 1945 (although certain *ad hoc* definitions had been formulated in the inter-war years) (Melander 1988: 7–10). This legal definition was constructed simultaneously with the development of the 'Cold War', with the result that in western capitalist societies, it was concluded that the post-1945 refugee crisis had been created in Europe largely because of the imposition of communism by the Soviet Union in eastern Europe. Thus, the United Nations definition of

1951 tended to identify as refugees those individual asylum seekers originating from the countries of eastern Europe. This definition has since been modified to include not only individuals who have left a country as a result of having a well-founded fear of persecution but also groups of people who have left because of political events or circumstances. The legal notion of refugee was therefore structured by ideological considerations which refracted the domination of capitalist interests in western Europe and the United States. These considerations are embodied in the common analytical dichotomy which contrasts refugee migrations as *forced* migrations with labour migrations as *free* migrations. This distinction is widely cited and used for analytical purposes (e.g. Richmond 1988a: 111–12). It presents migration in western capitalist economies as the outcome of the free choice of individuals seeking their individual optimal economic advantage. By way of contrast, refugee migrations are seen to result from the political tyranny of communism, a political regime in which individual freedom is said to be denied. Consequently, political repression forces people to migrate in search of freedom. Hence, given the ideological premium placed upon an individualised conception of freedom, this analytical distinction embodies the assumption that capitalism is a superior moral and economic principle of social organisation.

The inadequacy of the distinction is exposed by evidence which demonstrates that a great deal of labour migration is induced, indeed forced, by factors such as rural poverty, land dispossession, taxation and so on (see, for example, Adepoju 1988). Furthermore, taking the other pole of the dichotomy, in most situations which have created refugees, the individual nevertheless has a certain 'freedom' to determine whether or not to migrate. For example, in the case of the 'forced' migration of Jews from fascist Germany in the 1930s, less than a third of German Jews attempted to emigrate from Germany in the period up to November 1938, the majority choosing to remain in the country, despite the increasing repression (Fox 1988: 74).

But in addition to these conceptual considerations, there are empirical reasons to question this dichotomy. For example, between 1945 and the early 1950s, an average of over 20,000 refugees began work annually in the coal mines of the Ruhr, with the result that, by 1950, refugees formed 17 per cent of the mining work force (Roseman 1988: 185). Thus, people who became refugees as a result of political and military events were welcomed as suppliers of labour power by the mine owners of the Ruhr facing a serious labour shortage arising from the reconstruction of the capitalist economy in West Germany. This arrangement was a precursor of a broader trend within the post-war West German economy whereby the labour power of refugees from East Germany and eastern Europe was eagerly recruited by employers desperately short of labour (Herbert 1986).

A similar story can be told regarding the resettlement of the Polish armed forces in Britain in the late 1940s (Sword 1988). Many of these men, along with their dependents, were unwilling to return to Poland following the installation of a communist government in the country, and they therefore comprised in effect a refugee population resident in Britain. Initially, the Labour government was reluctant to grant them the right of settlement in Britain, but as evidence of the seriousness of the labour shortage and of the limited availability of labour elsewhere in western Europe accumulated during 1946, there was a change of policy. By the end of the year, the government had formulated a scheme for the resettlement of Poles in Britain and was actively persuading the trade union movement to accept the recruitment of Polish labour for the coal mines and the farms, and other sectors of the economy. Moreover, when it became apparent that the supply of Polish labour could not meet the demand, the government recruited labour under contract from European refugee camps to fill vacancies in sectors of production considered essential to post-war reconstruction (Kay and Miles 1992).

In these examples, people became spatially mobile primarily as a result of political processes. But their migration was additionally structured by the decision of states to seek an addition to the national labour force. Put another way, labour shortages within nations often lead to refugees being identified as a reserve army of labour by the state, but the origin of this status lies not in the capital accumulation process (as Marx's concept of the reserve army requires), but with political processes and conflicts (see Kay and Miles 1988). In other words, there is good reason to expand the concept of the reserve army to include that stratum of persons displaced by political relations.

The interleaving of the determination of the political and the economic in these latter examples indicates the importance of analysing international migration in a way which highlights the political mediation of the demands of capital. Moreover, the origin of many international migrations lies primarily either in the perceived political imperative on the part of the state to enforce a notion of cultural and 'racial' homogeneity or in the result of political conflict over the nature of the political order which results in the flight of a section of the population.

CONTEMPORARY PATTERNS OF INTERNATIONAL MIGRATION

In the early 1980s, the New York-based Center for Migration Research published a useful overview of evidence and trends concerning post-1945 international migration (Kritz *et al.* 1983). The passage of time and the ever intensifying integration of the capitalist world economy (which reinforces uneven economic development) warrants a new assessment of the continuities and changes that characterise the past decade (cf. Zolberg 1989). On the strength of its title, the two-volume survey jointly published by UNESCO and the University of Western Australia (Appleyard 1988a, Stahl 1988) suggests a comprehensive overview of migration trends, and therefore a more up-to-date foundation for empirical and theoretical discussion.

The content of Appleyard's volume is a disappointment. While a contemporary overview is promised, many of the chapters are as much concerned with (nevertheless helpful) historical analysis as they are with current trends and prospects. Seccombe's essay on the Middle East (1988) is a good example. While useful, this is not what was promised: large numbers of migrant labourers have been recruited to the Middle East since the early 1970s, especially from the Indian subcontinent and from Europe (e.g. Knerr 1990), but these migrations are commonly ignored or analysed in a perfunctory way, perhaps because their occurrence seems inconsistent with the argument that the crisis in the capitalist world system in the early 1970s led to the termination of international labour migration. As we shall see shortly, the crisis of the early 1970s resulted not so much in the termination of international labour migration as in its restructuring. Moreover, there are some significant silences in Appleyard's book which weaken the claim to comprehensiveness. There is no account of, for example, contemporary labour migrations within and into Israel, of migration from eastern Europe into (West) Germany, or of migration within the Indian subcontinent. And no attempt has been made to deal systematically with conceptual and theoretical issues.

Stahl's edited volume (1988) is more useful in so far as it is more tightly organised around a number of specific themes. These include the interrelation between internal and international migration, the position of migrants in the labour market, the effects of emigration and return on the countries of emigration, and female migration. However, many of the papers tread a well-worn path. For example, Gitmez (1988) retells a familiar story concerning the economic activity of returned migrant labourers to Turkey, demonstrating that the original economic objectives of the Turkish state in facilitating the emigration of its citizens have not been realised. Contrary to expectations and policy, returning migrant workers are more likely to purchase personal consumption goods or to invest in land, a café or a taxi business rather than to turn their earnings into industrial capital (cf. Schierup 1990). As a result, the export of labour by the state does little to assist indigenous capitalist development at the periphery of the world capitalist economy.

Moreover, several papers are concerned in various ways with migrant 'adaptation', an emphasis which explains the economic and social position of migrants primarily as the outcome of the migrant's culture or behaviour. The effect of racist ideologies held by, and exclusionary practices effected by, different classes and interest groups within the society in which migrants have settled are either ignored or regarded as minor, secondary determinants. The ideological assumptions involved in presenting the issue in terms of 'immigrant adaptation' are revealed by noting that neither Richmond (1988a) nor Appleyard (1988b), in their analyses of Canada and Australia respectively, consider whether the early European colonisers 'adapted' to the then dominant culture and mode of production of the indigenous populations amongst whom they 'settled'. Of course, we know that very few did. Rather, they legitimated their intervention and exploitation through an articulation of the ideologies of civilisation and racism in the course of suppressing the indigenous cultures and, on certain occasions, of genocide.

Some of the contributors to Stahl's book present both new evidence and theoretically relevant argument. Sassen-Koob's paper is one example, and her argument is developed at greater length in an important book published in the name of Sassen (1988). She questions the prevalent view that, since (and as a result of) the economic crisis of the world capitalist system in the early 1970s, labour migration into the advanced capitalist economies has declined in favour of an export of capital to the peripheries of the system where large supplies of cheap labour have been available (see Fröbel et al. 1981). Her starting point is the empirical evidence that migration to the United States from the Caribbean and Asia has increased continuously since the 1960s, that this migration is composed largely of women, and that this increase has coincided with increasing unemployment within the USA as a result of a restructuring of capital within the country. The apparent paradox of a continuing inward migration coinciding with domestic unemployment is explained by Sassen using a world-systems analytical framework.

She argues that the internationalisation of production, and specifically the increasing levels of capital investment in the peripheries of the world system, have resulted in the proletarianisation of large numbers of women who enter factory wage labour for a few years. Thereafter, having been expelled from the labour force because of declining productivity, they find it difficult to re-enter the social relations of their region of origin, and migration to the USA becomes one of the alternative options. This is in part because the export of capital from the USA has established economic and cultural connections with a number of Caribbean and Asian nation states, and has therefore generated a knowledge of the possibility of a place to migrate to and of the opportunities therein. These 'opportunities' result from the restructuring of capital within the USA which has created a large number of 'new' low-paid service and manufacturing jobs which are unattractive to the indigenous population, including the unemployed, in global cities such as Los Angeles and New York.

While Sassen promises an analysis on a world scale, most of her data and argument concern the United States and the relationship between the economy of the USA and certain parts of the 'Third World'. Furthermore, despite her reservations about explanations for international migration flows which cite poverty and economic stagnation as key variables, her own analysis is largely economic (even economistic) in character, in so far as she explains the 'new immigration' in terms of the interplay of capital export, capital restructuring and female proletarianisation within the capitalist world economic system. Moreover, she reproduces the widespread assumption, central to much recent migration research and theory, that the only significant post-1945 international migration is that of persons seeking semi- and unskilled manual waged labour.

I have already argued that it is difficult to acknowledge and account for refugee migrations within a theory of migration which prioritises the capital accumulation process as the primary determinant. As a result, writers working with a migrant labour theory, including Sassen, pay little or no attention to such migrations. But they also tend to ignore the international migration of a category of persons which is in principle more easily accommodated within that theory. This category is discussed by a number of contributors to another recently edited collection of papers (Appleyard 1989) who refer to either the migration associated with the notion of 'brain drain' or to the migration of professional, technical and managerial labour. Richmond has defined this category of migrants as *transilients* (1988b: 2, see also Price 1989: 144).

Although there are a number of distinct migration flows referred to here, they are all stimulated by a demand for non-manual, mental and/or managerial labour of various kinds. For example, there are migration flows from the periphery to the centre of the world system of young professional, technical and academic workers who live for several years, and often permanently, in the advanced capitalist nation states. They possess skills which are in short supply in both the 'Third' and the 'First' worlds, but they can earn considerably more in the latter than in the former. There are also increasingly large movements of professional and managerial workers between social formations of the centre of the world capitalist system. These include employees of transnational companies, each of which constitutes a form of closed labour market which crosses national boundaries and within which managers and technical staff circulate as they move up the career hierarchy within the company, and self-employed professionals. Where these companies are active in the peripheral social formations of the world system, as in the case of mining and oil companies, there is an additional migration of managerial staff and self-employed professional workers from centre to periphery. Salt and Findlay (1989) offer a useful empirical summary of the available evidence concerning these migrations as well as a series of theoretical reflections which repay further study.

Despite these limitations, Sassen's book represents a major contribution to the debate about the nature and determinants of contemporary migration flows within the capitalist world system because it demonstrates the complexity of the relationship between capitalist crisis, capital accumulation and international migration. Moreover, her analysis of the interplay between international migration and the feminisation of many sectors of wage labour reminds us to ensure that the gender-neutral category of 'migrant' does not lead to an analysis which is gender blind. Since the publication of the pioneering book *One-Way Ticket: Migration and Female Labour* (Phizacklea 1983), the literature on the importance of recent and contemporary female migration has grown considerably.

For example, Morokvasic (1988) and Wilpert (1988) document the significance of certain of the flows of female migration into post-1945 western Europe, exploring in particular the interplay between the entry into wage labour and gender relations in the domestic unit, and the consequent changes in the status and power of women. This is now a well-established theme in studies of female migration, although entry into wage labour is not a universal process. In the case of Pakistani migration to Britain, the early migrants were almost all men, and women generally migrated later (Shaw 1988), after which they tended to provide unpaid domestic labour. They rarely entered the labour market although many were, in addition to providing domestic labour, either directly or indirectly involved in the running of a family business, or were undertaking paid work which could be done in the home. Clearly, the proletarianisation of women through the medium of migration is neither a universal nor a one-dimensional process.

CONCLUSION

By exploring the themes and issues discussed above, the development of a sociology of migration would be an empirically and theoretically rewarding initiative. The contextualisation of post-1945 colonial migration to Britain is long overdue, and would allow consideration of important questions concerning the relative specificity and generality of the process and consequences of migration into advanced capitalist societies. For example, are migrant groups differentially signified by the state in the process of policing the spatial and cultural boundaries of the nation? This question prompts a comparative analysis of the determinants of, and state responses to, migration into Britain over the past two centuries. While parts of the picture have been completed, there is still much to do.

There is a growing awareness of the importance of a comparative European analysis. A body of work already exists (e.g. Castles *et al.* 1984, Hammar 1985), but much of it was published in the early and mid-1980s and the structure of the world capitalist system has changed in a number of important respects since then (see Chapter 8). The political agenda in all western European nation states is now structured by the consequences of post-1945 migration while the nature of the nation state, including the ability of the state to police its boundary and control migration, is being modified with the development of the European Community (EC) as a supranational entity. These changes have important implications for migration flows within and into the EC: the increasing internal mobility of EC 'citizens' is being countered by the erection of new barriers of exclusion at the border of the EC (although the precise position of that border remains an open question in the light of the potential for an increased membership of the EC). Moreover, the collapse of communism in central and eastern Europe has transformed political and economic relations, creating the potential for new migration flows into western Europe, alongside those from Africa and other parts of the periphery.

In order to explore all these developments comparatively, a conceptual framework is needed which utilises criteria of universality but which also allows the exploration of the specificity of developments in each nation state. For reasons set out elsewhere (Miles 1982, Bovenkerk *et al.* 1990), this is best found by means of a political economy of migration. Such a framework needs to take full account of the significance of political and ideological relations in the determination of internal and international migration. Refugee migrations constitute once more a considerable proportion of the sum total of international migration. However, as the argument of this chapter demonstrates, it is not only that many migrations are politically determined (although some are thereafter economically mediated), but also that international migrations determined by labour demand are necessarily mediated by the political institutions of nation and state. For these and other reasons, the dichotomy between refugee and labour migration, at least if simplistically applied, is of limited analytical value.

Moreover, the era of international labour migration is far from over. While the migration of semi- and unskilled (male and female) labour into western Europe has been largely terminated for the time being, similar migrations are under way or continuing elsewhere in the capitalist world system. Furthermore, by challenging the stereotypical equation of migrant with manual wage labourer, one can analyse other large-scale, international migrations of people whose managerial and technical work is more highly rewarded and whose migration is not defined as politically and ideologically problematic by the state. Again, the study of contemporary international migration flows may therefore tell us a great deal about the changing nature of work, and about the consequences of the ongoing circulation, concentration and centralisation of capital, in the world economy.

There is every reason to believe that these migrations will continue, and on an increased scale. Uneven economic development, class conflict and the political instability of many nation states all ensure that a large proportion of the world's population has good reason to consider migration across national boundaries. The continuing high level of capital and scientific investment in transportation technology and systems means that ever larger numbers of people can cross international borders and travel very large distances in very short periods of time. At the centres of the world capitalist system, the demand for certain kinds of labour power remains, and can be solved in principle by international migration. Finally, there were several warnings during the 1980s that the demographic profile of the advanced capitalist nation states will probably mean the intensification of labour shortages in certain sectors of the labour market and of the fiscal crisis of the state in the following two decades. There has never been a greater need for a political economy of international migration.

Chapter 5

Migration history and British racisms

There is nothing wicked in being a German – the Germans are a splendid people. But it is rank hypocrisy to pretend to be an Englishman if by race, tradition, instinct, and affection you are a German working for Germany though living in England.

(Leo Maxse, cited in Panayi 1991: 31)

INTRODUCTION

In Britain, use of the words 'immigration', 'migrant' and 'immigrant' have come to be understood to refer to migrants from the British Caribbean and the Indian subcontinent. Within popular discourse, an immigrant is, by definition, a 'coloured' or 'black' person, and vice versa. Following the public signification of New Commonwealth migration to Britain as a problem, or as giving rise to problems, since the late 1950s (there was a more secret signification within the institutions of the British state from 1947), researchers have analysed these processes. The output is now extensive and refracts the use of different theoretical paradigms.

Within sociology, this migration and its consequences have been widely conceptualised using notions of 'race' and 'race relations'. Attempts to gain a scientific status for these notions have entailed a legitimation of the common-sense discourse of 'race' which is grounded in nineteenth-century, European pseudo-science. This discourse was routinely employed during the nineteenth century to comprehend the British colonial enterprise and, more specifically, social relations between the colonisers and the colonised. Consequently, the colonial situation became understood as a 'race relations' situation: the colonised were usually understood to be an inferior 'race', a biologically distinct population whose future depended upon their assessed capacity for 'civilisation' under the tutelage of the superior 'white' British 'race'.

The post-1945 migrations from the Caribbean and the Indian subcontinent were movements of colonised people. The migrants, while being juridically British subjects, were signified publicly using the discourse generated to comprehend the colonial situation: they were conceived of as distinct 'races' and references to skin colour (usually by use of the descriptor 'coloured'), to blood and to 'stock' were common. But if these migrants were members of one or more 'races', then it followed that the British people too belonged to a 'race'. Hence, there was a simplistic logic to the conclusion that 'coloured immigration' had brought about a 'race relations' situation in Britain, and to the view that the problems of the colonial situation had been imported into Britain.

There has, therefore, been a close articulation between the public and the academic (notably but not exclusively within the discipline of sociology) responses to, and attempts to analyse, post-1945 migration to Britain from the New Commonwealth. Much of the sociological research and writing has consistently challenged the official discourses and the explanations that they implicitly and explicitly contain. But, in other respects, that articulation has taken the form of a legitimation of official discourses, accounts and explanations. In addition to the legitimation of the reification of 'race', there has also been a legitimation of official accounts of, and assumptions about, the composition of migration flows and of the British population of migrant origin. To a large extent, this has been by default rather than by intention.

For example, most sociological research and analysis since the mid-1960s has assumed that the post-1945 migration from the Caribbean and the Indian subcontinent has been either the most important or the only migration to Britain. Yet it is certainly not the only migration to have occurred and it can only be regarded as the most important in a rather specific sense. The occurrence of other migrations, along with the contextualisation of the importance of Caribbean and south Asian migration, is highlighted by adopting a longer-term, historical perspective on migration to Britain.

Broadening the historical canvas on which we work should not be inimical in principle to at least some of those who focus largely or exclusively on New Commonwealth migration as the sole and/or most important post-1945 migration to Britain. Important historical research has demonstrated that those migrants from the Caribbean and the Indian subcontinent who arrived after 1945 were not the first 'black' people to arrive and to settle in Britain. As a result, there is now a substantial body of work documenting the history of African, Indian and Caribbean migration to Britain, and the historicity of the African, Indian and

Caribbean presence in Britain (e.g. Fryer 1984, Visram 1986, Ramdin 1987). Thus, not only is the history of British intervention in the emergent world capitalist system intimately bound up with the labour power of colonised peoples in at least three different continents, but equally British domestic history is founded in part on the labour power and presence of these same colonised peoples. As the radical 'race' paradigm might express it, British domestic history is therefore not just a 'white' history but also a 'black' history.

But if historical analysis is considered to have important implications for the way in which we analyse post-1945 migration from the Caribbean and the Indian subcontinent, we can legitimately enquire about the history of other migrations. And once we begin to document these other migrations as social historians have begun to do, and to consider their impact, it becomes clear that this post-1945 migration from the Caribbean and the Indian subcontinent is anomalous in certain respects.

EUROPE IN BRITAIN

While British migration history is first a history of emigration (e.g. Baines 1985, Constantine 1991), it is one of the contradictions of capitalist development that the same forces that encourage the emigration from the nation state of the dispossessed and the politically unwanted also encourage the arrival of the dispossessed and the unwanted from other nation states. Thus, in the early nineteenth century, the boats that were sailing to various parts of the British Empire carrying Britain's surplus population were, at certain times, passing boats travelling to Britain carrying other surplus populations. Moreover, numerically speaking, the vast majority of migrants to Britain since the early nineteenth century have been of European origin (Miles and Solomos 1987): migrants originating from British colonies constitute only a very small proportion of the total number of migrants until the end of the 1950s.

Numerically, the most important migration originated from Ireland and has a history which extends back over several centuries. The scale of the migration increased substantially during the early and mid-nineteenth century (Miles 1982), and by 1861 805,717 Irish people were resident in Britain (Holmes 1988: 20). The volume of the migration decreased during the second half of the nineteenth century, but it nevertheless continued into the twentieth century: 631,629 Irish people were resident in 1901 (Holmes 1988: 21). By 1931, the number had fallen to 489,043 (Holmes 1988: 119–20). During the Second World War, migration from the Republic of Ireland was controlled for the first time by the British state and some 60,000 Irish people were employed under contract (Holmes 1988: 164). These controls were removed in 1947 and migration increased once more. The 1951 Census recorded 716,028 Irish people resident in Britain, and by 1971 this had expanded to 957,830 (Holmes 1988: 216). During the following decade, there was a decline in the total number of Irish-born people living in Britain: the 1981 Census recorded 607,000 Irish-born residents (Garvey 1985: 28). It is relevant to the subsequent argument to note that these statistics record only those people resident in Britain who were born in Ireland: they therefore exclude people born in Britain whose mother and/or father was born in Ireland (i.e. people who might be described as being of Irish ethnic origin).

The second largest migration from Europe has been of Jews, first from Russia at the end of the nineteenth century, and then from Germany during the 1930s. Assessing the scale of the first migration is difficult because not all those who arrived in Britain during the late nineteenth century from Russian Poland were Jews (although the majority were, their migration stimulated largely by persecution and only secondarily by material deprivation) and because many used Britain as a point of transit to the United States. In England, the largest number settled in London, while in Scotland, Glasgow was the main city of settlement (Lipman 1990: 50, Collins 1990). The 1901 Census records 82,844 Russian Poles resident in England and Wales, a figure that increased to 95,541 by 1911 (Holmes 1988: 26). The second migration, while also having its origin in political persecution, was composed of a very different Jewish population from Germany, a large proportion of whom were professionals and academics. Approximately 50,000 Jews entered Britain between 1933 and 1939 and a further 10,000 during the Second World War (Holmes 1988: 119, 163).

Several other European migrations have occurred at various times since the 1850s. During the latter half of the nineteenth century, there was a migration from Germany and, three years before the outbreak of the First World War, the Census recorded 53,324 Germans resident in England and Wales (Panayi 1991: 11). This population became the object of considerable hostility during the war: there were five separate outbreaks of anti-German rioting involving attacks on people and property, large numbers of Germans were interned and some were deported, German businesses were confiscated or destroyed and German employees were dismissed (Panayi 1988, 1989, 1991, Yarrow 1989). Further deportations were effected after the war was over in a political atmosphere of intense 'anti-alienism' which will be discussed further below (Cesarani 1987). Italian migration to Britain also increased during the nineteenth century, especially during the twenty years before the First World War: the 1911 Census recorded the presence of over 25,000 Italians in Britain (Sponza 1988: 13, Colpi 1991: 47–9). They, too, became the object of specific 'anti-foreigner' agitation at certain times, although this never cohered into an extensive political mobilisation against the Italian presence (Sponza 1988: 5–6, 267–9).

In the aftermath of the Second World War, the British government confronted a labour shortage which it regarded as a major obstacle to its reconstruction of British capitalism. At one point, the government calculated that more than a million additional workers would need to be found from outside Britain in order to resolve the shortage, although this estimate was later scaled down (Kay and Miles 1988: 215). But at the very same time that the government turned to various sources of European labour to resolve the problem, the first post-Second World War migrants from the British Caribbean began to arrive.

A number of different European sources were drawn upon (Miles 1990b) and these are described in more detail in Chapter 6. As a result of these various migrations and resettlement schemes, the number of aliens living in Britain increased substantially. In 1939, 239,000 aliens were estimated to be resident and by 1950 this had increased to 429,329 persons, although not all were of European origin (Holmes 1988: 214). Moreover, European migration to Britain continued after 1951, stimulated in part by state initiatives to recruit Italian labour for the coal- and tin-mining industries. Employers also initiated the recruitment of Italian labour (notably in the brick-making industry) and, in addition, the development of the catering industry led to the reopening of a more informal chain migration based on earlier Italian settlement (Colpi 1991: 136–58). As a result, between 1951 and 1971, the number of Italians living in Britain increased from 38,427 to 108,985 persons (Holmes 1988: 214, Colpi 1991: 135) The post-1945 increase in Irish migration has already been noted, and one should also refer to the migration from Cyprus and Malta that took place during the 1950s, although these people arrived as British subjects rather than aliens (Holmes 1988: 227). Finally, there has been a continuing migration under the terms of the work-permit system, although not all of these migrants originated from Europe.

Against the background of this outline history of European migration to Britain, in what senses is the New Commonwealth migration that began in the late 1940s anomalous? First, at the time that it began, it was a migration of British *subjects*. Within the context of British law, the various European migrants (with one important exception, detailed below) were all classified juridically as *aliens*. Because they were nationals of other states, they had no formal right to enter and settle in Britain and could only do so within the framework of a set of regulations and obligations drawn up and administered by the British state. The principle legislation governing the entry of aliens into Britain was introduced during the fifteen years between 1905 and 1920 (Dummett and Nicol 1990: 92–112).

But British subjects were exempt from these immigration controls. In itself, it is not unusual that nationals of a nation state are able to leave and enter without restriction (see Chapter 6 for further discussion of this point). However, the category of British subject included many millions of people living outside the United Kingdom: because the category referred to all those people who were *subject to* the authority of the British crown, it included not only the vast majority of the population ordinarily resident in the United Kingdom, but also the vast majority of the population of the British colonies and self-governing dominions. Although, under the terms of the British Nationality Act of 1948 this broad category had been subdivided into two, both citizens of the United Kingdom and colonies and citizens of independent Commonwealth nation states retained the right of entry into Britain. For certain categories of British subject (primarily those signified as 'coloured'), these rights were withdrawn by various Acts passed between 1962 and 1971 (Miles and Phizacklea 1984).

The exception concerns the Irish. Throughout the nineteenth century, the Irish were British subjects and were therefore exempt from immigration control. What is now the Republic of Ireland achieved political independence in 1921, although initially it remained within the Commonwealth, with the result that Irish citizens remained, in British law, British subjects and so retained the right of entry into Britain. Even after the Republic of Ireland declared itself a republic and left the Commonwealth, the British government granted the Republic a unique legal status by treating it as if it remained in the Commonwealth, with the result that its citizens retained the right to enter and settle in Britain without restriction (Dummett and Nicol 1990: 128–9). Furthermore, Irish citizens were exempted from the provisions of the Commonwealth Immigrants Act of 1962.

New Commonwealth migration may also be considered to be anomalous with respect to its scale. Between 1955 and 1960, 211,640 migrants from the Caribbean and the Indian subcontinent arrived in Britain (Deakin 1970: 50). This is considerably less than the number of Irish who migrated to Britain in the same period. Moreover, in 1961, the total number of aliens resident in Britain (415,700) was larger than the number of British subjects originating from the Caribbean and the Indian subcontinent (Walvin 1984: 111). Even in 1971, after the substantial increase in New Commonwealth immigration prompted by the threat and then the introduction of immigration controls on British subjects from Commonwealth countries (Walvin 1984: 110–14), the number of Irish-born resident in Britain was greater than the number of people born in the Caribbean and the Indian subcontinent (Holmes 1988: 216).

With immigration from the Caribbean and the Indian subcontinent strictly controlled by the mid-1960s, the focus of political attention shifted away from the level of migration *per se* and towards the size of the population of New Commonwealth origin, i.e. to include those born in Britain to parents who themselves originated from the Caribbean and the Indian subcontinent. In official discourse, the object of attention became 'ethnic minorities'. Thus, official data for the mid-1980s show that the average size of the ethnic minority population was 2.43 million persons (Shaw 1988: 5). But such a statistic is a product of the definitions used by the state to collect the information. To be considered as an 'ethnic minority', it is necessary to identify oneself as one of the following: West Indian, African, Pakistani, Bangladeshi, Chinese, Arab, Mixed or Other. Other than being an 'Other', the only remaining choice is to classify oneself as 'White' (Shaw 1988).

There is, therefore, no way of knowing whether, for example, the size of the population living in Britain of Irish origin is, collectively, greater than the total size of the 'ethnic minority' population. But, given the scale of Irish migration over the past century and a half, it almost certainly is. Significantly, there has been a campaign to have the Irish officially recognised as an 'ethnic group' and to make provision in the 1991 Census for people of Irish origin to define themselves as Irish rather than 'White' or 'Other' (*The Independent on Sunday*, 2 September 1990). Potentially, in the light of British migration history, there are other European 'ethnic groups' who might wish to make similar demands in the future.

POLICING THE FRONTIER: THE RACIALISATION OF EUROPEAN IMMIGRATION

The political and ideological response to New Commonwealth migration after 1945 is well documented (e.g. Miles and Phizacklea 1984, Solomos 1990). The racialisation (see Green and Carter 1987, Miles 1989a, 1989b) of this migration of British subjects was a key dimension of the ideological response which resulted in the hegemonic view that immigration had brought about a 'race relations' problem in Britain. By adopting a historical perspective, we can consider whether these post-1945 events have been unique. Was there a similarly hostile response to earlier migrations of European reaction? If so, what was the ideological content of that response? And what role did the state play? The role of the latter is crucial because it polices the national borders, identifying the populations which constitute an acceptable presence and those which constitute an unacceptable presence (Bovenkerk *et al.*).

I am particularly concerned here with political debates that have taken place in situations where agents of the state evaluate the potential sources of immigration or where agents of the state engage in debate about the introduction of restrictions on immigration or the deportation from its territory of a population of migration origin. These are all situations where the state defines what can be called the 'criteria of belonging', that is, the characteristics that are considered essential to become a member of the imagined community that is called the nation.

To varying degrees, all of these European migrations have been racialised: that is to say, the migrant population has been signified as a distinct category or type of human being by reference to real or alleged biological characteristics, a signification that has usually been accompanied by an explicit or implicit use of the discourse of 'race'. Elsewhere, I have shown how Irish migrants to Britain during the nineteenth and early twentieth centuries were racialised (Miles 1982). Similar processes of signification occurred in Britain in response to the migrations from eastern Europe and Germany in the late nineteenth century and again at the end of the First World War, as a result of which immigration was widely considered to have created an 'alien problem' in Britain.

Commencing halfway through the penultimate decade of the nineteenth century, a political campaign against the settlement of immigrants from eastern Europe achieved prominence (Garrard 1971: 23–47, Gainer 1972: 60–73). Those involved in the campaign consistently exaggerated the scale of the immigration (Gainer 1972: 6–14) and demanded the introduction of an immigration law which would permit the state to control and limit the entry of Jewish refugees from eastern Europe. Despite the fact that these refugees comprised only about one third of the total foreign population, the notions of 'immigrant' and 'alien' became synonymous in everyday life with that of Jew (Gainer 1972: 3, Lipman 1990: 67).

Moreover, Jewishness was increasingly interpreted as a quality determined by blood, and therefore as hereditary and ineradicable. References to the existence of a Jewish 'race' became common. This 'race' was signified as an alien presence that had the potential to destroy civilised society through the promotion of an international conspiracy: consequently, the Jews became the racialised 'enemy within' (Holmes 1979: 63–88, Lebselter 1981: 88–9, 92, Dummett and Nicol 1990: 98–9). Allegations that Jews were especially involved in criminal activity, that their life-style or their very nature encouraged disease and perversion (including venereal disease and sexual perversion), and that they were exclusive (Garrard 1971: 53, Gainer 1972: 46–52, Holmes 1979: 17–18, 37–46, Gilman 1990: 154–67) took on another level of meaning in this ideological context: such attributes became widely interpreted as 'racial' characteristics (cf. Pollak 1992: 77–107).

These racialised definitions were transformed and reinvigorated in the early decades of the twentieth century. I have already noted that legislation regulating the entry of aliens into Britain was introduced immediately preceding and after the First World War. This legislation was formulated and implemented in a conjuncture dominated by a process of defining another Other: given the events that led up to the war, and the war itself, one of the main objects of this struggle was people of German origin. Assertions about the existence of a German conspiracy multiplied, and myths about the German 'national character' which signified Germans as having certain (negatively evaluated) natural attributes were widely articulated (Panayi 1988). The categories of 'German' and 'Jew' were often used synonymously (Lebselter 1981: 96, Panayi 1988, Cesarani 1992), fusing the anti-Jewish racism of the late nineteenth century with nationalist stereotypes of Germans which themselves often contained a racialised (if not racist) content.

For example, Leo Maxse wrote repeatedly (in journals such as the *National Review*) about distinct German, and English 'races' and his evaluation of the qualities of the German 'race' became exceedingly negative as the war proceeded. Moreover, he fused the categories of German and Jew: 'The victory of Germany is for some mysterious reason a desideratum of almost the entire Jewish race' (cited in Panayi 1991: 163). An explanation was offered by another contributor to the *National Review* in 1915:

> The Jew understands the German . . . he is drawn towards a dream of universal empire, won by gold or iron, in which a religious clan, scattered through the nations, shall rule them by virtue of its racial excellence, or the 'master-folk'.
>
> (cited in Panayi 1991: 163)

Following the use of poison gas by the German armed forces in April 1915 and the sinking of the *Lusitania* in the following month, the stereotypes of the German 'race' became intensely hostile. Lord Derby was one of many leading public figures who made his views widely known. He declared that 'this country calls no longer for men to fight an honourable foe. It calls for men to hunt down and crush once and for all a race of cold-blooded murderers' (cited in Panayi 1991: 230). An articulation with colonial racist imagery occurred in the claim by the *Daily Express* that 'we must expect the Germans to fight like savages who have acquired a knowledge of chemistry' (cited in Panayi 1991: 231). This articulation was expressed even more vividly in an article by Horatio Bottomley, who called for a vendetta against Germans because 'you cannot naturalise an unnatural beast – a human abortion – a hellish freak. But you *can* exterminate it. And now the time has come'. He advocated fielding (cited in Panayi 1991: 233)

> an army of Zulus and Basutos and other native and half-civilised tribes – and let them run amok in the enemy's ranks. I would give them all the asphyxiating gas they wanted. I would allow no prisoners to be taken, on either land or sea; and I would do a lot of other things.

These racist conceptions can be explained in part by the events and nature of war involving a state (the British) that, since the end of the nineteenth century, had become increasingly concerned about the challenge to its industrial, political and military world supremacy (Summers 1981: 73–4). One such challenge came from Germany, and in this context hostility towards the German state and the 'German people' had been expressed and encouraged by various social forces before the war began. But while this explains the hostility and highly negative signification of Germans, it does not by itself explain the racialised form in which this hostility was expressed. The racist conception of the German population, both in Germany and in Britain, demonstrates that the discourse of 'race' remained central to conceptualising all 'Others' in the early twentieth century, whether of European or colonial origin. Concerning the former, the racialised conception of nation, a conception which typified each nation as *naturally* distinct, provided the ideological foundation for the expression of specific racisms (see Chapters 2 and 3).

During the war, right-wing groups called for changes to immigration and naturalisation legislation. For example, the British Empire Union campaigned for changes in naturalisation law in order to 'preserve effectively the heritage of British blood' from any 'foreign tramp who asks for it [i.e. naturalisation] at the Home Office' (cited in Panayi 1991: 203). Immediately after the war ended, the government pledged itself to expel 'enemy aliens' and, by April 1919, 19,000 Germans had been repatriated (Cesarani 1987: 6). But this repatriation marked the extension of the ideological and political offensive against 'aliens', and not its termination. Early in 1919, the government introduced the Aliens Restriction (Amendment) Bill in order to strengthen and to make permanent the temporary provisions of the Aliens Restriction Act of 1914 (Dummett and Nicol 1990). During the debate on the second reading of the bill, the discourse of 'blood' was introduced as justification for the legislation. One MP argued: 'They proved before the war and demonstrated to the satisfaction of every Briton that a German is always a German . . . . We do not want German blood any more in this country. We have had it in high places, and we want no more' (Hansard 1919, 114: col. 2799).

During the wider political debate about this legislation, three populations were signified as a problematic presence. First, there was a lingering desire to find additional ways of punishing the defeated foe, the 'Hun'. In addition, two 'new' enemies were found. These were trade union radicals or 'Bolshevik sympathisers', and Jews, including those who had arrived as refugees in the late nineteenth century as well as the longer-established Jewish community, a proportion of which formed part of the British bourgeoisie (Holmes 1979: 109, Lipman 1990: 60–1, 77–8). These three categories of people were all explicitly defined as 'aliens' and, in some discourses, the three distinct groups were merged into a single category. Collectively, this Other constituted the quintessential 'alien' (Cesarani 1987: 8, Dummett and Nicol 1990: 109–12).

This discourse revived the duality of 'alien' and Jew that had been constructed in the late nineteenth century in the course of the political agitation against the entry of Jewish refugees from Russia. Moreover, this duality signified the 'alien' as a distinct 'race'. For example, Sir John Pedder, in his capacity of Permanent Under-Secretary of State, and writing in May 1924, referred to 'Slavs, Jews and other races from Central and Eastern parts of Europe' (cited in Cesarani 1987: 17). In becoming effectively synonymous, the notions of alien and Jew were once more attributed with an additional level of meaning by being embedded in a discourse of 'race'.

Professor Karl Pearson went on to draw conclusions regarding immigration. Although Pearson was a professor of Applied Mathematics and Mechanics who made a major contribution to statistical analysis, his main passion was the study of human biology. In a lecture given in 1903, Pearson expressed the worry that 'the mentally better stock in the nation is not reproducing itself' (cited in Barkan 1992: 156). The task of improving the national 'stock' was, in Pearson's view, made more difficult by immigration. Concerned that Britain could be 'swamped by the influx of immigrants of an inferior race', Pearson identified the Jewish presence as an 'alien population' which was 'inferior physically and mentally to the native population', and proposed that Jewish immigrants be settled in Palestine or some other location far away from western Europe (cited in Holmes 1979: 36, 216–17). Pearson's interest in Jewish immigration continued into the 1920s, when he initiated a large-scale research project titled 'The Problem of Alien Immigration into Great Britain, Illustrated by an Examination of Russian and Polish Jewish Children', the results of which were published in five long articles in the *Annals of Eugenics* from 1925 onwards (Barkan 1992: 154–5). Pearson's racist claims were subsequently cited by those actively involved in fascist organisations during the 1930s.

Thus, from the 1870s through to 1939, the idea of 'race' was central to the signification of Jews in Britain as a distinct and alien population (Holmes 1979: 221, 227–9, see also Lebselter 1981, Cheyette 1989). The spurious idea of a Jewish conspiracy intent on world domination also gained ground, the immediate object being Jewish members of the bourgeoisie, but working-class and petit-bourgeois Jews were also the object of agitation on the grounds that they equally belonged to an alien 'race' which could not be 'assimilated', as we shall see shortly. Moreover, this racism did not disappear as a result of the war against German fascism and racism: it remained a significant ideological force during and after the Second World War (Kushner 1989, Cesarani 1992).

However, not all migrant populations have been racialised in an exclusively negative manner. Racialised discourses can attribute negative and/or positive attributes. Potentially, migrant populations can be racialised in such a way that they are evaluated as a beneficial presence, as populations possessing characteristics which are likely to make a positive contribution to the nation. One of the more remarkable examples of this form of racialisation occurred in the aftermath of the Second World War. Faced with a major labour shortage, the Labour government chose, with some reluctance, to resolve it, in part, by the large-scale recruitment of foreign labour (Kay and Miles 1992). By late 1946, a scheme for the resettlement of Poles had been formulated and implemented, and the European Volunteer Worker Scheme (EVW) was in its early phase of development (Tannahill 1958, Sword *et al.* 1989). The government remained hesitant, not least because there were signs of significant working-class opposition. But, as the economic and political crisis of 1947 escalated, a debate in the House of Commons was initiated on the subject of the displaced persons in European refugee camps, from whom volunteers were being sought for the EVW scheme.

The debate is remarkable for the vigour with which Labour and Conservative MPs called for an increase in immigration in order to expand the labour supply. It is equally remarkable because of the way in which the displaced persons were racialised. With the case for immigration established, the concern was to find the most suitable 'races and nationalities' that would not only provide labour power but also possess the kind of 'vigorous blood' that could be expected to benefit 'our stock'. The displaced persons were regarded as meeting these requirements, and so as likely to be transformed into 'good Britons' (Miles 1989c, 1990b).

Such a positive and unitary racialisation of displaced persons was not universal. For example, during the early phase of the EVW scheme, state officials distinguished between female recruits from the Baltic states, who were positively racialised and female recruits from the Ukraine, who were described as being of 'peasant stock' and so liable to age more quickly (Kay and Miles 1988: 220–1). This distinction was subsequently broadened in terms of a north/south divide: officials regarded those from the northern regions of eastern Europe to be 'superior types' who were eminently 'assimilable', while those from the south were often loosely described as being of the 'Slav race' and more 'racially distinct'. In the course of an investigation of what was seen to be the high rate of mental breakdown and suicides amongst certain EVWs, a Home Office psychiatrist referred to the likelihood that 'suicide came more easily to the Slav than to the Nordic races' (Kay and Miles 1992: 142–3).

The racialisation of migrant populations therefore has a history which precedes the post-1945 migration of British subjects from the Caribbean and the Indian subcontinent. Similarly, there is a long history of the British state responding to immigration using the discourse of 'assimilation'. As with the discourse of 'race', the notion is used as if its meaning and referent were a matter of common sense: the resulting imprecision and flexibility ensure that it can then effect powerful ideological work. In order to assess the meaning of the notion of 'assimilation' and the work that it does, I consider the same historical period as discussed in the immediately preceding paragraphs.

Parallel with the anti-alien agitation after the First World War, concern developed during the 1920s about the length of time the Home Office was taking to process applications by Jewish aliens for naturalisation. It was common for two years to pass between the original application being made and the request being granted. Although it did not make its rationale public, the principal reason was that the Home Office was operating a discriminatory policy based on racist beliefs about the 'assimilability' of

Jews. The practice was not to consider applications from certain 'races' until they had lived in Britain for a period that was considerably in excess of the statutory minimum of five years. This was justified by Sir John Pedder in the following way (cited in Cesarani 1987: 17):

> It rests on experience that different races display very different qualities and capabilities for identifying themselves with this country. Speaking roughly, the Latin, Teuton and Scandinavian races, starting some of them, with a certain kinship with British races, are prompt and eager to identify themselves with the life and habits of this country and are easily assimilated. On the other hand, Slavs, Jews and other races from Central and Eastern parts of Europe stand in a quite different position. They do not want to be assimilated in the same way and do not readily identify themselves with this country. Even the British born Jews, for instance, always speak of themselves as a 'community', separate to a considerable degree and different from the British people.

In addition to confirming that the idea of 'race' was a central structuring principle in official thinking about the consequences of immigration, this official memorandum equates assimilation with the willingness and capacity of immigrants to identify themselves with the British state and the idea of the British nation. The negative reference to the establishment of 'separate communities' also implies that assimilation is to be equated with the adoption of 'British values, customs and habits' (which are rarely specified) and the renunciation of a set of social relations and obligations in which people of a specific migrant and cultural origin are involved.

There are strong echoes here of the report of the Royal Commission on Alien Immigration, published in 1903, which chronicled the nature of official discourse that shaped the context in which the Aliens Act of 1905 was passed. The Commission had investigated the 'evil' of alien immigration, and had identified the migration of the Jewish 'race' from eastern Europe as the focus of its concern. Noting that, amongst the alleged 'evils', it was widely believed that alien immigrants had 'become a compact, non-assimilating community', that 'they do not assimilate and intermarry with the native race, and so remain a solid and distinct colony' (1903: 6), it concluded, *inter alia*, that 'the great bulk of Immigrants accumulate in the localities where men of their race and religion are dwelling, and where identity of language and habits mitigate the inconveniences and difficulties arising from dwelling in a foreign land' (1903: 10). The Commission also noted not only that 'the increase in the foreign population within these areas has caused the abandonment of houses almost of whole streets, by the English working classes, and their occupation by foreigners' (1903: 22), but that it had also led to the abandonment of shops because the 'Alien Immigrant prefers to deal with those who are of his race, speaking his own language, rather than with strangers' (1903: 25).

This report was referred to by state officials who initiated thinking in the late 1940s about the implications of the decision to grant Poles settlement rights in Britain and of the possibility of EVWs becoming permanent settlers. The recovery of this report ensured the persistence of the notion of assimilation as a determinant of state intervention. For once it had become accepted within the state that large numbers of first the Poles, and later the EVWs, were destined to become permanent settlers, the discourse of assimilation became widely used and assimilation became a policy objective. The crucial assumption was that, as was explicitly stated by the Dowager Marchioness of Reading in April 1948, 'we were a homogeneous nation and we must make every effort to assimilate the Poles and EVWs' (cited in Kay and Miles 1992: 133).

But the practice of assimilation was in fact primarily the responsibility of the Poles and the EVWs, for it was they who were expected to learn the English language and to behave in accordance with British ways and customs. As evidence accumulated showing that the Poles and the EVWs were not learning the English language, that they continued to identify themselves with the nation states from which they originated, and that they were forming 'exclusive communities', official concern increased. Such was the strength and persistence of this resistance to becoming 'British' that, by 1949, government and state officials began to acknowledge that the battle might have been lost. In some circles, it was concluded that the 'best elements of national character' should be retained and combined with those of the British (Kay and Miles 1992).

The internal discussion within the state about the Poles and EVWs in the late 1940s reveals another dimension of the discourse of assimilation. Officials were also concerned about what 'our own people will stand'. Thus, during the parliamentary debate on displaced persons in early 1947, one of the speakers suggested that it was necessary to bring about 'a complete mental readjustment on the part of the people of this country' because of their hostility to 'foreigners' (Miles 1989c). Concealed behind this evaluation was a concern about 'law and order': in other words, what was to be avoided at all costs was active resistance by British citizens to this foreign presence. One measure of whether or not assimilation had taken place, therefore, was the persistence of social order. And the best way of ensuring this was not only to require the foreigners to 'become just like us' so that they too subordinated themselves to the state, and to the hegemonic notion of the nation. In addition, 'our own people' had to accept their presence as legitimate and inevitable. In other words, assimilation policy was addressed not only to the Poles and the EVWs, but also to British citizens who had to learn that the migration of aliens was, if they did not already know it, 'in their own interests'.

In the course of policing the national frontier during the last one hundred and fifty years, the British state has persistently employed the interrelated discourses of 'race' and 'assimilation' to comprehend the consequences of opening the door to the nation to various Others on the other side. It is the continuity of this discourse, irrespective of the origin and specific attributed characteristics of the migrant population, that is remarkable, suggesting that we might seek for an explanation in the more general structural characteristics and processes of the social formation as much as in the historically specific circumstances in which the discourse has been employed.

RACISM, CLASS RELATIONS AND IMMIGRATION

Much ink has been used to discuss the articulation of racism and class relations in Britain following New Commonwealth migration to Britain but little attention has been devoted to earlier periods. In the light of the history of European migration to Britain, and of its racialisation, is there any value in reconsidering this history with this articulation in mind? I believe that there is.

Analyses of British immigration law conclude routinely that it is motivated by and expressive of racism. While most attention has been devoted to the period since 1945, it is not unusual for writers to search for continuities with the legislation passed in the first half of the twentieth century (e.g Gordon 1985, Dummett and Nicol 1990). This earlier period, and specifically the first British immigration act of the twentieth century (i.e. the Aliens Act of 1905), warrants examination because the main object of political debate and agitation was a population of European origin. The Aliens Act of 1905 was certainly motivated by racism but it simultaneously embodied another exclusionary principle (Miles 1991d): as a result, this legislation provides an example of the articulation of racism and class in the creation of a structure of exclusion.

For most of the nineteenth century, there were no state controls over people entering or leaving Britain and the British state proudly declaimed its acceptance of the principle of asylum (Porter 1979). Migrants, aliens as well as British subjects, crossed the national border in both directions

(Miles and Solomos 1987: 76–9), including many thousands of Jews from Russian Poland during the last quarter of the century (Lipman 1990: 43–4). The arguments deployed in favour of restricting or terminating the entry of these refugees were economic and ideological in character. In part, the refugees were identified as unnecessary competition with the indigenous population for access to scarce resources such as accommodation and jobs (Garrard 1971: 51, Holmes 1979: 15–16, 1988: 68, Lipman 1990: 68). This resulted in, so the argument continued, reduced living standards for 'our own people'. But they were also seen by some who participated in the agitation as an undesirable presence *per se* because, during the nineteenth century, Jews (like so many other populations) had been racialised.

We have seen that a Royal Commission on Aliens was appointed in 1902. Even though its report, published the following year, concluded that many of the allegations made against Jewish alien immigrants could not be supported by the evidence, it recommended that controls on immigration be introduced (Lipman 1990: 70–1). While previous attempts to legislate had failed for various reasons (Gainer 1972: 166–90), this recommendation strengthened the hand of those agitating in favour of restriction. The result was the Aliens Act of 1905 which gave powers to immigration officers to prevent 'undesirable immigrants' from entering Britain (Gainer 1972: 191).

The Act defined an 'immigrant' as an alien who travelled in a ship as a 'steerage passenger', a category that was distinguished from a 'cabin passenger'. The meaning and significance of this distinction will be discussed shortly. The Act also listed several criteria of undesirability, including lunacy, idiocy, and possession of a criminal record. Additionally, an immigrant could be designated as undesirable if 'he cannot show that he has in his possession or is in a position to obtain the means of decently supporting himself and his dependents (if any)' (Section 1[3]). The Act granted a right of appeal to those aliens refused entry on these grounds.

The Act did not attempt to regulate the entry of all aliens into Britain (only those defined as 'undesirable immigrants') and it excluded from its powers 'an immigrant who proves that he is seeking admission to this country solely to avoid prosecution or punishment on religious or political grounds' (Section 1[3]). The Act therefore had a very specific object. Significantly, the formal definition of that object did not include any explicit reference to either 'race' or Jews. And a large proportion of those who advocated control within and outside Parliament consistently claimed that they were not motivated by 'anti-semitism' (Garrard 1971: 57).

Yet, in so doing, they reproduced and legitimated a racialised discourse (e.g. Garrard 1971: 66).

Was the Act racist? If one conceives the concept of racism to refer to a theory of biological inferiority and superiority and if one takes the text of the legislation in isolation, the answer would have to be negative for the reasons already stated: the Act makes no reference to 'race' or to Jews (cf. Holmes 1979: 101). But if we analyse the Act in its political and ideological context, it is relevant that it was formulated and implemented at a time when a negative, racialised representation of Jews was widely reproduced. Whether intentionally or inadvertently, the Act legitimated this racist stereotype of Jews: the formal definition of 'undesirable immigrant' in the Act was understood in the everyday world to refer to Jews, a population that was signified as a 'race apart'.

Furthermore, irrespective of its formal content, the practical intention of the Act was to reduce the number of Jewish refugees from eastern Europe entering Britain. Whether or not it was successful in achieving this objective is difficult to assess. While there was a decline in the number of aliens from Russia and Poland who were admitted after 1906, the migration was not terminated by the Act: the Act deterred but did not prohibit alien immigration (Gainer 1972: 202, 210, Lipman 1990: 45, 73). Nevertheless, immigration controls on aliens were introduced at a time when the consequences were experienced by Jewish refugees in particular.

The significance of class relations is revealed by exploring further the content of the Aliens Act of 1905: we have not yet examined all the dimensions of the definition of 'undesirable immigrant'. Not all aliens seeking to enter Britain were defined by the Act as 'undesirable' or 'immigrants'. 'Undesirable' immigrants included aliens who could not show that they had sufficient money to support themselves or their 'dependents', but *not* those who could demonstrate that they did possess adequate financial resources. Furthermore, the definition of 'immigrant' included aliens travelling in the steerage section of a ship (that is, in the section containing the cheapest accommodation) but excluded those who could pay for a cabin. Hence, under the terms of the Act, aliens arriving in Britain who could afford to pay for a cabin and/or who could show that they were in a position to support themselves 'decently' were exempt from immigration control. This was acknowledged by the government after the end of the First World War when it was justifying an extension of controls over alien immigration in the form of the Aliens Restriction Bill in April 1919 (Hansard 1919, 114: cols 2748, 2775).

Analysis of the criteria embodied in the Act to define the object of control shows therefore that the primary criterion of 'undesirability' was economic. Wealthy aliens were not subject to the new procedures of immigration control but poor aliens were. Given that the majority of Jewish refugees arriving in Britain from eastern Europe in the latter quarter of the nineteenth century possessed few economic resources, they were subject to control under the terms of the Act. But the Act did not seek to control or prohibit Jewish immigration *per se*: alien Jews who could afford to pay for a cabin and/or who could show that they had sufficient resources to support themselves could enter Britain without restriction.

The concept of institutional racism has some utility in analysing these circumstances. In a conjuncture where anti-Jewish sentiment and practices were considered to be disreputable (Holmes 1979: 104), and yet where there was popular agitation for the state to control the entry of alien Jewish refugees, and where this particular category of migrants constituted a significant proportion of the total inward migration, it was possible for the state to implement and enforce controls to this end without identifying Jews by name. Given that most alien Jewish refugees from eastern Europe did not possess the means by which they could 'decently support themselves', use of this criterion of 'undesirability' could function effectively in practice to control their entry into Britain. The consequence of the Act, irrespective of its formal content, was to deliver to the state the power to control the entry of alien Jewish refugees from eastern Europe.

The racist dimension of the exclusion was therefore covert: the mechanism of exclusion was concealed in an articulation between the specific conjuncture in which the Aliens Act was formulated and the formal terms of the legislation. This obviated any need to define alien Jews explicitly as the object of legislation or to provide a legitimation which claimed that Jews were an 'inferior' or 'degenerate race'. Yet, many of those advocating control used explicitly racist arguments: Jews in general were increasingly signified as a distinct 'race' characterised by undesirable attributes, and the consequences of the Act were experienced primarily by alien Jewish refugees. Hence, the practice of exclusion was institutionalised in such a way that the racism that partly motivated and justified it was obscured (cf. Miles 1989a: 84–7).

Yet while the Aliens Act institutionalised an emergent modality of racism that had Jews as its object, it did not do so consistently or holistically. Specifically, the operating mechanism of the pivot of exclusion was not in itself an unmediated refraction of that racism. An exploration of these points exposes the contradictions of the conjuncture and the Act, and reveals an articulation of different instances of exclusion.

In its most extreme and 'consistent' form, the late-nineteenth-century modality of racism that signified Jews as a 'degenerate race' made no distinction between Jews who were aliens and Jews who were British subjects. It was Jews *in general* who were identified as an undesirable presence. Nevertheless, the ideology did refract in a particular way the reality of that presence because it recognised the class divisions within the Jewish population resident in Britain. The Jewish bourgeoisie and the Jewish working class were signified as equally threatening, but in different ways. The racists argued that both were part of an international Jewish conspiracy in which the Jewish bourgeoisie used its capital to advance Jewish financial interests, rather than the interests of 'our own people', while Jewish working-class revolutionaries sought to subvert and overthrow 'our civilised society'. The logic of this modality of racism led ultimately to the demand for some form of absolute exclusion of Jews from Britain (Holmes 1979: 117–19). But this logic was not embodied in the Aliens Act of 1905.

I have already noted that the Aliens Act did not function to exclude Jews *in general*. Jews who were British subjects were exempt from the provisions of the Act because it applied only to the entry into Britain of aliens. Moreover, alien Jews who had booked a cabin, and/or who could show that they had sufficient money to support themselves in Britain, were exempt from immigration control. They were exempt, not because they were Jews, but because the mechanism of exclusion was an economic one. Because the Aliens Act applied only to aliens who did not possess an independent means of subsistence, those who were in class terms members of the bourgeoisie or the aristocracy could enter Britain without being subject to any form of state regulation. The mechanism of control was structured around the *exclusion* of aliens who, by virtue of lacking money or resources that could generate a money income, could only reproduce themselves by means of the sale of their labour power.

In sum, the primary mechanism of inclusion and exclusion was located in the structure of class and class relations. In the first instance, the Aliens Act implemented a system of class discrimination in the procedures of immigration control. This was the shell within which racism had its effects. The moment of racism can be located at that point in the wider social relations of the social formation where Jewish immigrants, signified as part of a distinct Jewish 'race', were identified as an 'undesirable' presence. But, in institutionalising this racism in the Act, the state modified and diluted it: 'undesirability' gained a specific class content. 'Undesirable' Jews were alien Jews who were also potential or actual sellers of labour power. In signifying them as 'undesirable', their proletarian status was racialised. This was the point at which a class and a racist exclusion articulated.

The plotting of this articulation does not exhaust the analysis of the modes of exclusion embodied in the Aliens Act. Additional significations and exclusions were effected in association with this class differentiation between steerage and cabin passengers. The text of the Act gendered 'undesirable immigrants' as male and rendered females as invisible subjects of men by use of the category of 'dependent'. Moreover, the meaning of the category of alien derives from an implicit contrast with the category of national: nationals, unlike aliens, were not subject to immigration control. In other words, the Aliens Act also reinforced the significance of the national boundary and nationalism as a categorical distinction between human beings located in class relations.

CONCLUSION

The objective of broadening the historical perspective, of standing further back, is not only in order to see more. There are also theoretical and analytical implications. The historical analysis of migration to Britain since the nineteenth century outlined here demonstrates that racialisation and the expression of racism are not confined solely to conjunctures within western European nation states shaped by the consequences of colonial migrations. Hence, theories of racism which are grounded solely in the analysis of colonial history and which prioritise the single somatic characteristic of skin colour have a specific and limited explanatory power (cf. Cohen 1988).

A broader historical analysis of the political and ideological reaction to different migrations, including European migrations, to Britain necessarily requires that one seeks an additional set of analytical reference points to explain events and outcomes. The relevance of the task is further highlighted when one notes that racialisation has had internal as well as immigrant populations as its object (see Miles 1991c, also Chapter 3). What is common to all of the situations described in this chapter is that racialisation marks the boundary of the nation, defining who We are by reference to a racialised Other who may have either an internal or an external origin. This is a characteristic shared with the racialisation of post-1945 colonial migrations to Britain.

Consequently, we might more productively begin (but not conclude) our search for a theory of racism with the emergence of the nation state and with the growth of nationalism in Europe, historical developments that were inseparable from the evolution of the capitalist mode of production (cf. Miles 1989a: 111–21, see also Chapters 2 and 3). This captures the historical significance of that modality of racism that had Jews as its object, a form of racism that had greater significance elsewhere in Europe than in Britain (Mosse 1978) and that, until recently, has been barely mentioned (the work of historians such as Holmes is exceptional) in the recent British debate about racism. Moreover, it is more consistent with the historical evidence concerning the development of 'race' theory in Europe which shows that it has been as much concerned with explaining European history as with colonial situations (e.g. Benedict 1983, Banton 1987, Barkan 1992: 17). Yet, historically, colonialism has been central to the rise of capitalism and the construction and reproduction of certain European nation states, and so in these instances, the connections between racism and the colonial enterprise are of considerable significance.

Hence, it is not only 'black' people who are the object of racism. Such an interpretation constitutes a strange perversion of European history, a history in which the concept of racism was generated to comprehend the use of 'race' theory by the Nazis in the course of formulating a 'final solution' to the 'Jewish question' (Miles 1989a: 42, cf. Barkan 1992). However, the concept of *racisms* allows that the racisms expressed in different conjunctures could have different populations as their object and could have a different structure and content. One can then consider the possibility that certain racisms may be more effective in mobilising racist sentiment in one conjuncture than in another: in Britain, there is little doubt that contemporary racism which has as its object 'black' people coexists with other modalities which have Jews or people of Irish origin, while at the same time these latter modalities of racism have not been successfully employed recently to mobilise a racist social movement. But I have shown through historical analysis that they have had such an effect in earlier conjunctures.

Finally, the analysis has shown that the impact of racism is always mediated through a wider set of social relations, and this impact can be better understood, as we have seen, if those wider relations, including class relations, are identified and analysed simultaneously in relation to the expression of racism. The fact of mediation constitutes another reason why the expression of racism should not be interpreted as continuous and unchanging.

Chapter 6

Racialising subjects and aliens

> The problem of colonial immigration has not yet aroused public anxiety . . . [But] if immigration from the colonies, and, for that matter from India and Pakistan, were allowed to continue unchecked, there is a real danger that over the years there would be a significant change in the racial character of the English people.
>
> (Minute of Cabinet Meeting, 3 November 1955, cited in Carter, Harris and Joshi 1987: 335)

INTRODUCTION

A comprehensive survey of migration to Britain since 1871 has noted that, between 1945 and 1971, 'the Irish constituted the largest immigrant minority in postwar Britain' (Holmes 1988: 216) and that, over the past century, the majority of migrants to Britain originated from Europe. In the racialised language of the nineteenth century, most migrants to Britain have been members of 'white' rather than of 'coloured races' (Holmes 1988: 10–13, Miles and Solomos 1987). This fact is highlighted by a historical review of migration to Britain during the short period between 1945 and 1951. But the period is important for another reason. It also marked a point of transition: during these few years, we see the first indications of a shift from substantial migration flows originating from elsewhere in Europe to flows originating in British colonies and ex-colonies. This shift was marked by the occurrence of a political crisis within the British state, one which demonstrated its willingness to subordinate the principle of nationality to racism but also its hesitancy to institutionalise racism in law.

During the office of the post-1945 Labour government, there was a major labour shortage which the state attempted to resolve by organising a number of migrations of aliens from Europe. This decision was paralleled by a refusal to extend that recruitment to include British subjects resident in the colonies. This is a matter that has received little attention in recent general historical analyses of the period. The main history of the post-1945 Labour government ignores the former completely and makes only a passing reference to Cabinet discussion in 1950 about the consequences of Caribbean migration to Britain (Morgan 1984: 56). And the standard economic history of the period, although it refers briefly to the recruitment of European Volunteer Workers (EVWs), as well as to discussion about the possibilities of utilising prisoner-of-war (POW) and Polish labour, makes no reference to the migration to Britain from the Caribbean (Cairncross 1985: 56). Only in the past decade have researchers begun to recover this history (e.g. Joshi and Carter 1984, Carter *et al.* 1987, Kay and Miles 1992).

This virtual silence could be interpreted to mean that this historical recovery is of little significance. This is a problematic interpretation for two reasons. Labour shortages and the use of migrant labour to assist the solution of the problem were common to several north-western European nation states soon after the end of the Second World War (Castles and Kosack 1973, Hammar 1985). With the exception of Britain, all other north-west European nation states actively initiated or encouraged, to a varying extent and at different times, migration to assist the expansion of capitalist production. Yet, for the duration of the Labour government, we see it first confronting the possibility of utilising migrant labour, then failing to develop its limited initiative, and finally discussing ways to prevent the migration of British citizens seeking employment. In so far as the limited use of migrant labour is a factor which explains the comparatively slow rate of capitalist development in Britain since 1945 (Cairncross 1985: 275), the political decisions and ideological assumptions that lay behind this warrant explanation (Miles 1985).

Moreover, in absolute terms, the scale of the migration was notable. If all the migrants are enumerated collectively, more than half a million people entered Britain over a period of some five years: in the light of the scale of migration to Britain during the first half of the twentieth century, this represented a considerable level. Furthermore, while the majority arrived to fill vacant positions in the labour market, they were entering a nation state confronted by a scarcity of resources as a result of the war. There was an acute shortage of housing, while many basic foodstuffs, along with clothing, were rationed by the state for some or all of the period in question. If we are to believe anti-immigration campaigners who claim that immigration increases competition for scarce resources (with the 'natural' result that 'our own people' become hostile to migrants), then the period in question should have been characterised by a very high level of conflict. There was indeed conflict during this period, but neither state officials, government ministers, nor opposition politicians made any concerted attempt to mobilise the hostility expressed by 'our own people' towards European migrants.

Yet their reaction to the arrival of a few hundred British citizens from the colonies was different: this was a migration that they wanted to stop, despite the continuing labour shortage. This chapter identifies the reasons why this happened and, in so doing, demonstrates that the history of these few years tells us a great deal about the origins and effects of racism in Britain in the second half of the twentieth century.

MIGRATION TO BRITAIN, 1945–51

Historically, the legal concept of nationality and formal systems of immigration control are recent socio-political constructs in Europe. They have their origin in the premeditated formation of the nation state and of the conception that those who live within the boundaries of a nation state have certain rights and obligations which express their 'belonging' to the nation. It is for this reason that the origin of the conception of nationality lies, in part, with the French Revolution (Plender 1988: 9, also Parry 1957: 3). For paralleling the rise of the nation state has been the idea that those who live within its boundaries are members of an 'imagined community' (Anderson 1983) who have a set of collective interests which are grounded in a common heritage, the possession of common characteristics (e.g. language, 'blood', cuisine, etc.) and the universalisation of political rights. But this inclusive conception of community necessarily defined a constituency of Others who did not belong, who were members of other imagined communities with 'their own' collective interests. In other words, there developed a formal dichotomy between national and alien (or foreigner). The former, as citizens, were considered to have the right of residence and political participation within the nation state while the latter could enter only with the permission of the state which assumed sovereignty over the nation (Parry 1957: 4, also Brubaker 1989).

In the case of some European social formations (notably France and Britain), these formal systems distinguishing between those who belonged and those who did not were built on pre-existing foundations. In the case of England (later Britain), a succession of legislative acts from the seventeenth century onwards sought to specify the status of people resident in England who were born elsewhere, and of people born outside

England of parents who were 'natural born subjects' of England (Parry 1957: 28–91). While most of the Acts included the notion of nationality in their titles, this legislation neither formulated nor attributed legal status to nationality *per se*. Rather, it consistently opposed the categories of *subject* and *alien*, although the former category expressed the meaning of nationality as it is now understood (Parry 1957: 30–1). The feudal duality of *subject* and *alien* was reproduced in the British Nationality and Status of Aliens Act of 1914, which, *inter alia*, provided for children born outside Britain to be designated as British subjects if their father was a British subject, and specified that any person born within the dominions and allegiance of the Crown was a British subject. The latter provision included most of the population of the colonies and dominions as British subjects (Parry 1957: 82–3, 151, Macdonald 1983: 44).

This feudal demarcation in British law between subject and alien was made problematic by the desire of governments in the dominions (Australia, New Zealand, Canada, etc.) to establish independent criteria for the acquisition of nationality within their territories. The desire was endorsed by the Statute of Westminster of 1931, although it proposed that this right should be reconciled with the common status of British subject (Parry 1957: 88). Action was forced on the post-1945 Labour government, not by Indian independence as is commonly asserted (e.g. Walvin 1984: 118), but by the decision of the Canadian government in 1946 to establish its own citizenship law (Plender 1988: 21–2, Dummett and Nicol 1990: 134). The Labour government responded by passing the British Nationality Act of 1948, which sustained the common status of 'British subject' in an attenuated form.

This Act created a distinction between citizens of the UK and colonies, and citizens of Commonwealth countries, but stipulated that both categories of citizen had the status of British subject. All such persons were thereafter to be known as *either* British subjects *or* Commonwealth citizens, the two categories nevertheless being identical in terms of their rights (including the right of entry into and settlement in Britain). In practice, therefore, British law continued to divide the population of the world into British subjects and aliens, but the former category included those who were citizens of the UK and colonies as well as citizens of independent Commonwealth countries (Plender 1988: 92–5, Macdonald 1983: 45–6).

The British Nationality Act of 1948 was muddled (Dummett and Nicol 1990: 134–41), not least because it reinforced an extant anomaly, that concerning the legal status of the population of what is now the Republic of Ireland. As we have seen in Chapter 5, after independence, citizens of what was initially called the Irish Free State remained free to enter, and to take up residence in, Britain. And British subjects were accorded the same right with respect to the territory of the Irish Free State (Parry 1957: 928–30). No change was made to this situation by the British Nationality Act of 1948, with the consequence that, although an Irish citizen was not formally a British subject, neither was he or she an alien (Parry 1957: 936).

Thus, throughout the period of the post-1945 Labour government, the millions of British subjects, as well as all Irish citizens, living outside the United Kingdom were not subject to immigration control if they sought to enter the country. Only the entry of aliens was controlled by the British state in the light of legislation passed earlier in the century. The genesis of legislation concerning aliens began with the Aliens Act of 1905, its powers being amended and extended by further legislation in 1914 and 1919, and by the Aliens Order of 1920 (Parry 1957: 178–9, Macdonald 1983: 8, Bevan 1986: 70–3). As a result, an immigration officer could refuse entry to an alien if the person was mentally ill, medically unfit or unable to support himself or herself. And if an alien was seeking to enter Britain in order to work, he or she was required to possess a work permit issued by the Minister of Labour initially to the alien's employer (Isaac 1954: 166–7, Gordon 1985: 9).

This summary account of legislation concerning nationality and immigration provides a context for an account of the migration flows into Britain between 1945 and 1951: in 1945, British law defined the separate categories of British subject, Irish citizen and alien. Concerning the first category, approximately 319,800 British subjects entered Britain between 1946 and 1951, the vast majority originating from the British dominions. In addition, around 88,000 persons arrived from the colonies, the majority of whom were British subjects previously born in Britain who had served in the colonial administration or the armed forces. Also included in this latter figure were a small number of 'coloured' (to use the discourse of the period) British subjects from the Caribbean and West Africa. Many of these migrants were students, but several hundred of them were seeking paid work, and therefore at least temporary residence, in Britain. Some of them had played a role in the Allied war effort, either by serving in the armed forces or by working in the munitions factories (Isaac 1954: 146–51, Holmes 1988: 165–8, Pilkington 1988: 15–16, Bousquet and Douglas 1991).

Assessing the scale of Irish migration to Britain is more difficult. As a result of Irish neutrality, migration to Britain from Ireland had been rigidly controlled during the war, but it had continued because of labour demand within Britain. Those recruited by the state were directed to specific employment which could not be changed without permission. These controls were relaxed in mid-1946 and abolished at the end of 1947 (Isaac 1954: 194). Thereafter, evaluating the scale of the migration becomes problematic because the measurement of immigration was also terminated in 1947.

Estimates suggest that, in the period 1946–50, there was a net inflow of between 100,000 and 150,000 Irish citizens who intended to stay for more than one year (Isaac 1954: 196). This implies an annual net inflow of between 20,000 and 30,000 persons. A proportion of these migrants entered Britain within the framework of a continuing state recruitment policy and were guided into work in coal mining and agriculture, but the majority migrated without any official assistance or support (Isaac 1954: 194–5). These migrants added to an already substantial Irish presence in Britain: the Census recorded just over 716,000 Irish citizens living in Britain in 1951 (Holmes 1988: 216).

The category of alien migration includes a number of discrete flows. First, there were those who entered Britain in possession of a work permit issued under the provisions of the Aliens Order of 1920. Between 1946 and 1951, 173,037 permits were granted: with the exception of 1946 (when 10,744 permits were issued), between 27,000 and 37,000 were awarded annually. The majority were supplied to women of European origin for domestic service in private houses, hospitals and educational institutions (Isaac 1954: 167–9). This was a labour migration determined by the demands of certain sectors of the British economy for a gendered labour force.

The second flow consisted of members of the Polish Armed Forces and their dependents, many of whom had arrived in Britain during the war (Sword et al. 1989). In 1940, the Polish government and armed forces in exile had been allowed to enter Britain, and they were joined later by the Polish second corps and dependents in 1946. Given their military status in the context of the war and the subsequent imposition of communist rule in Poland, the provisions of the Aliens Order of 1920 did not apply to their entry. In May 1946, the War Office and the Air Ministry formed the Polish Resettlement Corps (PRC) with the intention of disbanding the armed forces and assisting, depending upon the Poles' individual choice, their return to Poland, their emigration to other countries or their resettlement and employment in Britain. The latter process was facilitated by the Polish Resettlement Act of 1947 (Sword et al. 1989: 245–55, 326–31).

Against a background of government hesitation, a number of factors led to the decision to offer resettlement in Britain. In addition to general humanitarian considerations, there was sympathy for the anti-communist sentiment of many of the Poles and there was a desire to use their labour power in sectors of the economy facing labour shortages (Holmes 1988: 212). Thus, members of the PRC who opted for employment in Britain were initially directed by the Ministry of Labour into certain kinds of work, especially coal mining and agriculture (Sword 1988: 236–7). As a result of this state initiative, the Polish population resident in Britain in 1949 numbered 127,900 persons, although this fell to around 115,000 by 1950 in the light of further emigration and repatriation (Zubryzcki 1956: 62, Isaac 1954: 176).

The third alien migration flow consisted of those persons recruited collectively by the British state under contract to work in designated employment. The main scheme recruited refugees from displaced persons' camps in West Germany and Austria (Marrus 1985: 340–5), specifically in order to enter sectors of the economy which were defined as essential to capitalist reconstruction and which were facing labour shortages. Those refugees who volunteered and were accepted (and who became known as European Volunteer Workers) were required to sign a contract, under which they accepted a job selected by the Minister of Labour, a job that they could only change with the permission of the Minister. They were initially admitted for one year, although they were later allowed to settle permanently.

The conditions of placement in employment varied somewhat, but they usually included the requirements that no British labour was available, that the EVWs would be the first to be made unemployed in the event of redundancy, that EVWs should join the appropriate trade union, and that they should work under the same conditions as British workers (Tannahill 1958, Kay and Miles 1988, 1992). EVWs (both female and male) were recruited in two phases between 1946 and 1950, and the total number resident in Britain in 1950 was 80,811 persons (Isaac 1954: 179–81). Large numbers were directed to employment in agriculture, textile production, coal mining and domestic service. All were restricted in the work that they could do until January 1951, when it was announced that, after three years of residence, all restrictions would be lifted (Stadulis 1951/2: 213, Tannahill 1958: 81, 133).

In addition to the EVW scheme, there were a number of smaller state programmes for the recruitment of alien labour under contract. Between 1948 and 1950, the 'Blue Danube' scheme recruited 2,341 Austrian women for textile work and nursing, and the 'North Sea' scheme recruited 9,713 German women for domestic work. Another programme, which began in late 1949 and ended in 1951, recruited 1,655 Italian women for factory and domestic work (Isaac 1954: 180). These were supplemented by additional schemes involving the recruitment of 900 Belgian female domestic workers between July 1945 and early 1946; of 250 Belgian male building workers between May 1946 and April 1947; of 440 Italian male skilled foundry workers in 1947 and 1948; and of 324 German scientists and technicians between November 1945 and late 1949 (Isaac 1954: 177).

The fourth category of aliens consisted of former POWs who were granted civilian status after 1945, largely in the hope that they would remain in employment in agriculture where many POWs had been employed during the war. By the end of 1949, this included some 25,000 aliens (mainly from the Ukraine, Germany and Italy) who either entered Britain during the war or who were brought to Britain after the war was over (Isaac 1954: 183–5, Holmes 1988: 211, Colpi 1991: 128–9, 137).

THE SIGNIFICATION OF MIGRATION FLOWS

Against the background of this overview of migration flows, the significance of nationality and citizenship can be contextualised by discussion of three interrelated themes. First, these post-war migrations occurred in a context where it was noted that economic circumstances required large-scale migration into Britain. Second, this evaluation led to discussion about the sources from which migrants might be drawn, in the course of which there was a racialisation (Miles 1982, 1989a, Green and Carter 1987) of all potential migrant populations. Third, while the issue of migration did not intrude into the racialised political debate about the transformation in the nature of British subjecthood (or nationality), nevertheless, in the light of the racialisation of migration, there were secret discussions within the state about the possibility of preventing 'coloured' British subjects from migrating to Britain.

The Labour government came to office with a reforming programme and facing a series of major economic problems, several of which were related to a serious weakening of the national economy and of its competitive position in the capitalist world economy, partly as a result of the war. The government was committed to nationalisation, the creation of a welfare state, full employment and, more generally, 'fair shares' for all, a notion reinforced by the collective experience of deprivation and resistance during the war. But while the government talked of socialism, and while it consolidated and to some extent strengthened many of the arenas of state intervention which had been established during the war, most of its actions were dedicated to the reconstruction of a capitalist economy. That reconstruction involved rebuilding the industrial infrastructure, increasing export production and ensuring an adequate labour supply (Miliband 1972, Eatwell 1979, Morgan 1984, Cairncross 1985).

Early in its period of office, the Labour government conservatively estimated the labour shortage to be in the order of one million persons (Kay and Miles 1988: 215), although official estimates did vary over time (Cairncross 1985: 386–93). The problem was considered to be especially acute in agriculture, coal mining and textile production because of the contribution that these sectors could make to easing the balance of payments problem (Cairncross 1985: 394) or, in the case of coal, because of its central role in sustaining industrial production generally (Wilson 1952: 226). In a situation of labour shortage, there are a number of options available to the state and capital, including mechanisation as a form of labour substitution and the improvement of wages and conditions in sectors experiencing shortages. A further option is to increase the size of the active, paid labour force by drawing on a surplus population either within or from outside the nation state (Harris 1987, Duffield 1988, Kay and Miles 1992).

In practice, the government sought to resolve the problem by increasing both the size of the working population and labour productivity, although the former strategy predominated for much of the period up to 1951. Thus, considerable effort was expended in persuading women and people of retirement age to enter or re-enter the labour market; women and the elderly were the main elements of the *internal* relative surplus population. But the government also decided early in 1946 to draw upon an *external* surplus population, that is, to recruit foreign labour from Europe, a decision that was given great prominence in its *Economic Survey for 1947* (Cmd. 7046).

While the government tended to see the problem of labour shortage as a short-term one, some commentators believed (correctly) that it was a structural problem which would continue for the foreseeable future. The Royal Commission on Population noted in 1949 the low rate of natural increase in the size of the British population and anticipated a fall in the population aged 15–40 years of 1.4 million persons over the following fifteen years. It concluded that this decline would require a net inward migration balance of 140,000 young migrants each year for ten years to prevent a decline in the size of the young working population (Royal Commission on Population 1949: 122, see also PEP 1948).

Migration became a political issue and was discussed as such in Parliament in the light of the government's initially hesitant efforts to recruit foreign labour. In February 1947, during a debate on displaced persons, there was bipartisan support for increased immigration. One of the main supporting arguments claimed that immigration was necessary to resolve the labour shortage and to accompany a policy of full employment (Hansard 1947, 433: col. 756). The same economic argument ran through the debate on the Polish Resettlement Bill later in the same month. While the government initially hoped that many of the Poles would return to 'their own country' (Sword 1988: 234), it also believed that it had a special responsibility to those in the Polish armed forces as a result of their contribution to the Allied war effort. This sense of obligation was strengthened by the continuing labour shortage (Hansard 1947, 433: cols. 373–87). This latter view was largely endorsed by the Conservative opposition, who criticised the government for its tardiness in placing demobilised Poles in employment (Hansard 1947, 433: cols. 396, 423).

But Parliamentary debate about migration was not concerned exclusively with economics. Attention was also paid to the biological and social implications of immigration: as a result, all migration flows were racialised. During the debate on displaced persons, one Conservative MP claimed that 'there are the strongest possible ethnographical reasons for having an infusion of vigorous new blood from overseas at the present time', noting that 'we have very greatly benefited . . . from other foreign blood at different times in the course of our history' (Hansard 1947, 433: col. 758). There were references to related notions of 'stock' and 'race' by other speakers, all of whom claimed that there were biological advantages to be gained from immigration, especially if, as one MP put it, 'we act quickly, get the best of the pick, and a very good best it is' (Hansard 1947, 433: col. 762).

A similar discourse was evident in the debate on the Polish Resettlement Bill. In introducing the Bill, the Secretary of State for the Home Department claimed 'We have . . . had great experience in this country of the benefits that come from the assimilation of virile, active and industrious people into our stock' and he went on to suggest that there was good reason to believe that 'a great part of our strength comes from the fact that we, more than any other of the ancient nations of the earth, have been able to assimilate these people and get them into the mainstream of our civic life' (Hansard 1947, 433: col. 387). This view was echoed by another MP who claimed that 'on the whole, it is a good thing for this race, which is a mongrel race, to be able to absorb into itself this great body of men [sic]' (Hansard 1947, 433: col. 399). The idea of 'race' was also articulated in the debate on the British Nationality Bill (Hansard 1948, 453: cols. 394, 403).

In all this discourse, it was assumed or argued that the world's population consisted of a number of discrete biological 'races' and that 'racial' characteristics were an important determinant of the political and economic prominence, indeed domination (although this was becoming illusory by the late 1940s), of the British nation on the world stage. Consequently, the presumed 'racial' characteristics of immigrants were widely considered to be a relevant criterion when deciding which particular immigrants should be admitted to Britain. This signification also created a hierarchy within the category of British subject.

For example, one contributor to the debate on the British Nationality Bill grounded his conception of British nationality in the idea of 'race'. David Renton referred to the existence of different categories within British communities resident outside the British Empire. He claimed, referring to Egypt, that one group 'are British in the full sense. Mostly British born, they are racially British and are recognisable as such.' They could be distinguished from a second category who were legally British nationals but who

> have little or no British blood in them. They do not often speak English or, for that matter, Scottish [sic], Irish or Welsh. They cannot claim to have served the King and the British people; and they have no real right to our protection.

> (Hansard 1948, 453: col. 476–7)

Thus, for this MP, Britishness was grounded firmly in biology rather than in the criteria established by the legal system to determine nationality and, as a result, 'race' became the foundation for 'nation'. And so racism articulated with nationalism (Miles 1987d). While Enoch Powell is infamous for his remark that a West Indian does not become English by being born in England and by carrying a United Kingdom passport, he was only reiterating a longer-established distinction: the 'logic' of Powell's argument can be found in the political debate of earlier conjunctures, as this example shows.

Not all those who contributed to the debate about the implications and value of immigration in the early years of the Labour government were positive about the anticipated consequences. Their reservations were grounded in part in a racialisation of potential migrant populations. Within Parliament, various objections were raised by a small number of MPs (e.g. Hansard 1947, 433: cols. 413–20) while the Royal Commission on Population drew negative conclusions. It claimed that it was difficult to identify a source which could supply the number of immigrants required. With the exceptions of Ireland, Italy and the Netherlands, the

Commission believed that no European country contained a surplus population available for emigration. Furthermore, it identified 'assimilation' as a major problem, and continued (1949: 124)

Immigration on a large scale into a fully established society like ours could only be welcomed without reserve if the immigrants were of good human stock and were not prevented by their religion or race from intermarrying with the host population and becoming merged in it.

On the basis of this racialised criterion of assimilation, the Commission believed that 'the sources of supply of suitable immigrants for Great Britain are limited' and concluded that 'continuous large-scale immigration would possibly be impractical and would certainly be undesirable' (1949: 125, 130). A similar conclusion had been reached in a PEP report published in the previous year (PEP 1948, Miles 1990b). Significantly, the Royal Commission's review of the possible 'sources of supply' was limited to Europe and therefore (with the exception of Ireland) to people who were aliens. However, potentially as well as in reality (because a small migration did occur), British subjects in the colonies and the Commonwealth constituted another source of migrants. This source was ignored by the Commission, presumably because they were not considered to be of 'good human stock'.

The silence of the Royal Commission on this matter was echoed during the debate on the British Nationality Bill. While political debate on nationality legislation has, since the early 1960s, become intimately intertwined with the question of immigration from the Caribbean and the Indian subcontinent, this was not the case in the late 1940s. The migration of British subjects from the colonies into Britain was not problematised by either the advocates or the opponents of the bill, although there were some abstract references to the rights of British subjects in this respect. This suggests that there was no public conception of the possibility of a migration of British subjects from the colonies at this time. Yet the debate about the Bill is of interest because, during its evolution, there was a conjunction of a racialised content with a formal reaffirmation of the right of entry into the 'Mother Country' of all British subjects.

Above, I have shown that the bill introduced a distinction between citizenship of the United Kingdom and colonies and of each independent Commonwealth country, although all persons who fell into each of these categories were also designated as British subjects. During the debates, arguments were advanced against this change, including the claim that this disadvantaged citizens of Commonwealth countries (relative to the populations resident in British colonies) because they would not possess the status of citizen of the UK and colonies as of right, but rather would have to register for it. Additionally, it was argued that the diminution of the conception of British subjecthood removed a key conception that had held the British Empire together in the past.

For example, David Renton referred to the 'immense diversity of native peoples within the Colonies' and argued that 'it has not been an easy matter to keep together so many of the diverse and often primitive races of the world under the British flag'. He believed that this had only been possible by giving them (Hansard 1948, 453: cols. 475–6)

> an easy conception . . . of a great Queen in a distant land, who would give them protection, who would give them prosperity, who no doubt would expect them to work in return, but whose subjects they were. It was in that way that we got loyalty and obedience from them.

His conclusion was that the idea of 'citizen' could not embody this 'easy conception' (presumably, 'primitive races' were not capable of understanding more complex conceptions) which flowed from 'subjecthood' under colonial domination. This view was echoed by Major Maxwell Fyfe (Hansard 1948, 453: col. 410).

But these advocates of a racialised (and racist), romanticised and idealised notion of Empire did not propose the removal of the rights (which included the right of entry in Britain) that accrued to subjecthood. Indeed, in this respect, their common conservatism was consistent in retaining the legal statutes and relations of the past. Thus, Sir Maxwell Fyfe referred to 'our proud boast of the open door in this country to people from all the Colonies' and argued that (Hansard 1948, 453: cols. 405, 411)

> there ought to be an open door and a reception for every type. If we create a distinctive citizenship for Britain and Colonies, inevitably such differentiation will creep in. We must maintain our great metropolitan tradition of hospitality to everyone from every part of our Empire.

But under the surface of this universal concern about the rights of all British subjects to experience the hospitality of the 'Mother Land' was a more specific concern about 'our own kith and kin'. Many of the critics of the British Nationality Bill were primarily concerned that the new distinction that the bill created could result eventually in the withdrawal of the right of Commonwealth citizens (i.e. those with British rather than 'primitive' blood in their veins) to migrate to Britain.

That this was a central subtext of the discussion is demonstrated by the fact that the Attorney-General, in summing up the debate on the second reading for the Labour government, denied that there was any such intention or implication. Referring specifically to the legal status of Commonwealth citizens under the provisions of the British Nationality Bill, he claimed that 'As a British subject, who is at the same time a citizen of a Commonwealth country, he will be entitled to come here and enjoy precisely the same rights as he has previously enjoyed' (Hansard 1948, 453: col. 495). Thus, whatever else divided the government and opposition in this debate, it had nothing to do with the right of British subjects (and especially Commonwealth citizens) to enter the United Kingdom. The rights of British subjects resident in the colonies were less secure.

Despite the public and apparently principled affirmation of this right in 1948, it was the subject of private discussion by state officials and the Labour Cabinet several times during the period 1945–51. There was an exchange of views between civil servants and ministers during 1947, during which it was recognised that aliens were being recruited to help resolve the labour shortage at a time when British subjects in the Caribbean were showing a desire to migrate to Britain to enter paid employment. Government ministers expressed opposition to this latter development (Harris 1987: 62).

Then, early in 1948, the Colonial Office initiated a discussion within the state about the possibility of using 'surplus colonial manpower' to resolve labour shortages. In the subsequent exchange of correspondence between civil servants, considerable reservations were again expressed (Joshi and Carter 1984: 58–9, Rich 1986b: 49–51). It is therefore not surprising that the Colonial Office finally recommended in July 1949 that the government should not establish any formal scheme to import British subjects from the colonies to work in Britain (Dean 1987: 318–24, Harris 1987: 65–7, Layton-Henry 1987: 64).

But before that report was written, the issue was raised again following the arrival by boat in June 1948 of 417 British subjects from Jamaica. The Colonial Secretary found himself under attack within the government for allowing this to happen. He replied by pointing out, correctly, that there were no legal powers to prevent the entry of British subjects but added (ominously and portentously) that 'every possible step has been taken by the Colonial Office and by the Jamaican Government to discourage these influxes' (cited in Harris 1987: 64, see also Dean 1987: 316–17). The Minister of Labour stated publicly in Parliament that he hoped that 'no encouragement will be given to others to follow their example' (cited in Pilkington 1988: 19).

The steps taken were insufficient to 'discourage' migration from the Caribbean. Further ships arrived, bringing a few hundred more British subjects to Britain. There was no public reaction on the part of the Labour government but the issue was discussed in secret on one further occasion. In June 1950, the Cabinet appointed a committee to undertake a review of 'the further means which might be adopted to check the immigration into this country of coloured people from the British Colonial Territories' (cited in Joshi and Carter 1984: 61). The committee identified three methods of restricting the entry of 'coloured' British subjects, but they all contradicted the long-established principle of the 'open-door' policy (which had been reaffirmed during the debate on the British Nationality Bill) and required that a distinction be drawn between 'coloured' citizens of the United Kingdom and colonies and all others.

Concerning this distinction, the committee commented that 'any solution depending on an apparent or concealed colour test would be so invidious as to make it impossible of adoption' but concluded that 'Nevertheless, the use of any powers taken to restrict the free entry of British subjects to this country would, as a general rule, be more or less confined to coloured persons' (cited in Joshi and Carter 1984: 63). Having racialised British subjects, this recommendation to bifurcate the unitary category resulted in a distinction between 'coloured' and 'white' subjects and an inferiorisation of the rights of the former.

However, the latter was not immediately embodied in practice and the government made no attempt at this point in time to mobilise public opinion in favour of racist legislation (cf. Lunn 1989). Moreover, no attempt was made to legislate in 1950 because, so the government reasoned, the number of 'coloured' British subjects migrating to Britain remained small (Joshi and Carter 1984: 64). Legislation to achieve this objective was eventually passed by Parliament in 1962, following a decade of hesitation motivated by concern about the consequences of the accusation of racism (Miles and Phizacklea 1984, Carter *et al.* 1987).

CONCLUSION

We can now return to the paradox identified in the opening paragraphs of this chapter. In the context of labour shortage, and of a policy to help resolve that shortage by the recruitment of migrant labour, the Labour government facilitated the migration of aliens (many of whom were refugees) from Europe, but sought to prevent the entry of British citizens from the colonies whose migration was motivated primarily by the desire to work. The explanation of this paradox demonstrates that the outcome of the racialisation of the potential sources of migrant labour displaced the formal significance of nationality and citizenship, although this does not, by itself, explain why the Labour government opted for alien rather than British labour. This explanation therefore takes issue with those accounts of the period which explain government opposition in largely economistic terms and which play down or deny the impact of racism on the decision (e.g. Layton-Henry 1984: 22).

I have emphasised that the discourse of 'race' permeated political debate about all migrations. It was not only British colonial subjects who were signified as members of a different 'race'. European aliens were similarly signified, a fact often ignored by accounts of this period (Layton-Henry 1984: 16–22). Within this political debate, racialisation was therefore universal (see Miles 1989c). But it functioned to construct a hierarchy of superiority and inferiority. Certain European migrants were signified positively as being of 'vigorous stock' which would strengthen what one MP defined as the British 'mongrel race'. Although the Labour government retained reservations, it nevertheless (in association with other advocates of immigration) consented to the view that European migrants were biologically acceptable and could be expected to 'assimilate' to the British way of life.

As far as 'coloured' British subjects were concerned, ministers and officials were more discreet about describing their racialised attributes, not least because the post-war period was shaped, as we have seen in Chapter 1, by revelations about the consequences of anti-Jewish racism in Europe. Certainly, no politician or state official argued publicly that the presence of colonial 'races' would result in the degeneration of the British 'race'. But there was a clear presumption (expressed explicitly but secretly within the walls of Whitehall) that, because of their 'race', 'coloured people' (irrespective of their status as British subjects) would not be able to 'assimilate' to the 'British way of life'. The reasoning was considered to be a matter of common-sense understanding. But this obscures as much as it reveals, unless it was believed that colonial British subjects did actually possess some biological characteristic which prevented their 'assimilation'. In fact, this aspect of the racialisation of migrant populations systematically obscured the most important factor.

A state official involved with the Working Party on the Employment in the United Kingdom of Surplus Colonial Labour (which was established in 1948) declared that it was the 'social implications' of introducing 'other races' which is the 'real answer to the question . . . and no amount of fencing will in the end lead the Working Party to any other conclusion'. What mattered most was not the principle of common nationality and citizenship of 'coloured' British subjects but rather the racist beliefs of British citizens resident in Britain about such 'races'. The Labour government and state officials were especially concerned that this racism would lead to discriminatory practices (see Dean 1987: 319–20, 322–5, Harris 1987: 60), a concern that was expressed fleetingly in parliamentary debates (e.g. Hansard 1947, 433: col. 759).

But the government was not prepared to confront racism and the exclusion that would follow. Or, more precisely, they were not prepared to challenge it when its object was 'coloured' British subjects: we have seen that it was prepared to do so in the case of European 'races' (who had been positively signified as 'vigorous stock' even if they did not carry 'British blood' in their veins). Consequently, government discourse and actions served to legitimate that racism. The nature and extent of it amongst the British population resident in the United Kingdom at that time is difficult to ascertain, although there is reason to believe that the Labour government overestimated its significance and strength (Banton 1983). If this is so, the later increase in the public expression of racism during the 1950s can be explained partly as the result of state intervention.

But the reluctance of the state to confront the racism of the British population was not the only factor that led to the state's legitimation of racism and to the subordination of the principles of nationality and citizenship to racism. From the rights of citizenship, and therefore from the inferiorised position of aliens resident in or permitted to enter Britain, flowed other consequences which concerned the commodification of labour power. Under the work-permit system and the contractual arrangements governing the entry of EVWs, the alien worker was subject to state control over to whom he or she sold his or her labour power. This restriction of the freedom of the worker to dispose of his or her labour power (Miles 1987a) had a special value in the context of labour shortage, as state officials recognised (see Harris 1987: 61, 65, Duffield 1988: 11–14).

This is because it allowed the state to retain workers in sectors of employment where it was difficult to recruit and retain labour in a situation of effective full employment. Further, at least in the case of the work-permit system, the state was not required to finance the production and reproduction costs of the labourer, the worker being recruited by a contract which stipulated a temporary and limited period of residence. These restrictions were legitimated by the fact that the workers were aliens rather than citizens. Hence, they could not be applied to workers from the Caribbean because they were British subjects, a legal status that required that they enjoy all the rights of British citizens, including that of the freedom to dispose of their labour power within the market-place.

This apparently simple duality between *subject* and *alien* was blurred by the specific circumstances of the Poles and the EVWs. This is because, to take the case of the EVWs, although deportation was formally possible, the practicality of deportation was constrained by the fact that they had been recruited from displaced persons' camps, and many were stateless. They therefore lacked a 'home' to which they could be 'repatriated'. In effect, their refugee status ensured that, despite the contractual character of the terms of their migration to Britain, they were destined to settle. This was even more clear in the case of the Poles, whose insertion into British social relations was seen by the government to involve settlement because of their unwillingness to return to Poland under a communist government. Thus, in both cases, the migrants were not British subjects and their presence was legitimated on the grounds that they provided a source of labour power. Yet the outcome was, for the vast majority, permanent settlement, with the result that there could not be any long-term positive economic consequences arising from temporary residence or from some permanent status as contractual, directed wage labour.

Thus, in post-1945 Britain, the status of refugee in the context of labour shortage also blurred the common distinction between 'free' migrants who are mobile across national borders in search of a buyer for their labour power (migrant labour), and 'forced' migrants whose mobility is determined by political persecution (refugee migrants) (Kay and Miles 1988, 1992). In addition to the more general difficulty of determining the ambiguous character of the 'freedom' of the labourer whose migration is forced by virtue of the necessity to obtain a money income, the evidence demonstrates that the admission of refugees to Britain in this period was not determined principally by humanitarian considerations, but rather shaped by the perceived economic value of their presence.

In order to state this argument more precisely, let us consider the claim that it is mistaken to equate 'the importation of foreign workers with the incorporation of blacks as different ways of satisfying the same labour shortage' (Duffield 1988: 12). It has been argued that the period between 1945 and 1951 was characterised by a shortage of skilled labour for a work process that was largely unchanged, whereas during the 1950s, mechanisation reduced the skill content of the labour that was required. Thus, during the former period, the recruitment of foreign labour was characterised by attempts to fit the skills of the labourer with the demand for skilled labour in the understaffed industries, while during the latter period semi- and unskilled labour was sought. For this reason, it is concluded that 'black' labour was recruited during the 1950s to solve the continuing labour shortage (Duffield 1988: 11–14).

The argument is problematic for the following reasons. First, many of the vacancies for which alien migrant labour was destined in the late 1940s were for semi- and unskilled jobs, especially in agriculture and domestic service: little training was required to dig potatoes or wash floors. Second, while an attempt was made to link the experience and skills of foreign labour with the skill content of vacant jobs, a large proportion (perhaps even a majority) of foreign migrants had either to be trained to undertake the skilled work in which they were placed or were placed in jobs which did not correspond to their qualifications and experience (Sword 1988: 238, 248). Third, a large proportion of Caribbean migrants had experience of skilled manual work before their migration (Glass and Pollins 1960: 24, Pilkington 1988: 23–4). Fourth, as I have shown, foreign migrants from Europe as well as British colonial migrants were racialised and became the object of hostility. Indeed, the possibility of such resistance was a key factor in the Labour government's hesitancy in initiating the recruitment of foreign migrant labour, while the reality of such resistance was a factor determining the demise of the migrant labour solution to labour shortage (Sword 1988: 237–41, Kay and Miles 1988: n. 34).

Yet, the British state did distinguish between European and colonial labour migration. But it is more accurate to conceive the categorisation of migration flows in terms of the state-imposed duality of national and alien, from which flow differential rights of entry and settlement and which has differential implications for the imposition of restrictions on the commodification of labour power. It is this complex of judicial inclusion and exclusion which the British state racialised in the period 1945–51. It expressed a clear preference for the recruitment of alien migrants over British subjects from the colonies to fill vacant positions in the labour market for two reasons. First, the differential racialisation of migrants signified the presence of 'coloured' British subjects as more likely to lead to social disorder because of the racism of British subjects resident in Britain. Second, British citizens from the colonies could not be deprived of the freedom to commodify their labour power in the way that aliens could: alien labour power was therefore more controllable because the state could deny to aliens the right of citizens to sell their labour power 'freely'.

Consequently, the years 1945–51 constitute a period of transition (Kay and Miles 1993). They mark the beginning of the shift away from Europe being the major source of migration to Britain, to be replaced by migration from British colonies and ex-colonies. The racialisation of potential migrants, in association with the duality of national and alien, constructed a hierarchy of desirability in which alien European labour was initially favoured over British subjects of colonial origin whose legal Britishness was cancelled by their attributed negative characteristics as a 'coloured race'. But because the British state proved unwilling to realise its racism in law at this time, the rights of British colonial and ex-colonial subjects to enter and settle in Britain were not withdrawn. Migration from the Caribbean (as well as from Ireland) continued and increased through the 1950s, and was paralleled by migration from India and Pakistan. It was not until 1962 that the British state imposed controls on the entry of British subjects from what had become known as the New Commonwealth.

Part III

European perspectives

Chapter 7

Integrating immigrants in Europe?

L'intégration se mesure-t-elle au nombre de mariages mixtes et d'acquisitions de nationalité ou au nombre d'élus et de leaders des «minorités»?

(Costa-Lascoux 1991a: 107)

Cette indétermination du vocabulaire est sans doute l'une des raisons qui explique que la «question de l'immigration» fonctionne aussi bien comme instrument de mobilisation et de polémiques politiques.

(Beaud and Noiriel 1991: 261)

INTRODUCTION

The problematic of integration occupies a central place in contemporary analyses (by officials and government ministers as well as academics) of the consequences of post-1945 migration into Europe. To cite just one example, an OECD review of international migration at the end of the 1980s identified, as one of the major features of the conjuncture, the 'growth of foreign populations and the problems posed by the social and economic integration of migrants in the main OECD host countries' (OECD 1990: 1). And the report noted that many European governments were actively pursing policies intended to achieve the integration of migrants.

This is indeed the case. In December 1989, the French government announced the formation of a *secrétariat général à l'intégration* and of an *Haut Conseil à l'intégration*. Inter-ministerial committees were asked to assess the potential for new policies for immigration control, housing, education and employment (*Libération*, 6 December 1989, *Le Monde*, 9 February 1990, 12 July 1990). This initiative occurred in a context of a political crisis concerning immigration which had continued for much of the 1980s, a decade during which immigration became the focus of conflict between parties of the left and right and during which the *Front National* became a major political force (Mayer and Perrineau 1989, Husbands 1991, Perrineau 1991), its prominence due in part to its manipulation and legitimation of everyday racism in France. For French governments during the 1980s, and especially for those of the Left, *intégration* was part of the solution to racism. Consequently, official and semi-official organisations have utilised the notion of integration to comprehend not only the situation in France but in Europe as a whole (e.g. ADRI 1991). The other key area for action was immigration control (Wihtol de Wenden 1988, 1991).

In the Netherlands in the late 1980s, a review of government policy was conducted in the light of what some regard as the failure of a preceding 'ethnic minorities' policy. This latter policy had been implemented in 1983 following lengthy debate about a report prepared by the Netherlands Scientific Council for Government Policy (NSCGP) which had been published in 1979. As the decade of the 1980s drew to a close, the Dutch government again passed on the task of analysis and policy formation to the NSCGP and its report was published early in 1989 (NSCGP 1990). Without accounting for the alleged failure, it called for the replacement of the 'ethnic minorities policy' by a new 'immigrant policy' (NSCGP 1990: 63), within which a high priority was placed upon the introduction of an integration policy (NSCGP 1990: 58, 60). The report proved to be highly controversial and, by the early 1990s, the government had done little more than accept its main principles.

Seen from Köln or Berlin, these attempts to 'integrate' immigrants into French and Dutch societies seem to have a progressive quality: the German government, for reasons that have a certain internal political logic (although there is no logic at all in terms of the reality of situation of the migrant communities), continues to insist that Germany is not a 'country of immigration'. While certain state initiatives appear to suggest acceptance of the integration problematic, the German government's formal definition of the situation obviates the need for a policy of integration (e.g. Heckmann 1985, Korte 1985, Mehrländer 1985, Hollifield 1986). But seen from London or Glasgow, there is a strong sense of *déjà vu* about the promotion of a policy of integration: successive British governments since the mid-1960s have promoted such a policy. Yet its effects have been limited, at least if we take account of the evidence concerning the extent of exclusionary practices inspired by racism and the structural position of certain groups of migrant origin (e.g. Brown 1984, see also Jenkins and Solomos 1989).

I am not suggesting that, because some argue that a policy of integration has failed in Britain, it can therefore be expected to fail elsewhere in western Europe. Such a purpose would presume too much. Not least, it assumes that integration is a meaningful concept, that it refers to a clearly identifiable condition or process that can be brought about by state intervention. This chapter questions this assumption (cf. Beaud and Noiriel 1991).

THE IDEA OF INTEGRATION

The notion of integration refers generally to a process of mixing or amalgamation of a previously external population with another, pre-existing population in a nation state. The process is defined a priori as problematic, if not conflictual. The assumption is that the former population is not yet a participant, or not yet an equal participant, in social relations. Herein lies the origin of the problematic status of the concept. For, in suggesting that immigrant populations, or rather populations of recent immigrant origin, resident in the nation states of western Europe should *now* be integrated into the nation state by means of state intervention, it is denied that they have been, from the very instant of their arrival in western Europe, an integral part of these social formations.

The main determinant of many of these migrations to western Europe was a labour shortage and, as a result, many millions of migrants have filled vacant positions in the labour market. From the moment of their arrival, therefore, they have participated in commodity production and exchange and, through the taxation of their wages and of the expenditure of their income, they have sustained the welfare (not to mention the 'law and order' and 'warfare') state. Moreover, migrant workers have reproduced their labour power and themselves: they required accommodation and food, they engaged in leisure practices, and they organised social relations within which to reproduce themselves. While many of these practices were accomplished in a culturally distinct manner, they were nevertheless an immediately present part of the social fabric of the social formation. The notion of integration therefore *exteriorises* in thought, and in politics, those populations which are already, indeed have always been, a constituent element of the social formation.

There is another dimension to the problematic status of the concept. The notion not only has a subject ('the immigrants') but also an object, namely the social formation into which they are supposed to be 'mixed'. While all the social formations of western Europe are dominated by the capitalist mode of production, the cultural and political form taken by the nation state varies. This is in part a difference of language, of political institutions and systems of representation, of symbols and themes that constitute the imagination of the nation form. In particular, it is also a difference in the mode of belonging, of affinity, to the nation: the way in which the nation is imagined therefore presumes a certain mode of being, a particular profile of cultural practices, on the part of its members.

Thus, not only is the concept of integration implicitly prescriptive (in the sense that 'the immigrants' are required to 'belong' in the culturally prescribed manner), but in addition, it is nationally variable in the sense that, within Europe, what it means to 'belong' varies from one nation state to another. As a result, while the word might be the same in translation, and might have the same general object, the idea of integration has discrete nuances and refers to distinct practices in each nation state. In other words, while the French, Dutch and British states all claim to be implementing a policy of integration, what is meant differs because the structure of the nation, and the nature of its imagining, varies.

For example, French researchers often distinguish between the French 'way of doing things' and the 'Anglo-Saxon tradition'. Behind this dichotomy lies a conception of the distinctiveness of the nature of the French nation state which is seen to originate in the French Revolution at the end of the eighteenth century, a distinctiveness which is expressed in the contemporary nature of the mode of affinity to the French nation. One French sociologist has concluded 'La France est l'Etat-nation par excellence, et, part conséquent, la nation de l'intégration individuelle (Schnapper 1992: 114). Thus, in concluding a comparative analysis of the legislation against racism in several member states of the European Community (EC), Costa-Lascoux argues that there is a legal and political choice to be made between 'une Europe des citoyens et une Europe des minorités' (1991a: 131, see also Schnapper 1992: 151–78), the former being derived from the French national tradition and the latter from the British and Dutch national traditions.

This distinction is structured by universalism, by the notion of the French nation as the expression of the collectivity of equal and active citizens, a structuring that is thought to be absent in Britain and the Netherlands, which are characterised alternatively (and in polar opposition) as social formations shaped by institutional pluralism and decentralisation. The validity of this distinction is not relevant here (but see Lloyd 1991). It is cited to demonstrate that a specific conception of the nation will lead to a specific set of nuances to the meaning of integration. While this theme is not explored in detail below, its significance should be remembered.

INTEGRATION AS AN IDEOLOGICAL PROJECT

To what social phenomenon or process does the notion of integration refer in official discourses? What are the parameters or conditions of a state of integration? Given, so it is argued, that integration is something that is or should be happening, it follows that the condition cannot exist at present. Hence, how would we recognise it once it had been brought about?

Because the previously cited OECD report defines integration as one of the major issues arising from post-1945 international migration, one anticipates that its authors will have answered these questions. No answers are provided. We are offered only certain 'yardsticks' of integration, which are identified as the rates of naturalisation and 'mixed marriages' (OECD 1990: 17, 19). Why these are adequate measures of integration is not explained. Moreover, an explanation could not make any sense without a formal definition of integration. Hence, in this official report, the notion of integration has an ideological character and role: because it has no specific object, it can only mystify existing social relations.

This failure to define integration is neither universal nor necessary. There has been a long academic debate on the meaning of the concept (e.g. Hammar and Lithman 1987) which would require an extensive, but not an absolutely indispensable, diversion. There is more reason to consider here the definition offered by the NSCGP report to the Dutch government because of its potential significance in shaping state policy in the Netherlands and because it claims a scientific status. It distinguishes between cultural and structural integration, and it prioritises the latter, which refers to the 'inclusion of immigrants into the institutions of the host society' (1990: 45). Immigrants are 'integrated', therefore, when one can show their 'equivalent participation in the leading social sectors and institutions' (1990: 45).

Much depends upon what is meant by 'equivalent participation' and 'leading' social institutions. The report does not offer any clarification and so, for analytical purposes, some definitions must be surmised. One can interpret the latter to refer to those social institutions which have a persistent presence in the social formation, and either entail the participation of large numbers of people or have significant consequences for the functioning of other institutions within the same formation. Regarding the former, one can assume that this means that the proportion of immigrants present in each institution is the same or very similar to the proportion of immigrants, or of a specific immigrant group, in the total population. The boundary of the definition of immigrant is therefore of central importance.

If the Scientific Council considered the situation to be sufficiently serious to call upon the Dutch government to act quickly to bring about integration, it follows that integration cannot exist currently. In other words, immigrants must be excluded from the 'host institutions'. But if they are excluded, where do they live out their lives, where do they obtain the means of subsistence and reproduction, and where do they manifest their cultural distinctiveness? In short, if immigrants are excluded from the host institutions of Dutch society, where are they?

Yet, the immigrants are self-evidently present in the Netherlands because, otherwise, there would not need to be an official report which urges the state to do something about them. And action is required because immigrants are to be found in certain 'host institutions'. The Scientific Council suggests that, as a result of a dramatic increase in unemployment amongst immigrants, marginalisation is occurring (1990: 3): although no supporting evidence is offered, the Council suggests that over-representation amongst the unemployed leads to over-representation in crime and drug use, and amongst those in receipt of state welfare payments. Furthermore, a protracted state of high un-employment amongst immigrants 'tends to be passed on to succeeding generations' (1990: 51). If the state does not intervene, the report predicts 'the further growth of an ethnic sub-proletariat, with rising crime and costly welfare facilities' (1990: 10, also 58). By implication, Dutch citizens are increasingly likely to be the victims of crimes perpetrated by immigrants and to have to pay increased taxes to sustain the welfare state.

So, contrary to the initial intimation that immigrants somehow exist in a social vacuum, 'outside society', we discover that they are (reputedly) over-represented amongst the unemployed, criminals, drug users and recipients of welfare payments: immigrants are, after all, represented in certain of the 'host institutions' of Dutch society. All capitalist societies generate and require the existence of a pool of unemployed, and the state in all capitalist societies defines (and denigrates) certain kinds of practice as 'criminal'. Furthermore, during the twentieth century, the state in all European social formations has constructed a system of welfare payments and services which is available to its citizens. In other words, the reserve army of labour, the criminal justice system and state welfare systems are 'host institutions' of Dutch society, and they existed prior to the arrival of immigrants after 1945.

However, if the authors of the report are to be believed, the immigrants are not *equally* represented within these institutions. Rather, they are *over-represented.* But, if exclusion is taken as the measure of the absence of integration, it follows that inclusion to the point of over-representation must mean that a condition of *excessive* integration exists in Dutch society. After all, as the report puts it, 'genuine integration can only be said to have taken place if institutions both within and outside the sphere of government influence are in fact open to these people' (1990: 53). It would seem that the Dutch reserve army of labour and Dutch prisons are very open to 'these people'. In which case, there seems little for the state to do in promoting integration because immigrants are very well represented in certain of the central institutions.

This report to the Dutch government demonstrates very well the analytical poverty of the concept of integration: it does not have a clearly demarcated object. But, as a result, the concept has an important ideological role. If immigrants have to be integrated into society, then they must first be outside of it. Intentionally or otherwise, the ideological consequence is a legitimation of the notion that immigrants are apart from, or outside, 'our' nation state, that they do not 'belong'. Yet, where particular populations of migrant origin are over-represented amongst the unemployed or the criminalised, the proposal that this justifies a policy of integration mystifies the ever present realities and determinants of surplus and criminalised populations. Mistakenly, it suggests that these 'social problems' are a consequence of immigration, and therefore that crime and unemployment can be reduced by means of an integration policy. Thereby, the structural determination of unemployment and acts considered by the state to be illegal is obscured.

Having highlighted the involvement of immigrants in criminal activity and their over-representation amongst the unemployed, the Scientific Council is required to provide an explanation. Let us consider the example of unemployment. Since the early 1970s, this has become a central issue in political debate in the Netherlands, and in north-west Europe generally, about the consequences and necessity of international migration. It is commonly argued, as in the OECD report (1990: 19), that an integration policy should seek to reduce the level of unemployment amongst migrants or foreigners. As a result, the nature of the explanation offered for the levels of unemployment experienced by particular groups of migrants or people of migrant origin is of considerable political significance: the nature of the 'cause' should shape the solution of the problem.

The OECD report (1990: 19–21) offers a number of explanations. The immigrant labour force is described as lacking skills and progressively ageing, and so less in demand. Unemployment is also said to result from an increase in the numbers of asylum seekers and refugees. And unemployment amongst immigrant women (as well as amongst indigenous women) is said to result from 'their desire to remain on the labour market'. All of these formulations locate the explanation for unemployment either with attributed characteristics (which may or may not be valid) of the migrants (that is, lack of skills, age, desire to sell their labour power) or with the migration process (specifically, the arrival of yet other migrants). In other words, unemployment results from the migrants' own characteristics or desires, or from the arrival of other migrants. Logically, the conclusion of such an argument is that these migrants should 'go home' with their undesirable characteristics and desires, and that asylum seekers and refugees should be prevented from entering the country.

There is a silence in this argument. No attention is given to the structure, ideology and practices of the social formation into which the migrants are considered to have the obligation of integrating. For example, having few skills to sell on the labour market is only problematic if the demand for semi- or unskilled labour falls below the available supply: thus, contemporary unemployment is less a function of the possession or absence of skills and more a result of the changing structure of production and distribution, of the reconstitution of the capital accumulation process, which leads to fewer semi- and unskilled vacancies on the labour market. Increasing unemployment is the result of structural transformations within the social formation and not of individual attributes

Furthermore, the OECD report ignores the possibility that forms of exclusion (of which the ideology of racism is one) might confine migrants to inferior conditions and subordinate positions. While the report comes close to considering such a possibility when its authors refer to 'the difficulty that young second-generation immigrants are finding in gaining access to the job market' (OECD 1990: 21), the reasons for this difficulty are not explored, leaving open the possibility that it arises from some individualised attributes of the 'second generation'.

Unemployment is also discussed in the report of the Scientific Council to the Dutch government. Indeed, it is the increasing level of unemployment amongst immigrants that is identified as one of the two changes requiring the replacement of the existing 'ethnic minority' policy in the Netherlands (NSCGP 1990: 9, 51). Unlike the OECD report, this explains increasing unemployment primarily as the result of a restructuring of the Dutch economy which has led to the elimination of many semi- and unskilled jobs. It is in this sector of the labour market that certain immigrant populations have been over-represented. Furthermore, it is argued that these same immigrant populations, lacking education and relevant training, do not possess the qualifications that would permit their alternative employment in the growth sectors of the economy (1990: 51, 52).

The possibility that racism and related exclusionary practices might be another determinant of unemployment is considered tangentially. Elsewhere in the report, the Scientific Council claims that, while there has been a gradual decline in 'prejudice' during the 1980s, there is a limited amount of direct discrimination and a greater quantity of indirect discrimination 'on the grounds of race or ethnic origin' (1990: 47). The state is seen to be responsible for the elimination of discrimination and, to this end, the report recommends the introduction of a system of contract compliance and legislation which is modelled on recent Canadian law (1990: 75–7).

In this subterranean manner, racism and discrimination are conceded to be part of the explanation for the high rate of unemployment. But in the absence of an evaluation of the relative significance of these factors for an explanation for the high rate of unemployment, their significance is marginalised. Consequently, the specific need for legislation on contract compliance, etc., is not explained and the proposal appears secondary, even superfluous. This contrasts sharply with the first NSCGP report which took systematic account of the evidence concerning 'prejudice' and discrimination (1979: 60–3), and which identified the elimination of discrimination as one of the central dimensions of its recommended 'ethnic minorities' policy (1979: XXV–XXVI).

This official report to the Dutch government demonstrates that the integration problematic signifies the immigrant presence and attributed immigrant characteristics as the primary, if not the sole, reason for their subordinate social position. This is an interpretation which leaves the existing structure of political and economic relations largely undisturbed. If the processes of exclusion were shown to arise from ideologies (for example, from racism) and practices within the main institutions of the social formation, then those ideologies and practices would need to become the object of policy and action. This is avoided by locating the origin of the 'problem of integration' in the immigrant presence and by transferring the burden of the solution onto the immigrants. This is reinforced by predicating an integration policy upon a policy of strict control over, if not the termination of, immigration. This dualism was an ideological cornerstone of state intervention in Britain in the mid-1960s (Miles and Phizacklea 1984, Solomos 1990) and has been central to policy initiatives by the state in France and the Netherlands (as well as, more recently, in Italy) in the 1980s and early 1990s.

In France in December 1989, immigration control was reconfirmed as central to the policy of *intégration*. And it was the subject of discussion at a *table ronde* on 29 May 1990. All this ensured a high public profile for the state's definition of the problem and its preferred solution. The government announced later that stricter immigration controls would be necessary and outlined a series of initiatives that were being considered to achieve this (e.g. controls on individuals entering for purposes of family reunification after their arrival in France). It also expressed concern about immigration statistics, on the grounds that they were imprecise and created misunderstanding. A commitment to publish improved immigration statistics annually was given (*Le Monde*, 12 July 1990).

A similar conjunction of integration and immigration control is evident in the NSCGP report to the Dutch government. Whilst it acknowledged that immigration cannot be stopped and, indeed, that it is likely to increase (1990: 57), the report nevertheless recommended further restrictions. It proposed that labour migration from countries *other* than member states of the EC should be reduced. This, it continued, could be achieved by, *inter alia,* more thorough checks on the issue of employment permits, a prohibition on the issue of permits for semi- and unskilled work, and stricter measures to prevent the employment of illegal residents. It also recommended action to prevent the entry of asylum seekers becoming a disguised labour migration (1990: 66–7).

This interdependence of integration policy with increased controls on immigration in the report of the Scientific Council has been over-determined in several respects. First, integration policy was presented as one dimension of immigration policy. In other words, the introduction of an immigration policy was the primary objective of the state and integration was conceived as a secondary consideration. Given that the Scientific Council suggested that an immigration policy should replace the existing ethnic minorities policy, this was a significant shift in discourse and practice in that it constituted an explicit attempt from within the state to problematise immigration and the immigrant presence and to invent them as a political issue.

This was facilitated and magnified by inflating the number of people included by the category of immigrant: if immigration is *the* problem, the scale of the problem is enlarged and dramatised in proportion to the numbers of people defined as immigrants. The Scientific Council defined the concept of *immigrant* to refer to all persons of either non-indigenous or non-Dutch origin and their descendants up to and including a 'third generation' if they define themselves as non-indigenous (1990: 10, 43, 49). Thus, people born in the Netherlands of parents born outside the Netherlands were categorised as immigrants, even though they may never have crossed the border of the Dutch nation state in either direction.

This inflation was augmented by homogenising different legal statuses. The formal definition of immigrant included people who entered the Netherlands as Dutch citizens, aliens who are citizens of other member states of the EC, and aliens from other nation states. While the first two categories could be conceived of as immigrants in the limited sense that they were born outside the Netherlands, such a totalising definition nevertheless marginalised their specific legal status. For different reasons, both categories of people had or have a wholly or largely unrestricted right of entry into, and right of residence within, the Netherlands. In the case of the former category, that right followed from the fact that they possess (or possessed) the same legal status, as nationals and citizens, as people born in the Netherlands. In migrating to the Netherlands, they were moving from Dutch territory in one part of the world to Dutch territory in another. Their spatial mobility was (and is), therefore, no more than an expression of the reality of Dutch colonialism which ensured that Dutch territory was located in different parts of the world. Dutch citizens had no choice but to be 'immigrants' if they wished to move around within Dutch territory. But to categorise these Dutch citizens as immigrants along with people of non-Dutch nationality (i.e. aliens) is to marginalise and devalue this common nationality. It is an ideological process of exclusion which masquerades as science.

The homogenisation of the category of immigrant leads to deceptive conclusions about the scale and nature of immigration flows. Given that there can be few or no state-imposed and state-enforced controls on the inward movement of Dutch citizens and of citizens of other EC nation states, and in so far as there are good reasons to anticipate that inward flows of such people are likely to be sustained at current levels, or even to increase, the overall level of immigration into the Netherlands must necessarily be maintained or increased. The case for an intensification of immigration control is therefore grounded in part in an analysis which obscures the legitimacy of (and the inability of the state to control) the entry and presence of a large proportion of those collectively defined as immigrants (a point that is discussed further in Chapter 8).

Nevertheless, the Scientific Council noted that the main countries of immigrant origin were Morocco, Turkey and Surinam. Using data for 1989 cited in the Report, and a narrower definition of immigrant to include only those people resident in the Netherlands who do not possess Dutch citizenship, these three countries account for 53 per cent of immigrants (NSCGP 1990: 15). The Scientific Council predicted that 'Greater numbers of migrants may . . . be expected to start arriving from *other* countries' (1990: 57, my emphasis). The sources were identified as eastern Europe, other EC member states and 'especially' Africa (1990: 57). No attempt was made to calculate the proportions originating from these different parts of the world. Moreover, it is not clear on what basis the Council singles out Africa.

The decision to do so is difficult to defend in terms of recent migration flows and the current relative sizes of immigrant populations in the Netherlands. The number of African immigrants resident in the Netherlands in the late 1980s constituted 26 per cent of the total, which is exactly equivalent to the proportion originating from the EC. But the figure for Africa included citizens of Morocco, and the Report explicitly predicted arrivals from countries *other* than Morocco, Turkey and Surinam. If we therefore exclude Moroccan immigrants from the total for Africa, the proportion of African immigrants resident in the Netherlands is 3.5 per cent (that is, 22,087 persons).

Using an admittedly simple predictor (i.e. the relative proportion of current immigrants from different regions of origin), there is good reason to expect a much greater numerical (and probably proportionate) increase in immigration from other EC countries than from African countries (with the exception of Morocco). Moreover, the grounds for using such a predictor are consistent with the Council's assertion that migration is 'self-sustaining' by virtue of 'bridges' established between countries of origin and the Netherlands (1990: 57): the existing 'bridge' with Africa is very narrow indeed. One is left to speculate as to why, having identified increasing immigration as the primary problem, the Scientific Council chose to highlight and exaggerate African immigration when, on its own admission, immigration from elsewhere in Europe will increase and cannot be controlled.

The predication of an integration policy upon strict immigration control not only reinforces the definition of the immigrant presence as the source of the problem to be solved by state intervention. It also leads to political debate about immigration statistics, in the course of which certain interest groups often exaggerate the scale of particular migration flows. The result is not just an arid debate about 'numbers', because the statistics can be used to reinforce the claims of those who argue for more extreme solutions to the 'problem' of the immigrant presence. A similar outcome is likely in France. In the context of the focus upon *les immigrées clandestin*, the decision to publish annually 'improved' immigration statistics can be expected to result in an annual political row about numbers of immigrants which, as in the Netherlands, has become a code word for only certain 'Third World' immigrants. It is this transformation which is discussed next.

DEFINING THE IMMIGRANTS

The preceding section has concluded by suggesting that, despite appearances of universality, the integration problematic is not concerned with the integration of immigrants generally (that is, with *all* immigrants), but rather with a certain category of immigrant. In other words, the problematic is legitimated by a selective presentation of post-1945 migration into north-west Europe. And, as a result, only certain immigrants become the subject of state policies of integration.

Analyses of post-1945 migration tend to tell a similar story. While the explanation for the 'facts' often differs, depending upon the theoretical orientation of the writer (compare, for example, the work of Böhning (1984), Castles *et al.* (1984) and Verhaeren (1990)), there is general agreement on what the 'facts' are. Post–1945 migration history is presented primarily or exclusively as a movement of people from 'Third World' nation states who arrived before the crisis in the early 1970s to become semi- and unskilled manual workers in western Europe. Subsequently, a large proportion of these temporary migrants have become permanent settlers and have been joined by dependents. Thus a labour migration has been succeeded by a migration of spouses and children (e.g. Maillat 1987a). As a result of these two phases of migration, there are more than 14 million people resident in Europe who retain the legal status of *foreigner* (Maillat 1987a: 40, Layton-Henry 1990c: 2).

There is no doubt that post-1945 migration into Europe, at least up until the early 1970s, was dominated by a migration of semi- and unskilled manual labour and was determined by uneven capitalist development. Broadly speaking, the migrants originated from two distinct politico-legal contexts. First, there were those from colonies and ex-colonies of the north-west European nation states who were citizens of the latter when they migrated. Second, the Mediterranean periphery (along with Ireland in the case of Britain) provided another source of labour: again with the exception of Ireland (see Miles 1989d, Dummett and Nicol 1990: 127–9), migrants from these regions were nationals and citizens of independent nation states who therefore arrived in north-west Europe as *aliens* or *foreigners*. They were admitted by the state conditionally and temporarily but, for now well-known reasons, permanent settlement was in fact the outcome (e.g. Miles 1986). Of course, not all the migrants have remained and settled, and there is a continuing return migration even now (OECD 1990: 15–16), but a very large proportion have in fact done so.

However, this is not an exhaustive account of post-1945 migration into north-west Europe. As I have shown in Chapter 4, the composition of international migration is more complex. Other migrations have occurred and continue to occur, but they are rarely noted or analysed. This silence expresses the assumptions that the only significant migrations are those that originate from the 'Third World' and result in settlement, that labour migration is a category that includes only those who are spatially mobile in order to provide manual labour, and that the category of 'foreigner' is homogeneous (cf. Miles and Satzewich 1990). In addition to refugee migrations, there are two others that are relevant here although, in reality, it is difficult to disentangle one completely from another.

First, there has been, and there continues to be, a migration of managerial, professional, technical and scientific workers, a large proportion of whom originate from other advanced capitalist nation states. These, too, are foreign migrant workers, although in comparison to the movement of manual labourers they are a very privileged category. There is also an associated, shorter-term migration of business persons. In Britain, during the mid-1980s, the number of work permits issued by the Overseas Labour Division of the Department of Employment increased from 15,700 in 1984 to 26,000 in 1988 (OECD 1990: 127, Salt and Kitching 1990). The number of applications is probably in excess of the number issued: a consultant who established a company to make applications for work permits on behalf of clients has estimated that the annual total is more than 35,000 (*The Independent on Sunday*, 8 July 1990). These work permits are of three kinds (long-term, short-term and for trainees), with the majority of long-term permits being issued to 'highly skilled workers'. Between 1984 and 1988, the number of long-term permits issued annually increased from 6,800 to 10,400. In 1988, 3,400 (or 33 per cent of the total) were issued to nationals of the USA and 2,100 (or 20 per cent) to nationals of Japan. A further 1,300 (12.5 per cent) were issued to nationals of European countries other than member states of the EC.

Foreigners are also permitted to enter Britain 'for business purposes', without a work permit, for up to twelve months. The number of such admissions has increased steadily from 548,491 in 1974 to 987,000 in 1986, with a peak of 1,024,000 in 1985 (*Control of Immigration*

Statistics, United Kingdom, 1974–1986, London: HMSO, 1975–87). Nationals of EC member states are excluded from these statistics. It is not clear what criteria are employed in determining whether or not an individual is seeking entry for 'business purposes' and there are no published statistics concerning the country of origin, the length of stay or the numbers who fail to leave the country. A large proportion of this migration probably consists of employees engaged in temporary company business (sales, administration, planning, etc.) as well as self-employed professional and technical persons.

Evidence concerning the scale of these migrations to other European countries is limited. The OECD survey of migration noted, as the decade of the 1990s began, that one of the main features of international migration was an increased flow of skilled workers between the highly industrialised countries (OECD 1990: 1). However, in addition to Britain, evidence was cited for only two other countries. In Belgium, 2,790 work permits were issued in 1988 to migrants, 32 per cent of which were to nationals of the United States, Canada and Japan (OECD 1990: 33). In 1988, 27 per cent of the foreign workers admitted to France were from North America and Asia-Oceana (which includes Japan) (OECD 1990: 124). In the absence of further data, we cannot be certain that these migrants are in fact providing skilled non-manual labour, although these countries have no significant tradition of emigrants seeking semi- and unskilled manual work in Europe. Additionally, data for the Netherlands have shown that there were 10,826 nationals of the United States, 2,674 nationals of Canada and 3,466 nationals of Japan resident in the country in 1988 (Muus 1990: 14), although again no information was provided about their employment status.

Against the background of this statistical evidence, it is relevant to note also the privileged position within European immigration law of migrants from other advanced capitalist nation states: the conditions governing the entry of such migrants into western European nation states are generally less restrictive than for nationals of other nation states. In France, for example, a visa requirement for entry into the country was reintroduced in September 1986 for nationals of all nation states other than those belonging to the EC and Switzerland. This, however, was subsequently relaxed. In December 1988, the requirement was removed in the case of nationals of other western European nation states and, during 1989, for nationals of the USA, Canada and Japan (OECD 1990: 38).

These recent changes in France assume greater significance in the light of the signing by the French government of the Schengen Treaty in 1985.

With the governments of Germany, Belgium, Luxembourg and the Netherlands (later joined by the Italian government), it agreed to abolish frontier control at the internal borders between these five countries and to harmonise visa policies (Groenendijk 1989). Detailed discussion about the latter includes other EC member states and has been taking place within the framework of the Trevi Groups of EC ministers and the Immigration Group of EC ministers (Cruz 1990). The objective is to agree on a list of countries from which all member states of the EC will require nationals to obtain a visa prior to departure and on another list of countries whose nationals will not require a visa. The latter list includes 25 countries. In addition to the EC member states, these include the EFTA (European Free Trade Association) countries (Norway, Sweden, Switzerland, Austria and Iceland), the five European mini-states and probably Australia, Canada and Japan. While agreement has not been reached as to which list all other countries will be placed on, all of those on the former (negative) list are from eastern Europe, Africa, Asia, and south and central America (Groenendijk 1989: 34). However, since German unification, the visa requirement for certain east European countries has been abolished. In this way, the category of foreigner or alien is being (re)divided into two classes, one of which is attributed with a more privileged status than the other.

The second migration to which little attention is paid is intra-EC migration. This silence cannot be justified in terms of numbers. Moreover, it has resulted in temporary and permanent settlement. In the mid-1980s, there were approximately 4.75 million people resident in EC member states who were nationals of other EC member states (Petri-Guasco 1989: 16, see also Venturini 1989, Lebon 1990). Excluding Spain and Portugal, around 2 million wage-earners live and work in an EC member state other than the one in which they are defined as a national. The nation states with the largest number of residents originating from other EC member states were, in descending order, France (1,577,860 persons), Germany (1,364,800 persons) and Britain (742,000 persons).

Analysis of the country of origin of the majority of these contemporary foreign residents suggests at least a partial explanation for this migration. For example, there were 764,860 Portuguese, 333,740 Italians and 321,440 Spaniards resident in France in 1982. In Germany, in 1986, there were 537,100 Italians, 278,500 Greeks and 150,500 Spaniards. Italy, Portugal, Spain and Greece were the most important sources of foreign manual labour during the first phase of capitalist reconstruction in north-west Europe after 1945. Britain is the exception in so far as the majority of residents of other EC countries originate from Ireland, but it is Ireland which has traditionally supplied (and continues to supply) the reserve army of manual labour for capital (Miles 1982).

This is not a complete explanation. It does not explain, for example, why it is that there are just over one million French, German, British, Belgian and Dutch citizens resident in other EC countries (Petri-Guasco 1989: 16). Moreover, the vast majority of these citizens are resident in other advanced capitalist nation states within the EC. For example, of the 289,842 French citizens resident elsewhere in the EC, 103,215 are resident in Belgium, 76,700 in Germany and 37,000 in Britain (i.e. 216,915 persons or 74.84 per cent of the total). More recent data for the Netherlands (Muus 1990) underline the significance of this intra-EC migration. During the 1980s, there was a small, but continuing, increase in the number of Dutch citizens residing in other European countries, from 293,400 in 1984 to 304,100 in 1988. In 1988, 113,900 Dutch citizens were resident in West Germany, 76,400 in Belgium, 30,600 in Britain and 20,000 in France. Indeed, overall, the number of Dutch nationals residing abroad in 1988 (642,800) was higher than the number of foreign residents living in the Netherlands (591,800).

Given the limited evidence, one can offer only a preliminary explanation for this category of intra-EC migration. The determinants are likely to include marriage to a citizen of another EC nation state, advanced educational study, and service in the diplomatic corps abroad. Moreover, given the terms of the Treaty of Rome, it will also include labour migrants, both manual as well as managerial, professional, scientific and technical employees. A further determinant will be the pursuit of business interests within the EC by owners of large and small capital. Finally, certain migrations and settlements are likely to be the result of decisions to live in another EC country after retirement from paid employment or business activity. This would partially explain the fact that, for example, there were 35,263 British nationals resident in Spain in 1984 (Petri-Guasco 1989: 16).

Selective accounts of post-1945 European migration history should be challenged, not only to sustain the tradition of a critical scientific analysis, but also to identify the political interests that are served by the legitimation of such accounts. Without such a challenge, one becomes complicit in the official image that the nation is 'under seige' as a result of uncontrolled migration from 'Third World' countries. The reality is that, as a result of state decisions, it is intra-EC migration that is increasingly uncontrolled by the state, and that certain migrations from other centres of the world capitalist system are also increasing. It is these migrations that we do not see and that the state does not signify as a problem.

Moreover, there are migrations which the state used to interpret as problematic but which are no longer signified as such. The example of Portuguese and Spanish migration to France illustrates this very well: migrants from these countries are the previously racialised Other that has been redefined as European. Thus, when the state in north-west Europe advances an integration policy for immigrants, it does not problematise all immigrants, but only certain categories of immigrant. State definitions can only be challenged adequately if the categories and the manner of their employment can be deconstructed: challenging the referent of the category of immigrant is therefore an essential analytical task.

'STANDING ON THEIR OWN FEET'

The adoption of a selective policy of integration by the state has political and ideological consequences which can have at least a conjunctural, and perhaps a strategic, utility from the point of view of the interests of the state and of capital. The integration problematic refracts certain real problems and resignifies 'ordinary' processes which are integral to the reproduction of capital and the nation state. This is evident in the report of the Scientific Council to the Dutch government, which expresses two main concerns.

The first concerns the maintenance of social order. Criminal behaviour is, from the perspective of the state, a condition of disorder and requires the use of scarce resources to restore order (NSCGP 1990: 58). The Scientific Council anticipated (without an explicit justification) a rising crime rate, and increasing immigrant participation in crime (NSCGP 1990: 10). Furthermore, the Council foresaw some kind of open conflict, or 'social polarisation' as the authors preferred to describe it (NSCGP 1990: 52), between immigrants and the Dutch population. Concern was also expressed that Dutch freedoms 'can sometimes be subject to militant attack' as a result of cultural diversity and confrontation (NSCGP 1990: 59).

Conflicts between immigrant and indigenous populations are not illusory. But the integration problematic signifies these conflicts 'immigrant conflicts'. Hence, conflicts that have their source in the ever present processes that create surplus and criminalised populations are ideologically subverted and resignified in such a way that their origin is externalised, in the sense that they are interpreted as having arisen from the presence of a population which originated from beyond the boundary of the nation state. The integration problematic thereby constitutes a symbolic statement by the state to 'its own people' that 'their concerns' about 'immigrant crime', for example, have been acknowledged and will be dealt with by ensuring that the numbers of immigrants entering the nation state will be reduced and by requiring those 'immigrants' allowed to remain to behave in an acceptable manner.

Second, the report of the Scientific Council to the Dutch government conceived of immigrants as a contingent category (1990: 53), a category which is 'poorly placed to contribute effectively towards Dutch society' (1990: 58). This alleged failure to contribute, to 'pay their way' (and so the necessity that, in the future, they 'stand on their own feet' (NSCGP 1990: 9)), should be rectified to ensure 'social justice' (NSCGP 1990: 58). Simultaneously, it was claimed that immigrants constitute assets, the 'development of which is in society's interests' (NSCGP 1990: 58). The Council concluded that immigrants can best show their intention to contribute to Dutch society by participating in the 'host institution' of wage labour, with petit-bourgeois enterprise as a secondary option (NSCGP 1990: 77). Rather than be over-represented in the 'host institutions' of crime and welfare state dependency, the immigrants should be selling their labour power. This was thought to be especially necessary because Dutch employers, eager to compete successfully in the international economy, face a shortage of skilled labour (1990: 59). So, in order to ensure the survival of Dutch capitalists and to continue to attract international capital to the Netherlands, immigrants should be trained to provide a quality of labour power suitable for the new phase of capitalist development.

The Scientific Council saw such an outcome as having another benefit. It claimed that immigrants, having become 'dependent', thereby constitute a drain on the resources of the welfare state. Dependency means that the Dutch population provides the material resources to support the immigrants who, by failing to work, prove they are not conforming to Dutch standards and are therefore not worthy members of the nation. Training and entry into wage labour were portrayed as a solution to what are real problems (the fiscal crisis and reproducing the sense of nation), because immigrants would then become net contributors to the welfare state and in this way would prove themselves to be worthy members of the nation.

Despite having stressed the liberalism and tolerance of Dutch society (NSCGP 1990: 59), the Scientific Council's recommendations had a distinctly authoritarian character. It suggested that, where immigrants refused to accept suitable training, basic education and/or work experience, sanctions should be applied (1990: 86). By making training available, it proposed that the Dutch state had 'the right to demand of immigrants in the Netherlands at public expense that they acquire the necessary skills to function in Dutch society and to impose penalties where people fail to cooperate' (NSCGP 1990: 99). Reference to this 'right' contradicted the claim made elsewhere in the Report that 'Public coercion has proved a poor substitute for the spontaneous acceptance of responsibility and accountability' (NSCGP 1990: 75). This 'general principle' was used by the Council to explain why it was not recommending that employers be required by law to employ a quota of immigrants. Furthermore, the Council stressed that its recommended legislative obligations on employers should be non-punishable. Clearly, what is good enough for capitalists is not good enough for immigrant labour.

CONCLUSION

Much of the content of this chapter has taken the form of a critique of a report submitted to the Dutch government. This is, in part, because of the report's potential to influence state policy and the wider political debate in the Netherlands. But it is also because the circumstances in which the report was written prevail elsewhere in Europe. The reconstruction of the capital accumulation process, the fiscal crisis of the state and the reproduction of the nation are ongoing throughout Europe. It is not only the Dutch state that has to oversee the restructuring of the economy, the social order and the welfare state in a political context where the expression of racism is increasing. Whether or not the Dutch government, or other European government, will follow the path identified by the NSCGP report remains to be seen. While there are good reasons to anticipate varying political and ideological reactions on the part of the state in different countries to these tasks (Bovenkerk *et al.* 1990), recent events may nevertheless be taken by other states as a model. Certainly the linking of the policy objective of strict immigration control with that of integration has happened in Britain, France and (more recently) Italy.

There is another reason to focus on this official report. The ideological work required to ensure this particular articulation between integration and immigration was undertaken in the name of science. A critical analysis of the report of the Scientific Council is therefore justified in order to assess its scientific status, its 'truth value'. I have shown that the report contains unwarranted assumptions and a series of arguments which are founded on a problematic analysis of immigration statistics.

Moreover, the use of the integration problematic has the result (if not the intention) of removing the issues of racism and discrimination from the political agenda. These issues have been replaced with an alternative conceptualisation which alleges that immigrants (meaning, in fact, only certain groups of immigrants) have become a disintegrative force within the Dutch social formation.

Such a suggestion not only provides an ideological explanation for certain features of the current conjuncture but also generates a 'solution' in the form of compulsion upon unemployed and 'criminal' immigrants to become skilled manual labourers in the Dutch economy, and in the form of a strengthening of the system of strict immigration control. As a result, with the dichotomy between Dutch citizens and the immigrant Other renewed and reworked, Dutch citizens have been assured that the crisis of 'their own society' will be solved in their own interests by 'their state'. Thus, the integration problematic constitutes an important ideological moment in the ongoing process of nationalising the Dutch social formation, of reconstituting the nation form as a bourgeois institution of domination.

But this is a moment in a wider struggle: a combination of social forces is challenging this integration problematic and the immigration policy that derives from it. Underlying these challenges is another way of interpreting the situation, an alternative to the integration problematic. Rather than view the subjects of integration strategies from the perspective of the state, as the objects of the state as it seeks to renegotiate the conditions for the reproduction of capital and of the nation state, one can see them as social actors seeking ways to respond to the disadvantaged position in which so many find themselves. In attempting to define the terms of their inclusion within the nation states of Europe, they are continuing a historical struggle for equality and for a widening of the scope of the category of citizenship, political principles which accompanied the birth of the bourgeois nation state. The problem, therefore, is not a problem of integration, but rather a problem of inequality and exclusion, a problem which tests the capacity of capitalism and of the nation state to realise in practice the values of universalism and equality.

Chapter 8

Migration and the nation state in Europe: contradictions and transformations

Few people in the United Kingdom seem yet to have grasped that the British government no longer has absolute control over entry and settlement in the United Kingdom, and that what power it has now will diminish within the bounds of Community law.

(Dummett and Nicol 1990: 258)

A propos des «étrangers», les Etats membres de la Communauté, qui envisagent l'abolition des frontières communes et la création d'un espace commun, ne pourront plus légiférer en matière d'entrée et même de séjour sans se concerter au préalable entre eux, sous peine de laisser se développer des pratiques ou des inégalités de traitement incompatibles avec la définition d'un espace commun.

(de Lary 1989: 107)

INTRODUCTION

The crisis in the world capitalist economy of the early 1970s brought an end to a large-scale labour migration into north-west Europe that had begun soon after the end of the Second World War. But the emergence of that crisis was followed by neither the termination of inward migration nor the elimination of immigration as a theme in political debate. Indeed, since the early 1970s, immigration has continued (as it has to other centres of the capitalist world economy, including the United States: see Sassen 1988) and migration, as the object of political struggle, has moved increasingly to the centre of the political stage of most nation states in western Europe (cf. Schnapper 1992: 29–61).

Immigration became an increasingly important item on the political agenda in the nation states of western Europe during the 1970s, and in most of them, it became pivotal during the 1980s, especially in France and Germany (e.g. Hollifield 1986, Wihtol de Wenden 1988, Wieviorka 1992). During the latter decade, the same debate spread to the southern nation states of Europe, especially Italy (Palidda and Campani 1990). The widely publicised racist attacks on migrants from Africa in Firenze in March 1990 occurred in a context where new immigration controls were under discussion, controls that were intended to limit migration from Africa in particular (*The Guardian*, 13 April 1990, *The Independent on Sunday*, 15 April 1990).

This interrelationship between immigration legislation and physical attacks on migrants has parallels in other European countries: throughout the region, the increasing level of public hostility to certain categories of migrant, the evidence of material disadvantage experienced by certain populations of migrant origin, and the evolution of the single market within the European Community (EC) are amongst the factors ensuring that migration has become the focus of conflict between different political forces. Threaded through (although subordinate to) that conflict has been another debate, one concerning the nature and effects of racism in western Europe. It, too, is now firmly placed on the political agenda, as is demonstrated by, *inter alia*, the two investigations conducted by the European Parliament into the extent of racism within the EC (e.g. Runnymede Trust 1987).

This chapter will focus on the twelve nation states which collectively constitute the EC rather than Europe as a whole, although mention will be made of eastern Europe in the light of certain of the consequences of the collapse of 'really existing socialism'. Furthermore, for reasons argued elsewhere (Bovenkerk *et al.* 1990, 1991), analytical priority will be given to the role of the state. The intention is to identify the main contradictions in the contemporary conjuncture between the reality of migration flows and their determinants, the evolution of state and suprastate policies concerning immigration and its various consequences, and the ideological content of the political debate about migration.

MIGRATION AND THE DISSOLUTION OF THE NATION STATE

The continuing international movement of capital and labour and political displacement of populations have intensified a developing contradiction in contemporary Europe, the underlying causes of which lie in the ongoing internationalisation of capital. That contradiction is between, on the one hand, the reproduction of the ideology and institutional reality of the nation state and, on the other, its partial dissolution within Europe as a result of its inability to accommodate itself to certain consequences of the reproduction of the capitalist mode of production. This is manifested in a number of interconnected migration-related processes and events.

During the era of post-1945 mass labour migration, a large proportion of those recruited to fill vacancies in national labour markets in Europe were juridically foreigners. They lacked the requisite nationality and rights of citizenship awarded by the state in the national territory which they had entered in order to become sellers of labour power. For several million of these 'birds of passage', their intended temporariness was transformed into effective permanent settlement. Where they were not encouraged, or where they were not willing, to undergo naturalisation, they (and often their children) have remained (or, in the case of the children, they became) juridically foreigners. As a result, they continue to be deprived of a variety of civil and political rights and obligations while having become permanent residents within Europe (Rogers 1986, Hammar 1990, Layton-Henry 1990b).

Juridically, they 'belong' elsewhere. Given a political world order where, since the nineteenth century, each nation is supposed to have its own sovereign territory wherein the population has been granted by the state the status of national and also (usually as a result of political struggle) the right to political expression and representation (that is, citizenship), it follows that those who 'belong' to a nation should reside within its territory. The presence of a large proportion of these migrants and their descendants within the nation states of the EC, sustained by the continuing demand for the labour power of the majority, is therefore anomalous: they are a permanent presence but they have limited rights of political participation and a qualified right of residence within Europe.

The legal distinction between *national* and *foreigner* (which only evolved in its current form during the nineteenth century) is therefore blurred, demonstrating that the existing political structures seem to be unable to contain the political consequences of the earlier migration of labour that was necessary to sustain the capital accumulation process. As a result, there is an evolving crisis of bourgeois democracy within the European nation state (cf. Balibar 1992). For example, in France, there is an ongoing struggle to dissociate the rights of citizenship from the juridical category of nationality in order to permit those permanent residents in France who do not possess French nationality to exercise in full the right of political and social participation (Silverman 1991, 1992). Specifically, the demand for voting rights for permanent residents of EC nation states who possess the nationality of a non-EC nation state is being raised throughout the EC (Rath 1990).

This contradiction is intensified by the consequences of the implementation *within* the EC of the principle of the free movement of labour. Since 1968, nationals of each member nation state have had the right to seek work and to take up residence in any other, subject to certain restrictions and limitations (Straubhaar 1984, Molle and Van Mourik 1988: 336, Leonard 1988: 117–8, 173, Penninx and Muus 1989: 377, European Commission 1990: 40–1). As a result, nationals of a member state have the right to seek and be offered work, and to take up residence, in any other member nation state of the EC (but not yet the right to vote, although this possibility has been discussed (Leonard 1988: 155) and there is a clause to this effect in the Maastricht Treaty). In enacting this right, EC member states have accepted that, as far as the circulation and recruitment of labour *within* the EC is concerned, it should not be subject to any substantial state regulation where the worker is a national of one of the member states.

The result is a European labour market which is now bounded by a supranational institution and a supranational territorial border. This, too, blurs the duality of national and foreigner: within each of these nation states, the juridical dichotomy between 'our own people' and foreigners has been partially dissolved because the nationals and citizens of other member nation states of the EC have been granted a set of rights which are identical to those of its own nationals and citizens, at least as far as the labour market, residence and social security provisions, etc., are concerned.

The contradiction is overdetermined by the intersection of the two processes, which are moving in different directions. For nationals of member nation states of the EC, the partial dissolution of the duality between national and foreigner reinforces the disadvantaged position of those migrants, and their descendants, who originate from nation states beyond the boundaries of Europe and who have become permanent residents within the EC (a population often described as 'third country nationals'). Where they have not been (or have been unable to be) naturalised, their juridical status as foreigner is reproduced and reinforced by those EC provisions which apply only to the nationals and citizens of each member nation state. The ongoing dissolution of the significance of the distinction between national and foreigner for nationals of member nation states of the EC refracts the increasing rightlessness (although this too is a relative rather than an absolute condition) of the foreign population of non-EC origin which is permanently resident within the EC. Hence, the principle of a single market within the EC is contradicted by the presence of several million people who are not free to live and work where they wish, as is the right of nationals of EC member states. This contradiction has become an issue for debate within the EC and proposals have been made to transcend it partially (Böhning and Werquin 1990).

A further measure of the partial dissolution of the nation state is provided by the attempt to abolish border controls between member nation states of the EC, and to formulate and implement a common immigration policy for the EC. However, there is a struggle within the EC over these initiatives because certain EC states wish to retain specific powers to regulate migration across their national borders. This struggle, in turn, refracts the attempt of certain political forces to sustain the powers of the nation state against the encroaching power of supranational political structures.

The logic of the provisions for the free movement of labour within the EC leads inexorably to the proposal to abolish state regulation of the movement of all people (and not just those seeking paid work) across the internal, national borders of the EC. Article 2 of the Treaty of Rome, signed on 25 March 1957, committed its signatories to 'the abolition, as between Member States, of obstacles to the freedom of movement for persons, services and capital' (cited in Leonard 1988: 24). Few initiatives were made to this end until the mid-1980s when member states committed themselves to the completion of the internal market by the end of 1992. A White Paper was then drawn up which outlined proposals for the removal of physical, technical and fiscal barriers to the completion of this market. The result was the Single European Act which came into force on 1 July 1987 with the objective of creating a single market within the EC from 1 January 1993 (Venturini 1989: 26–7, 77–8). This entailed the creation of 'a Europe without frontiers', a Europe without controls on the internal movement of people, capital, services and commodities (European Commission 1988: 31–59).

The decision to abolish internal barriers to the free movement of nationals of EC member states has led to an attempt to harmonise national immigration policies and practices. This has proven difficult to achieve (e.g. *Social Europe* 1988: 31–3). A European Commission decision of 1985 to establish a communication and consultation procedure on migration policies within the EC was declared void by the European Court of Justice in 1987 following an appeal by five member states (Simmonds 1988). Since then, the initiative has been taken, not by the European Commission, but by a number of separate intergovernmental bodies whose members are nevertheless members of the EC (Cruz 1990). The most important of these has been the Schengen group (formed in

1985) whose original members were the governments of France, Germany, Belgium, Luxembourg and the Netherlands. Italy joined the Group later. Their deliberations led to the signing of a formal agreement in June 1990 on a common policy abolishing border controls between the respective territories from 1 January 1993 (*The Independent*, 7 June 1990).

From what is known about the Schengen Treaty (Baldwin-Edwards 1991, Costa-Lascoux 1991b), and from related discussion in other semi-secret intergovernmental bodies, it is clear that a corollary of free movement of EC nationals within the European Community will be the introduction and policing of far stricter controls at the external borders and the harmonisation of visa policies (Gordon 1989, Greater Manchester Immigration Aid Unit 1990). Yet there has been considerable opposition within the EC to the abolition of internal border controls. The British government has been at the forefront, supported by the Irish, Danish and Greek governments, claiming that the Single European Act did not impose an obligation to abolish internal border controls on the movement of people from other EC countries as from 1 January 1993 (*The Independent*, 27 November 1990, *The Guardian* 10 January 1991). They argue that economic and political factors will make illegal migration from outside the EC an even greater problem and that it will become more difficult to control if border controls are abolished.

For geo-spatial and ideological reasons, the greatest apprehension originally concerned migration from the southern edge of the EC. The fear was, and is, that the Mediterranean Sea will become Europe's Rio Grande, no more than a minor obstacle for the 'millions' of Africans seeking to enter the EC illegally (e.g. NSCGP 1990: 57), with the result that member states such as Italy, Spain and Portugal occupy the first lines of 'defence'. Since 1989, new fears have been articulated: speculation has increased about a large-scale migration from eastern Europe, one that places Germany (and Austria) in the front line against an 'invasion' from the east.

Alongside the collapse of 'really existing socialism', there has been a dismantling of the physical barriers and military patrols that divided eastern from western Europe. With the introduction of bourgeois democracy, there has been the promise, if not yet the practice, of issuing passports to the nationals of all east European nation states. And with the introduction of capitalist market relations, there have been large increases in unemployment and an intensification of material disadvantage. As a result, eastern Europe, and especially Russia, has become a large reservoir of potential migrants, although opinion differs on the scale of that potential (Cohen 1991, Okolski 1991, Vichnevski and Zayontch-kovskaia 1991). During 1990, for example, officials in what was then the Soviet Union reported that up to 3 million Soviet citizens could migrate annually to western Europe from 1991 (*The Independent* 25 September 1990, 1 December 1990).

While it is doubtful whether such large numbers of people have the resources needed to migrate to the EC, it is certain that eastern Europe has become a major site of emigration (SOPEMI 1991: 8–18) and that the architects of control are no longer the communist-controlled states of eastern Europe but those of western Europe (Zolberg 1989: 412–14). There is the additional possibility of large refugee migrations in the event of the disintegration of extant nation states in central and eastern Europe. The attempt by Albanian refugees to enter Italy during 1991 was a small example of this potential. The civil war in what was Yugoslavia is a more dramatic example.

The potential for new or increased migration into the EC (which is discussed further below) from the south *and* the east is central to the political struggle within the EC over the advisability and possibility of a common immigration policy and the form that a Europe without barriers to internal mobility (for nationals of member nation states) should take. However those struggles are resolved, the signing of the Schengen Treaty nevertheless reinforced the abolition of a key dimension of state power, the power to regulate the movement of citizens of other nation states across national boundaries. The abolition is far from absolute as yet: internal controls remain, and the freedom of movement is restricted formally to nationals of the other signatory member nation states. Yet it is another indication that the political structures that have evolved in parallel with the development of capitalism within Europe for the past one hundred years or more are increasingly incompatible with its future development.

THE DISCOURSE OF CONTROL AND THE REALITY OF IMMIGRATION

Broadly speaking, the twenty years from the early 1950s to the early 1970s constituted a period of large-scale labour migration into western Europe (Castles and Kosack 1973, Castles *et al*. 1984, Cohen 1987, Miles 1987a). The origin of the migrants, their legal status, and the role of the state in the processes of recruitment, travel, admission, residence and employment varied from one nation state to another (Hammar 1985). But, with certain exceptions, the state explicitly promoted and legitimated immigration as a political and economic necessity. Since the early 1970s, this discourse has been replaced by one which stresses the necessity for strict (and stricter) immigration controls. Thus, during 1991 alone, three large international conferences were held in Europe to discuss migration trends and methods of regulation (SOPEMI 1991: 15).

As we have seen in Chapter 7, this policy change has been accompanied by the adoption of integration as a related objective. Throughout the EC, politicians and state officials argue that a central precondition for the 'integration' of migrants is that 'our own people' feel assured that immigration either has been stopped or is strictly controlled. But the interrelated discourses of immigration control and integration coexist with the continuation of a number of migration flows into the nation states of the EC. The result is a contradiction, one that is intensified in so far as the ability of the state to control migration is constrained in a number of ways. At the beginning of the 1990s, this continuing migration included the following categories, most of which are likely to continue at some level throughout this decade (cf. Baldwin-Edwards 1991).

First, there are the spouses, children and other family relatives of earlier migrants (a large proportion of whom were aliens who were originally granted temporary entry on the basis of a legal contract in order that they might sell their labour power) who retain and exercise a legal right of entry in order to facilitate 'family reunion' (Maillat 1987b: 43–9, SOPEMI 1990: 7, 1991: 19). Most, if not all, EC states are considering or seeking to reduce the scope of the legal criteria of eligibility of these 'dependents'. This has been a central objective of immigration policy in Britain since 1962, the most recent legislation having been passed in 1988 (Miles and Phizacklea 1984, Gordon 1989: 16). A report to the Dutch government published in 1989, while opposing any new restrictions on immigration for the purpose of 'family reunion', nevertheless indicated the initiatives that could be taken if the government so desired. These included redefining the existing boundary of 'family dependent' and introducing the requirement that family members would only be admitted where it had been demonstrated that they would be supported by the family without recourse to state funds (NSCGP 1990: 66–7). These criteria have been used elsewhere in the EC, including France (e.g. Wihtol de Wenden 1991: 324), to reduce the migration of family members.

The scope for restriction is not absolute, however. Humanitarian and moral considerations constitute a limit on the action of the state, as do existing national and international laws and formal commitments to human rights' principles and charters. While these do not prevent the introduction of further restrictions, they do provide a standard against which to evaluate a state's intentions and actions, and therefore a site from which opposition can be organised. Within the EC, agreed common policies, laws and principles can be enforced by means of appeals to the European Court of Justice or to the European Court of Human Rights.

Second, foreigners continue to be recruited (both legally and illegally) to fill specific positions in the labour market. Indeed, there has been an increase in such recruitment and migration since the early 1980s (Maillat 1987b: 54, Salt and Kitching 1990, SOPEMI 1990: 7–13) and there are reasons, both economic and demographic (OECD 1991), to expect this to continue through the 1990s. In part, the labour shortages have been for semi- and unskilled manual labour. The recent growth of the construction industry and the service sector in Italy, Spain, Portugal and Greece has occurred partly on the basis of the recruitment of 'Third World' migrants, often from north Africa, who have entered southern Europe illegally (Simon 1987: 284–9, Calvaruso 1987, Soulis 1987, *Social Europe* 1988: 22, Penninx and Muus 1989: 378, SOPEMI 1991: 21–5, Venturini 1991). Attempts have been made by the state in these countries to restrict and regulate this migration (e.g. Martiniello 1991, SOPEMI 1991: 24, 36). In the case of Italy, the 'Martelli' law of 30 December 1989 granted an amnesty for illegal migrants and introduced quotas for the issue of work permits to non-EC citizens (*The Independent on Sunday*, 6 January 1991). Its objective was to bring Italian immigration law and practice into line with that of the majority of other EC nation states, and thereby facilitate Italian entry into the Schengen Group.

In Germany, the recruitment of semi- and unskilled foreign labour has continued, in part, in the form of subcontracting agreements between German and foreign firms, as a result of which foreign workers enter Germany to work on the basis of temporary work contracts (SOPEMI 1990: 11). Furthermore, the increasing migration of *aussiedler* and *übersiedler* (see below) during the late 1980s was a disguised labour migration. In addition, there has been an increasing semi-legal and illegal migration from eastern Europe (and especially from Poland) into Germany (Martin *et al.* 1990: 601): most of the migrants are seeking paid work or entry into some kind of trading activity. The German state (along with those of France and Belgium) signed bilateral agreements with the Polish and/or Czechoslovak states governing the migration of short-term and/or seasonal labour following the collapse of communism in central and eastern Europe (SOPEMI 1991: 18, 32). These short-term shortages of semiskilled labour are recurrent in most EC countries, where they are also solved by the recruitment of foreign labour: for example, small numbers of foreign workers were recruited in the Netherlands in 1990 to fill jobs in the metal industry and for seasonal work in the bulb industry (SOPEMI 1991: 58).

As we have seen in Chapter 7, there has also been an increasing demand for, and recruitment of, skilled professional and managerial labour from countries outside Europe (e.g. Penninx and Muus 1989: 384, SOPEMI 1990: 11, 1991: 32–3, Miles 1990c: 294–5, Miles and Satzewich 1990, Salt and Kitching 1990). Assessing the scale of the resulting migration is difficult because of the lack of published statistics. But it is evident, for example, in the issue of work permits by the Belgian, Dutch and British states to nationals of countries such as the United States, Canada and Japan (e.g. SOPEMI 1990: 33, 57, 1991: 42). This is a consequence of the inward capital investment by international companies based outside the EC, an investment that is often managed by nationals from the country of origin. To take another (and different) example, in 1990 local authorities in Britain were recruiting foreign labour from outside as well as inside Europe to help solve a shortage of school teachers (*The Independent*, 3 September 1990).

Formally, these labour migrations can be closely controlled because non-EC foreigners continue to be permitted to enter an EC nation state on conditions set by, and at the will of, the state. There are two senses in which this control is mediated in practice. In situations of labour shortage, employers are likely to demand that the state sanctions or organises labour migration on an appropriate scale. Moreover, even in situations of high internal unemployment, some fractions of capital prefer or even require the employment of cheap and illegal migrant labour, and this demand sustains a continuing illegal migration, as has been especially evident in the 'new immigration countries' of southern Europe during the 1980s.

Third, there is a continuing migration of people seeking political asylum in Europe. The number of people entering the EC with the intention of claiming the right of asylum increased during the 1980s (e.g. Cohen and Joly 1989: 11, SOPEMI 1990: 3). Between 200,000 and 300,000 asylum seekers arrived during 1990 (Martin *et al.* 1990: 601). Descriptions of this as a 'massive influx' are increasingly common (e.g. SOPEMI 1990: 2) even though the scale of the migration remains small when measured in relation to the size of the total population of the individual nation states and the scale of other migrations (Cohen and Joly 1989: 8). Most EC governments have argued that many of those seeking refugee status are, in reality, economic migrants seeking entry solely in order to find paid work. Such interpretations are often legitimated in the reports of international organisations such as the OECD (e.g. SOPEMI 1990: 2). During 1990 and 1991, there has been an emergent consensus amongst EC states that measures must be taken to restrict and reduce these flows.

Again, the scope for state intervention is constrained by international law and conventions: for example, the 1951 United Nations Convention on the Status of Refugees defined a refugee as a person who has a 'well-founded fear of being persecuted for reasons of race, religion, nationality, membership of a particular social group or political opinion' (cited in Greater Manchester Immigration Aid Unit 1990: 15). The fact that all EC governments have signed this Convention means that there is a formal limit to their increasingly restrictive interpretation of this definition and, as a result, it is impossible to terminate absolutely the migration of refugees. However, with new initiatives under active discussion in an attempt to reduce the number of people seeking asylum actually entering EC nation states, there are increasing fears that refugees will be unable to leave, or will be returned to, situations where their fear of persecution is well founded (e.g. *The Guardian* 4 January 1991). And, in 1990 and 1991, a number of EC states have rescinded the eligibility for refugee status in the case of at least some of the east European nation states which have reintroduced capitalist market relations (SOPEMI 1991: 31).

Fourth, there is a continuing migration of nationals of other EC member nation states. Compared with the previous three categories, and for reasons previously discussed, this migration is subject to even less political control by the state, and the degree of control is likely to decrease in the future. Despite certain obstacles (Simon 1991), migration *within* the EC is already considerable, as I have shown in Chapter 7. The largest part of this population of migrant origin is the result of earlier migrations of manual labour from the periphery to the centre of Europe. Although it is expected that there will be a net increase in jobs in the period up until the year 2000, few European commentators or officials anticipate a repetition in the foreseeable future of this large-scale semi- and unskilled labour migration *within* the EC (Penninx and Muus 1989: 381–2, Martin *et al.* 1990: 595). This is largely because of the restructuring of the capitalist economies which has resulted in the elimination of large numbers of semi- and unskilled manual jobs, and the creation of a large reserve army of labour within each of the EC nation states.

However, it is expected that there will be an increase in the short-term migration of skilled managerial, technical and professional persons, especially those employed by large multinational companies (*Social*

Europe 1988: 18–20, Penninx and Muus 1989: 381–2, Ardittis 1990: 464). This is a result of various trends, including the continuing concentration and centralisation of capital, resulting in transnational company operations in different parts of the EC (Venturini 1989: 36, Salt and Kitching 1990). The anticipated increase in this migration is regarded by many commentators as the main feature of internal EC migration in the immediate future. Migration flows will take place in several directions simultaneously and the migrants will probably be resident in other EC nation states for periods of a few years at most.

A fifth category of migration includes all those persons who, while possessing the juridical status of national in another nation state wherein they are resident, have the right to the nationality of one of the member states of the European Community. Having been granted this nationality, the individual then has the right to live in that nation state as a full citizen. I cite two examples. In British law, a person having a parent or grand-parent born in the United Kingdom has the right to British nationality, and thereby the right to enter and settle in Britain, irrespective of his or her current nationality status (Dummett and Nicol 1990: 216–9, 245). The number of people included in this legal category is difficult to estimate precisely, but it is several million persons. Most of them are resident in, and are citizens of, Commonwealth countries such as Canada, Australia and New Zealand. Significantly, around a million 'white' people resident in South Africa also have such a right (Dummett and Nicol 1990: 279).

Under the terms of the German Constitution, nationals of other nation states who can demonstrate that they have German 'ancestry' have the right to claim German nationality and to enter and settle in Germany (Hailbronner 1989: 67–8, 73). The majority of these *aussiedler* or 'ethnic Germans' are resident in Poland, Rumania and the former Soviet Union and they have been migrating to Germany in increasing numbers since the early 1980s: in 1983, 37,900 *aussiedler* entered what was then the Federal Republic of Germany, and the number increased to 377,000 in 1989 (SOPEMI 1990: 6).

There is scope for the state to revise the law on nationality and citizenship in such a way as either to remove the right of entry of these populations, or to establish annual quotas for the number of people permitted to enter and settle. For example, in 1990, restrictions were imposed by the German state on the entry of *aussiedler* (Räthzel 1991: 41). But significant political constraints remain. In Britain, there would be political opposition to an attempt to remove or limit the right of 'our kith and kin' in, for example, South Africa to enter Britain and take up British nationality, especially if the political situation there were to deteriorate dramatically. And, in Germany, any attempt at the formal revision of the guarantees regarding the entry of *ausseidler* would probably lead to a constitutional crisis.

The political objective of strict immigration control conflicts with the reality of these continuing migration flows and with the constraints on the ability of the state to enforce further controls. Every official statement expressing support for the 'principle' of increased control therefore legitimates political opposition to immigration within the electorate in circumstances where the state faces structural constraints on its ability to deliver what it promises: this contradiction will ensure that immigration remains at the centre of political conflict within most European nation states and within the European Commission during the 1990s and beyond.

The contradiction is overdetermined by the reality of the EC as a political entity: because of the attempt to create a European immigration policy, the politicisation of immigration as a problem in one member state can have immediate repercussions in the others. Moreover, in so far as a consequence of continuing immigration is a magnification of political opposition to it, and in so far as that opposition is grounded in, or expressive of, racism, the intervention of the state reinforces that racism.

The contradiction between the objective of immigration policy and the reality of immigration flows is partially mediated ideologically by a closure on the meaning of the categories of 'immigration' and 'immigrant'. As we have seen in earlier chapters, these categories are used in European political discourse in such a way that they do not refer to *all* people who are mobile across national boundaries in order to settle temporarily or permanently in another nation state. That is, they do not necessarily include all of the preceding categories of migration. Rather, in popular and political discourse, the notion of 'immigrant' identifies only specific migrant populations.

The language employed to name the immigrants, and the categories of person included, varies from one country to another. But in all countries, a notion that appears to have a universal reference is used in such a way as to identify only particular groups of people. For example, in Britain for much of the period since 1945, the notion of immigrant has referred exclusively to people of Caribbean and south Asian origin, that is to 'black people' (e.g. Miles and Phizacklea 1984, Solomos 1990). It does not refer, for example, to the hundreds of thousands of citizens of the Republic of Ireland who are now 'legitimate' migrants under the conditions permitting the free movement of labour within the EC. In France, the notion refers primarily to '*les Arabes*', many of whom are

French nationals and citizens, but not to the Spanish and Portuguese migrant workers who have been present in France in large numbers since the 1950s and who were and are juridically *étrangers* (Ogden 1991: 301–2, Silverman 1991: 337). And, in Germany, the notion of immigrant refers specifically to 'Turks', although during 1990 a significant proportion of public opinion extended the scope of the category to include not only the *ausseidler* but also the *überseidler*, that is, to those who were previously citizens of the German Democratic Republic.

There is a further level of meaning in this discourse. While in each of the European nation states, a different migrant population or populations is signified as a problematic presence, they tend to share two characteristics. They originate from nation states beyond the European definition of the boundary of Europe and from nation states which are included in the diffuse notion of the 'Third World'. In other words, as we have seen in Chapter 7, within the EC, an immigrant is by definition a person who was previously a poor peasant producer, a (at best) semiskilled wage labourer, or unemployed in the periphery of the world capitalist system. This spatial and material origin is overdetermined by a set of signified cultural (e.g. Muslim) and somatic (e.g. 'black' skin) characteristics which constitute further signs of difference, if not inferiority. It is because of this particular set of attributes that political debate about immigration rarely includes reference to migrants originating from other European nation states or to professional, technical and managerial migrants, a significant proportion of whom originate from Japan and the United States.

Consequently, the ideological notion of migrant, once embedded in the common sense of a particular nation state as a reference to a specific population or populations, becomes a moment in the reproduction of hegemony. Once 'we' all know who 'the immigrants' are, and once the state has indicated that their presence is undesirable and that their numbers should be controlled or reduced, all uncritical and unreflexive use of the category legitimates that official definition and the related conspiracy of silence about all the other immigrants whom the state does not 'see' and who are excluded from public view.

THE INCOMPLETE PROCESS OF NATIONALISATION

The third contradiction evident in contemporary Europe is that between the state's discourse, which represents the nation as a historically continuous and culturally homogeneous political unit, and the reality of nation-state formation, of *nationalisation* as a historically specific process which has yet to overcome cultural heterogeneity within national territories.

The concept of nationalisation (see also Chapters 2 and 3) refers to the process by which a particular territorially bound, but culturally diverse and class- and gender-divided, population is mobilised to develop a sense of 'belonging', of membership, of a nation state. This entails an attempt to create (if necessary by force) both cultural homogeneity in various arenas of social life, and the imagination that one belongs to a culturally and spatially unique community, to a nation, wherein all participate equally in a democratic political process and wherein all are expected to perform 'sacred acts' for the state as well as be granted certain privileges which are denied to non-members (cf. Anderson 1983, Brubaker 1990: 380–1). Apart from circumstances of acute crisis when direct force may be employed, it is now to a large extent a process of self-subordination, not only to an ideal (of the nation), but also to a set of political institutions (that is, to the state). That is to say, given that Europe is now divided into nation states with agreed borders, each with its structure of social reproduction (e.g. education system, political institutions), the notion of belonging to a nation is, for large numbers of people, part of the 'natural order of things': the process of nationalisation is thereby effected through the 'unremarkable' working of the education and political systems, reinforced by institutions such as the mass media.

The process of nationalisation does not necessarily have as its objective the creation of cultural homogeneity in an absolute sense. Degrees of cultural pluralism are possible so long as they are validated by cultural homogeneity at a superordinate level, by an over-arching commitment to a set of 'common' beliefs, values and practices which serve as symbols of national origin and identity and which thereby unite these differences on another terrain. This is evident in European nation states such as Belgium, the Netherlands and Switzerland where particular cultural differences (e.g. of language, of religion) have been recognised and legitimated, but have also been institutionalised in different ways (e.g. the structure of 'pillarisation' in the Netherlands, the canton system in Switzerland), within a context of a commitment to a more inclusive set of common attributes which supposedly embody the essence of the nation. Indeed, the differences may be constructed as specific instances of a common value, belief or practice (as for example where Protestantism and Catholicism are represented as different forms of Christianity so that the nation may be signified as a Christian nation).

The theme (indeed the myth) of national homogeneity has been central to the manner in which the state in western Europe has responded to the social consequences of post-1945 migration. I have already noted that integration has become a policy objective of the state: the society into which the immigrants are expected to integrate is commonly assumed, or is explicitly claimed, to be a cultural unity. The result is that 'they' are expected to learn to behave like 'us' because cultural homogeneity is considered to be a necessary precondition for the survival of the nation. The specificity of this discourse is revealed when it is compared with the discourse of multiculturalism which is central to the hegemonic strategy of the state in 'new nation states' such as Canada and Australia (Kallen 1982, Jakubowicz 1984, Bolaria and Li 1985: 30–1).

This official discourse of cultural homogeneity has not gone unchallenged in European nation states. Within Britain, notions such as the 'multiethnic' or 'multicultural society' have gained increasing currency and even pass the lips of government ministers. They have been embedded in such state initiatives as the creation of the Community Relations Commission in 1968, and in the partial substitution of the discourse of 'race relations' by that of 'ethnic relations'. Nevertheless, this shift in discourse simultaneously legitimates the notion that Britain *was* a culturally homogeneous nation before post-1945 immigration began. The same assumption is implicit in those academic analyses of the consequences of post-1945 migration which suggest that one of them is the creation of 'multi-national and multicultural societies' (Layton-Henry 1990a: 186). If immigration has effected such a novel transformation, the society must have been mononational and monocultural beforehand (see Chapter 4).

The scope for a similar shift in discourse and practice to occur in other nation states in Europe varies. In France, the Jacobin tradition of universalism, and the associated idea that the doorway to *civilisation* is open to all who immerse themselves in the French language and culture (that is, the tradition of *assimilation*), is more resistant to the notion that 'the nation' has the potential to be transformed into a culturally heterogeneous political unit. Ironically, it was partly because of a fear about the potential of populations of migrant origin to form culturally distinct groups, 'different nations within the French nation', that a law of 1889 awarded French citizenship to all persons born in France of foreign-born parents if they were resident in France when they reached the age of majority (Brubaker 1990: 394–5, also GISTI 1992).

In Germany, within the current dominant ideology, there is little space for the notion of the nation as a multicultural unit. The German nation is officially conceived as an organic, linguistic and cultural community, a unique 'natural' and historically continuous community (or *Volk*): in certain versions of this discourse, this is underpinned by the idea of 'race'. It follows that the German nation is a community of descent to which one belongs naturally through the possession and expression of the designated signifiers (Brubaker 1990: 386, 396). People who lack those characteristics, and express others, must therefore belong to another, distinct, community of descent. The possibility of *becoming* German is either ruled out, or considered extremely difficult. Once this conception of the German nation is combined with the nationalist tenet that a nation has a natural right to self-expression and sovereignty within a specified territory, the space for the conception of the German nation state as a multicultural unit is extremely limited. Yet, official ideology is contradicted by the reality of the historical development of different nation states structured around Germanness and by the fact that in the past, within Germany, non-German-speaking minorities have been guaranteed certain rights to sustain their distinctiveness (Räthzel 1991: 41).

The discourse of cultural homogeneity derives from the idea that the world's population is naturally divided into discrete nations, each with its own unique set of cultural attributes. This was a key component of the nationalist ideology that was formulated and reproduced in Europe in the late eighteenth, and throughout the nineteenth, centuries in parallel with the ongoing struggle between different pre-existing and emergent states (supported by different bourgeois classes) for economic and political supremacy (Smith 1979: 1–13). In reality, in certain parts of Europe (e.g. Britain, France) an already existing and powerful state was faced with the task of bringing reality into line with ideology by creating cultural homogeneity. In other parts (e.g. Italy), regionally based proto-states were engaged in a struggle to present themselves as the foundation for the 'really existing' nation that still had to be 'born'.

Viewed from the end of the twentieth century, and putting on one side the cultural consequences of immigration and of class and gender differentiation, this process of nationalisation is far from complete within Europe. While the extent of cultural homogenisation brought about, for example, by national systems of education might be considered to be impressive (as in the example of the diffusion of the French language in France), considerable cultural differentiation remains. Moreover, that difference often coincides with economic inequalities and with the existence of previously established political institutions indicative of some degree of negotiated regional autonomy.

This has constituted, in part, the foundation for the evolution of new nationalist movements (Watson 1990, Coakley 1992). During the 1960s and 1970s, political movements demanding political and economic autonomy for 'nations' believed to have been illegitimately incorporated into the existing nation states of western Europe mobilised large numbers of people. These often revived and built upon earlier nationalist movements and struggles. While these movements declined during the 1980s, they have continued and there is evidence of a more recent resurgence. Their existence is a measure of the incompleteness of the process of nationalisation within extant national boundaries and of the identification of another route by which to gain greater political control over the wider forces of political and economic change.

The contradiction between the discourse of national homogeneity and the incomplete process of nationalisation is simultaneously deepened and mediated by the consequences of post-1945 migration to western Europe. On the one hand, as a result of new (or renewed) cultural presences, the existing cultural heterogeneity of the nation can be further exposed: these new presences only deepen and extend a pre-existing reality. On the other hand, these presences can be signified in such a way as to reinforce and extend the ongoing process of nationalisation: 'their' presence can be used to signify what 'we' have in common against 'them', indeed what 'we' might lose to 'them'. The contemporary debate about immigration, integration and the nation within Europe cannot therefore be isolated from ongoing processes of hegemony and domination, processes that are sustained by nationalisation.

RACISM AND THE SINGLE MARKET

The continuation of migration, the development of the European single market and the moves towards the abolition of internal border controls have all become the focus of increasing political attention and conflict in Europe since the latter half of the 1980s. Within Britain, one particular reading of these developments has become especially prominent on the left. This interprets them as leading to the creation of a 'Fortress Europe', a political unit which is erecting insurmountable barriers to those who live beyond its boundary. This process is considered to be either motivated by or expressive of racism (e.g. Webber 1991). Concerning the Single European Act, it has been suggested (Greater Manchester Immigration Aid Unit 1990: 5, 12):

> What it will mean for black people is not freedom of movement but its opposite. It will mean the establishment of a 'Fortress Europe' in which they will have no part except as a rigidly controlled work force

... the main issue being confronted by the EC in opening the borders is how to close them to black people, not to lose their labour but to control it along with their lives.

Others have identified another 'new racism' at work, a European or Eurocentric racism which is 'directed against the migrants, refugees and asylum-seekers displaced from their own countries by the depredations of international capital' (Sivanandan 1988: 8).

The creation of the single market within the EC is motivated primarily by the interests of capital, and especially international capital. This is not an interpretation that is peculiar to Marxist analysis. For example, Harrop has argued (1989: 49, 55–6, see also Emerson *et al.* 1988):

Modern industry is characterised by the growth of giant firms which are able to reap static and dynamic economies of scale within a large market such as the EC ... the aim of the EC has been to provide a market size to try to match the economies of scale, standardisation and productivity levels of the USA .... Fragmentation of the market has prevented European firms from exploiting their competitiveness to the full. The lack of a single internal market has been estimated on average to have added some 15 per cent to total costs.

The logic of capitalist production on a world scale, the tendency for capital to centralise and concentrate, and the need for ever expanding markets all require the removal of barriers to the movement of capital, labour and commodities at the national boundaries within the EC. The influence of these forces has been working in this direction within Europe since the early nineteenth century (Pollard 1981): 'economic integration' is now essential if capital with its base in Europe is to remain competitive with that based in Japan and the United States.

Thus, the primary motive behind the Single European Act is the creation of the economic and political conditions for capital based and/or located in Europe to remain competitive within the wider world capitalist economy (e.g. Commission of the European Communities 1982). But to what extent are these developments also expressive of, or determined by, a new Eurocentric racism? Much depends on what is meant by racism. Unfortunately, the concept is rarely defined by those advancing this interpretation. From the context of its use, one can presume that it refers to the discriminatory exclusion of 'Third World' immigrants and refugees on the grounds that they are 'black'. I have argued in earlier chapters and elsewhere (Miles 1989a) that such a definition is problematic, but the difficulty is more than a matter of definition (c.f. Miles 1992). The moment of racism is identified in the effect or outcome of a decision-making process which, intentionally or otherwise, has consequences for 'black' people which are different from, and inferior to, those for 'white people'. But are 'black people' universally excluded as a result of the completion of the internal market?

The reality is that many millions of people of Caribbean, south Asian and north African origin (i.e. 'blacks') living in the EC have the juridical freedom to work and reside anywhere within the EC because they are nationals of EC member nation states. Consequently, they have the formal freedom of movement within the EC that follows from the (partial) removal of border controls between EC member nation states, and there is no attempt to impose legal restrictions on this freedom. Their situation contrasts sharply with, for example, many millions of people in Germany who were born in Turkey or who were born in Germany of Turkish parents. These, and other 'third country nationals' from the southern periphery of the Mediterranean, Africa and elsewhere, have been excluded from equal participation in the single market of the EC. If these latter populations are included within the definition of 'black' (itself a problematic assumption), then it is clear that 'black people' are not a universally excluded category. The basis of the discriminatory treatment of the latter lies, in the first instance, in their legal status as nationals of non-EC nation states, a status that is shared with the populations of all other non-EC nation states. The struggle against their exclusion is therefore a struggle to redefine the scope of, and the relationship between, nationality and citizenship in order to ensure their social inclusion within the EC.

Furthermore, the reinforcement of the external borders of the EC is not motivated by a strategic intention to exclude 'Third World' or 'black people' exclusively. One measure of this is the increasing concern within the EC since 1989 about migration from eastern Europe. Seen retrospectively, for states in western Europe, one of the advantages of the 'Iron Curtain' was that it was extremely effective in preventing east Europeans from migrating into western Europe: now that it has been dismantled in the name of 'freedom' and 'democracy', new methods (including stricter border controls and electronic forms of surveillance) are being sought to prevent an 'invasion' from the east. For example, the German state favours a high level of investment in the emergent capitalist economies of eastern Europe in order to minimise the potential for large-scale migration into the EC (*The Guardian* 8 February 1991) and the creation of an autonomous region in Russia to discourage further migration of 'ethnic Germans' into Germany (*The Independent* 22

November 1991), but intensified controls and policing of the border will also be put in place. The objective of the latter is to reinforce immigration control at the external borders for all people who are not nationals of EC member nation states. This category of non-EC national includes 'black people' (in the sense previously referred to) but also east Europeans and nationals of advanced capitalist nation states such as the USA and Japan.

The problems of the 'Euro-racism' argument originate partly in the assumption that all migrants seeking to enter, and circulating within, the EC are 'Third World' immigrants and refugees (i.e. 'black'). This homogenisation of migration flows is factually mistaken and analytically problematic. It has been shown above that large numbers of recent migrants originate from eastern Europe (the migration of the *aussiedler* into Germany being of special significance), that the most important category of internal labour migration within the EC is that of skilled professional and managerial labour, and that one of the fastest growing categories of non-EC migration into the EC includes similarly highly skilled non-manual labour from other sectors of the advanced capitalist world economy. In the light of the evidence of the 'new immigration', the stereotyping of immigrants as 'blacks' originating from the 'Third World' ironically mirrors and legitimates the official discourse of EC states about 'the problem of immigration'.

The diversity and complexity of contemporary migration flows, and the juridical decisions and procedures that sustain them, are closely related to the restructuring of the world capitalist economy and the relocation of an increasing proportion of industrial commodity production in the periphery and semi-periphery of that economy. In other words, class interests are playing a more important role in the reorganisation of international migration than the advocates of the thesis of the 'new Euro-racism' would have us believe. The barriers to migration from the south and east have their origin first in the fact that the demand for semi- and unskilled manual labour within the EC is in decline and there is now an internal reserve army of semi- and unskilled manual labour upon which to draw. There are important exceptions, as the example of southern EC countries demonstrates. But of equal, if not greater, importance for the determination of migration flows within and into the EC is the flexible demand of European-based capital for professional, skilled non-manual labour, and inward capital investment from the USA and Japan (Harrop 1989: 90), an investment that is accompanied by the migration of high-level managerial and technical labour and of self-employed professionals from the USA and Japan.

Of course, the privileged position of, for example, US and Japanese nationals (evident in the attempt to harmonise visa policy in such a way that nationals of most advanced capitalist nation states will not be required to possess a visa to enter the EC (Groenendijk 1989: 34), as well as in the relative ease with which these same nationals can be granted a work permit) contrasts with the treatment of nationals of 'Third World' nation states as well as nationals from eastern Europe. But the exclusion of the latter groups is determined primarily by the interests of capital (and especially international capital): the era characterised by a large-scale shortage of semi- and unskilled wage labour in western Europe is over, at least for the immediate future. Where specific needs for migrants to fill such positions arise, the structures and procedures (both legal and illegal) exist to facilitate such a migration.

Consequently, the creation of the single market in the EC, and the associated regulation of the migration flows into and within the EC, is determined by capitalist interests. These interests structure the context within which racism has specific effects. For racism has been, and remains, an important influence on decisions taken by EC states about immigration, and is a determinant of aspects of the immigration control procedures that already exist and those that are being established. Racist agitation was an increasingly important influence in the period leading up to the termination of labour immigration in the early 1970s, and it remains an influence in the official legitimation of contemporary immigration policies, as well as in political agitation for 'strict immigration control'. But the space within which racism has these effects has been created by the changing demands for labour: in the same way that racist reservations were overcome in the 1950s when European governments considered how they might solve severe domestic labour shortages, they are likely to be overcome again in the future if 'Third World' peasants, workers and refugees are identified as a source of semi- and unskilled migrant labour.

Racism is also likely to have an increased influence in the practice of immigration control at the boundary of, and within, the EC. For example, the abolition of internal border controls will be accompanied by random checks within the EC. Racist stereotypes which associate migrant status with certain somatic characteristics will play an important part in the selection of the individuals and groups whose credentials are checked in public places (e.g. Bovenkerk 1989). Moreover, the use of racist criteria in the definition of the juridical status of national will continue to influence migration into the EC because nationals of EC member states will have the absolute right to enter the EC. Such criteria are present in both British and German nationality law.

CONCLUSION

A contextualised assessment of the specific impact of racism, one that seeks to identify its articulation with other structures of domination and exclusion, requires an analysis that recognises the different determining factors in the interplay between economic, political and ideological relations, and in the contradictions that result. This chapter has identified the main contradictions which are evident within the EC in relation to migration. And, while racism plays an important role in the evolution of immigration policy and practice within the EC, the transformations under way have other determinants and other consequences.

These transformations demonstrate that social forms and relations previously held to be natural or universal (such as the nation, the duality of national and foreigner, etc.) are, in fact, the product of the actions and interests of human beings organised in structured relations with one another. The evolution of the single market has problematised national boundaries and contributed to a further decline in the significance of the nation state. In that process, the *social* origin of the juridical duality between national and foreigner is exposed. Within each EC member nation state, people who remain in a formal sense foreigners, but who are nationals of another EC member nation state, have an increasing number of rights which they share with those who are nationals of that nation state. What were recently apparently rigid and fixed distinctions between national and foreigner have now become fluid, open to transformation. The status of being a national is therefore revealed as an attribute granted, indeed required, by a state in a particular historical conjuncture, rather than a natural or eternal attribute of each human being.

It is true that this transformation is partial and unequal: the status and position of 'third country nationals' within EC member nation states testifies to that, not to mention those who remain outside the EC, constructed by the state as 'fully foreign'. But the reality of the ongoing deconstruction of the duality opens up the possibility of advancing the process for quite different reasons and interests to those of capital and the ruling class. The Other of immigrant origin now occupies within Europe a social position which exposes the limits of bourgeois democracy, as well as the effects of racist exclusion: the reality of the contradiction means that there is an emergent European space within which to construct a new We against capital by further contesting the scope and meaning of the categories of national and citizen in the name of equality and democracy.

Bibliography

Adepoju, A. (1988) 'International migration in Africa south of the Sahara', in R. Appleyard (ed.) *International Migration Today Volume 1: Trends and Prospects*, Paris/Needlands: UNESCO/University of Western Australia.

ADRI (Agence pour le Développement des Relations Interculturelles) (1991) *L'Intégration des Minorités Immigrées en Europe Tome 1: Problématiques*, Paris: Centre National de la Fonction Publique Territorial.

Anderson, B. (1983) *Imagined Communities: Reflections on the Origin and Spread of Nationalism*, London: Verso.

Anne Frank Stichting (1985) *The Extreme Right in Europe and the United States*, Amsterdam: Anne Frank Stichting.

Anthias, F. (1990) 'Race and class revisited – conceptualising race and racisms', *Sociological Review*, 38(1): 19–42.

Appleyard, R. (ed.) (1988a) *International Migration Today Volume 1: Trends and Prospects*, Paris/Needlands: UNESCO/University of Western Australia.

—— (1988b) 'Issues of socio-cultural adaptation and conflict', in C. Stahl (ed.) *International Migration Today Volume 2: Emerging Issues*, Paris/Needlands: UNESCO/University of Western Australia.

—— (ed.) (1989) *The Impact of International Migration on Developing Countries*, Paris: OECD.

Ardittis, S (1990) 'Labour migration and the single European market: a synthetic and prospective note', *International Sociology*, 5(4): 461–74.

Ascherson, N. (1990) 'A breath of foul air', *The Independent on Sunday*, 11 November.

Baines, D. (1985) *Migration in a Mature Economy: Emigration and Internal Migration in England and Wales, 1861–1900*, Cambridge: Cambridge University Press.

—— (1991) *Emigration from Europe 1815–1930*, London: Macmillan.

Baldwin-Edwards, M. (1991) 'Immigration after 1992', *Policy and Politics*, 19(3): 199–211.

Balibar, E. (1988a) 'La forme nation: histoire et idéologie', in E. Balibar and I. Wallerstein, *Race, Nation, Classe: Les Identités Ambiguës*, Paris: Editions La Découverte.

—— (1988b) 'Le «racisme de classe»', in E. Balibar and I. Wallerstein, *Race,*

Nation, Classe: Les Identités Ambiguës, Paris: Editions La Découverte.

—— (1988c) 'Racisme et nationalisme', in E. Balibar and I. Wallerstein, *Race, Nation, Classe: Les Identités Ambiguës*, Paris: Editions La Découverte.

—— (1988d) 'De la lutte des classes à la lutte sans classes?', in E. Balibar and I. Wallerstein, *Race, Nation, Classe: Les Identités Ambiguës*, Paris: Editions La Découverte.

—— (1991) *'Es Gibt Keinen Staat in Europe*: Racism and politics in Europe Today', *New Left Review*, 186: 5–19.

—— (1992) *Les Frontières de la Démocratie*, Paris: Editions La Découverte.

—— and Wallerstein, I. (1988) Race, Nation, Class: Les Identités Ambiguës, Paris: Editions La Découverte.

—— and Wallerstein, I. (1991) *Race, Nation and Class: Ambiguous Identities*, London: Verso.

Ballard, R. (1990) 'Migration and kinship: the differential effect of marriage rules on the processes of Punjabi migration to Britain', in C. Clarke, C. Peach, and S. Vertovec (eds) *South Asians Overseas: Migration and Ethnicity*, Cambridge: Cambridge University Press.

Banton, M. (1967) *Race Relations*, London: Tavistock.

—— (1970) 'The concept of racism', in S. Zubaida (ed.) *Race and Racialism*, London: Tavistock.

—— (1977) *The Idea of Race*, London: Tavistock.

—— (1983) 'The influence of colonial status upon black-white relations in England, 1948–1958', *Sociololgy*, 17(4): 547–59.

—— (1987) *Racial Theories*, Cambridge: Cambridge University Press.

—— (1991) 'The race relations problematic', *British Journal of Sociology*, 42(1): 115–30.

—— (1992) 'The nature and causes of racism and racial discrimination', *International Sociology*, 7(1): 69–84.

Barkan, E. (1992) *The Retreat of Scientific Racism: Changing Concepts of Race in Britain and the United States Between the World Wars*, Cambridge: Cambridge University Press.

Barker, M. (1981) *The New Racism*, London: Junction Books.

Barnett, A. (1982) *Iron Britannia: Why Parliament Waged Its Falklands War*, London: Alison and Busby.

Barzun, J. (1938) *Race: A Study in Modern Superstition*, London: Methuen.

Beaud, S. and Noiriel, G. (1991) 'Penser l'«integration» des Immigrés', in P.-A. Taguieff (ed.) *Face au Racisme Tome 2: Analyses, Hypothèses, Perspectives*, Paris: Editions La Découverte.

Benedict, R. (1983) *Race and Racism*, London: Routledge and Kegan Paul.

Bevan, V. (1986) *The Development of British Immigration Law*, London: Croom Helm.

Biddiss, M.D. (ed.) (1970) *Gobineau: Selected Political Writings*, London: Jonathan Cape.

—— (1972) 'Racial ideas and the politics of prejudice 1850–1914', *Historical Journal*, 15: 570–82.

—— (ed.) (1979) *Images of Race*, Leicester: Leicester University Press.

Billig, M. (1978) *Fascists: A Social Psychological View of the National Front*, London: Harcourt Brace Jovanovich.

Blaut, J.M. (1987) *The National Question: Decolonising the Theory of Nationalism*, London: Zed Press.

Böhning, W.R. (1984) *Studies in International Labour Migration*, London: Macmillan.

—— and Werquin, J. (1990) *Some Economic, Social and Human Rights Considerations Concerning the Future Status of Third-country Nationals in the Single European Market*, Geneva: International Labour Office.

Bolaria, B.S. and Li, P. (1985) *Racial Oppression in Canada*, Toronto: Garamond Press.

Boshyk, Y. (1988) 'Repatriation and resistance: Ukranian refugees and displaced persons in occupied Germany and Austria, 1945–1948', in A.C. Bramwell (ed.) *Refugees in the Age of Total War*, London: Unwin Hyman.

Bousquet, B. and Douglas, C. (1991) *West Indian Women at War: British Racism in World War II*, London: Lawrence and Wishart.

Bovenkerk, F. (1989) *Er Zijn Grenzen*, Arnhem: Gouda Quint BV.

——, Miles, R. and Verbunt, G. (1990) 'Racism, migration and the state in western Europe: a case for comparative analysis', *International Sociology*, 5(4): 475–90.

——, Miles, R. and Verbunt, G. (1991) 'Comparative studies of migration and exclusion on the grounds of "race" and ethnic background in western Europe: a critical appraisal', *International Migration Review*, 25(2): 375–91.

Bramwell, A.C. (ed.) (1988) *Refugees in the Age of Total War*, London: Unwin Hyman.

Brown, C. (1984) *Black and White Britain: The Third PSI Survey*, London: Heinemann.

Brubaker, R. (ed.) (1989) *Immigration and the Politics of Citizenship in Europe and North America*, Lanham: University Press of America.

—— (1990) 'Immigration, citizenship, and the nation-state in France and Germany: a comparative historical analysis', *International Sociology*, 5(4): 461–74.

Burleigh, M. and Wippermann, W. (1991) *The Racial State: Germany 1933–1945*, Cambridge: Cambridge University Press.

Cain, A.M. (1986) *The Cornchest for Scotland: Scots in India*, Edinburgh: National Library of Scotland.

Cairncross, A. (1985) *Years of Recovery: British Economic Policy, 1945–1951*, London: Methuen.

Calder, J. (ed.) (1986) *The Enterprising Scot: Scottish Adventure and Achievement*, Edinburgh: HMSO.

Calvaruso, C. (1987) 'Illegal immigration to Italy', in OECD, *The Future of Migration*, Paris: OECD.

Carrothers, W.A. (1929) *Emigration from the British Isles, With Special Reference to the Development of the Overseas Dominions*, London: P.S. King and Son Ltd.

Carter, B., Harris, C. and Joshi, S. (1987) 'The 1951–55 Conservative government and the racialisation of black immigration', *Immigrants and Minorities*, 6: 335–47.

Castles, S. and Kosack, G. (1972) 'The function of labour immigration in western European capitalism', *New Left Review*, 73: 3–21.

—— and Kosack, G. (1973) *Immigrant Workers and Class Structure in Western Europe*, London: Oxford University Press.

——, Booth, H., and Wallace, T. (1984) *Here for Good: Western Europe's New Ethnic Minorities*, London: Pluto Press.

CCCS (Centre for Contemporary Cultural Studies) (1982) *The Empire Strikes Back: Race and Racism in 70s Britain*, London: Hutchinson.

Cesarani, D. (1987) 'Anti-alienism in England after the First World War', *Immigrants and Minorities*, 6: 5–29.

—— (1992) *Justice Delayed: How Britain Became a Refuge for Nazi War Criminals*, London: Heinemann.

Chevalier, L. (1973) *Laboring Classes and Dangerous Classes in Paris During the First Half of the Nineteenth Century*, Princeton: Princeton University Press.

Chevalier, Y. (1988) *L'anti-sémitisme*, Paris: Les Editions du Cerf.

Cheyette, B. (1989) 'Jewish stereotyping and English literature, 1875–1920: towards a political analysis', in T. Kushner and K. Lunn (eds) *Traditions of Intolerance: Historical Perspectives on Fascism and Race Discourse in Britain*, Manchester: Manchester University Press.

Christian, B. (1990) 'What Celie knows that you should know', in D.T. Goldberg (ed.) *Anatomy of Racism*, Minneapolis: University of Minnesota Press.

Clarke, C., Peach, C., and Vertovec, S. (eds) (1990) *South Asians Overseas: Migration and Ethnicity*, Cambridge: Cambridge University Press.

Coakley, J. (ed.) (1992) *The Social Origins of Nationalist Movements: the Contemporary West European Experience*, London: Sage.

Cohen, P. (1988) 'The perversions of inheritance: studies in the making of multi-racist Britain', in P. Cohen and H.S. Bains (eds) *Multi-Racist Britain*, London: Macmillan.

—— (1992) ' "It's racism what dunnit": hidden narratives in theories of racism', in J. Donald and A. Rattansi (eds) *'Race', Culture and Difference*, London: Sage.

Cohen, R. (1987) *The New Helots: Migrants in the International Division of Labour*, Farnborough: Avebury.

—— (1991) 'East–west and European migration in a global context', *New Community*, 18(1): 9–26.

—— and Joly, D. (1989) 'Introduction: the "new refugees" of Europe', in D. Joly and R. Cohen (eds) *Reluctant Hosts: Europe and its Refugees*, Aldershot: Avebury.

Colley, L. (1989) 'Radical patriotism in eighteenth-century England', in R. Samuel (ed.) *Patriotism Volume I: History and Politics*, London: Routledge.

Collins, K.E. (1990) *Second City Jewry: The Jews of Glasgow in the Age of Expansion, 1790–1919*, Glasgow: Scottish Jewish Archives.

Colls, R. (1986) 'Englishness and the political culture', in R. Colls and P. Dodd (eds) *Englishness: Politics and Culture 1880–1920*, London: Croom Helm.

—— and Dodd, P. (eds) (1986) *Englishness: Politics and Culture 1880–1920*, London: Croom Helm.

Colpi, T. (1991) *The Italian Factor: The Italian Community in Great Britain*, Edinburgh: Mainstream.

Comas, J. (1961) ' "Scientific" racism again?', *Current Anthropology*, 2: 303–40.

Commission of the European Communities (1982), *The Competitiveness of the Community Industry*, Luxembourg: Commission of the European Communities.

Condon, S. and Ogden, P.E. (1991a) 'Afro-Caribbean migrants in France: employment, state policy and the immigration process', *Transactions of the Institute of British Geographers*, 16: 440–57.

—— and Ogden, P.E. (1991b) 'Emigration from the French Caribbean: the origins of an organised migration', *International Journal of Urban and Regional Research*, 15(4): 505–23.

Connor, W. (1984) *The National Question in Marxist-Leninist Theory and Strategy*, Princeton: Princeton University Press.

—— (1990) 'When is a nation?', *Ethnic and Racial Studies*, 13(1): 92–103.

Constantine, S. (1991) 'Empire migration and social reform 1880–1950', in C.G. Pooley and I.D. Whyte (eds) *Migrants, Emigrants and Immigrants: A Social History of Migration*, London: Routledge.

Costa-Lascoux, J. (1991a) 'Des lois contre le racisme', in P.-A. Taguieff (ed.) *Face au Racisme Tome 2: Analyses, Hypothèses, Perspectives*, Paris: Editions La Découverte.

—— (1991b) 'L'espace Schengen', *Revue Européenne des Migrations Internationales*, 7(2): 163–8.

Cottrell, S. (1989) 'The devil on two sticks: Franco-phobia in 1803', in R. Samuel (ed.) *Patriotism Volume I: History and Politics*, London: Routledge.

Cox, O.C. (1970) *Caste, Class and Race*, New York: Monthly Review Press.

Cruz, A. (1990) *An Insight into Schengen, Trevi and other European Intergovernmental Bodies*, Brussels: Churches' Committee for Migrants in Europe.

Cummins, I. (1980) *Marx, Engels and National Movements*, London: Croom Helm.

Cunningham, H. (1989) 'The language of patriotism', in R. Samuel (ed.) *Patriotism Volume I: History and Politics*, London: Routledge.

Curtin, P.D. (1965) *The Image of Africa: British Ideas and British Action, 1780–1850*, London: Macmillan.

Davin, A. (1989) 'Imperialism and motherhood', in R. Samuel (ed.) *Patriotism Volume I: History and Politics*, London: Routledge.

Deakin, N. (1970) *Colour, Citizenship and British Society*, London: Panther.

Dean, D.W. (1987) 'Coping with colonial immigration, the Cold War and colonial policy: the Labour government and black communities in Great Britain 1945–51', *Immigrants and Minorities*, 6(3): 305–34.

Delacampagne, C. (1983) *L'Invention du Racisme*, Paris: Fayard.

Denoon, D. (1983) *Settler Capitalism: The Dynamics of Dependent Development in the Southern Hemisphere*, Oxford: Clarendon Press.

van Dijk, T.A. (1987) *Communicating Racism: Ethnic Prejudice in Thought and Talk*, Newbury Park: Sage.

Dixon, D. (1983) 'Thatcher's people: the British Nationality Act, 1981', *Journal of Law and Society*, 10: 161–80.

Duffield, M. (1988) *Black Radicalism and the Politics of De-industrialisation: The Hidden History of Indian Foundry Workers*, Farnborough: Avebury.

Dummett, A. (1973) *A Portrait of English Racism*, Harmondsworth: Penguin.

—— and Nicol, A. (1990) *Subjects, Citizens, Aliens and Others: Nationality and Immigration Law*, London: Weidenfeld and Nicolson.

Eatwell, R. (1979) *The 1945–1951 Labour Governments*, London: Batsford.

Elias, N. (1978) *The Civilising Process: The History of Manners*, Oxford: Basil Blackwell.

Emerson, M. (1988) *The Economics of 1992: The E.C. Commission's Assessment of the Economic Effects of Completing the Internal Market*, Oxford: Oxford University Press.

Essed, P. (1991) *Understanding Everyday Racism: An Interdisciplinary Theory*, Newbury Park: Sage.

European Commission (1988) *Europe Without Frontiers – Completing the Internal Market*, Luxembourg: Commission of the European Communities.

—— (1990) *European Unification: The Origins and Growth of the European Community*, Luxembourg: Commission of the European Communities.

Evans, N. (1991) 'Immigrants and minorities in Wales, 1840–1990: a comparative perspective', *Llafur*, 5(4): 5–26.

Fields, B.J. (1982) 'Ideology and race in American history', in J.M. Kousser and J.M. McPherson (eds) *Region, Race and Reconstruction: Essays in Honour of C. Vann Woodward*, New York: Oxford University Press.

—— (1990) 'Slavery, race and ideology in the United States of America', *New Left Review*, 181: 95–118.

Fleming, G. (1986) *Hitler and the Final Solution*, Oxford: Oxford University Press.

Foster, C.R. (1980) *Nations Without a State: Ethnic Minorities in Western Europe*, New York: Praeger.

Fox, J.P. (1988) 'German and European Jewish refugees 1933–45: reflections on the Jewish condition under Hitler and the western world's response to their expulsion and flight', in A.C. Bramwell (ed.) *Refugees in the Age of Total War*, London: Unwin Hyman.

Fröbel, F., Heinrichs, J., and Kreye, O. (1981) *The New International Division of Labour*, Cambridge: Cambridge University Press.

Fryer, P. (1984) *Staying Power: The History of Black People in Britain*, London: Pluto Press.

Gainer, B. (1972) *The Alien Invasion: The Origins of the Aliens Act of 1905*, London: Heinemann.

Garrard, J. (1971) *The English and Immigration 1880–1910*, London: Oxford University Press.

Garvey, D. (1985) 'The history of migration flows in the Republic of Ireland', *Population Trends*, 39: 22–30.

Geiss, I. (1988) *Geschichte des Rassismus*, Frankfurt am Main: Edition Suhrkamp.

Gellner, E. (1983) *Nations and Nationalism*, Oxford: Basil Blackwell.

George, H. (1984) *American Race Relations Theory: A Review of Four Models*, Lanham: University Press of America.

Gilman, S.L. (1990) ' "I'm down on whores": race and gender in Victorian London', in D.T. Goldberg (ed.) *Anatomy of Racism*, Minneapolis: University of Minnesota Press.

Gilroy, P. (1987) *'There Ain't No Black in the Union Jack': The Cultural Politics of Race and Nation*, London: Hutchinson.

GISTI (1992) *Le Guide de la Nationalité Francaise*, Paris: Editions La Découverte.

Gitmez, A.S. (1988) 'The socio-economic reintegration of returned workers: the case of Turkey', in C. Stahl (ed.) *International Migration Today Volume 2: Emerging Issues*, Paris/Needlands: UNESCO/University of Western Australia.

Glass, R. and Pollins, H. (1960) *The Newcomers: The West Indians in London*, London: George Allen and Unwin.

Glebe, G. and O'Loughlin, J. (eds) (1987) *Foreign Minorities in Continental European Cities*, Wiesbaden: Steiner Verlag.

Goldberg, D.T. (ed.) (1990a) *Anatomy of Racism*, Minneapolis: University of Minnesota Press.

—— (1990b) 'The social formation of racist discourse', in D.T. Goldberg (ed.) *Anatomy of Racism*, Minneapolis: University of Minnesota Press.

Gordon, P. (1985) *Policing Immigration: Britain's Internal Controls*, London: Pluto Press.

—— (1989) *Fortress Europe? The Meaning of 1992*, London: Runnymede Trust.

Gossett, E.F. (1965) *Race: The History of an Idea in America*, New York: Schocken Books.

Gould, S.J. (1984) *The Mismeasure of Man*, Harmondsworth: Penguin.

Greater Manchester Immigration Aid Unit (1990) *Imagine There's No Countries*, Manchester: Greater Manchester Immigration Aid Unit.

Green, M. and Carter, B. (1987) ' "Races" and "race-makers": the politics of racialisation', *Sage Race Relations Abstracts*, 13(2): 4–30.

Groenendijk, C.A. (1989) 'Schengen, refugees and human rights', in P. Gordon, *Fortress Europe? The Meaning of 1992*, London: Runnymede Trust.

—— (1992) 'Europa 1992: Realitäten, Mythen und Chancen', in A. Kalpaka and N. Räthzel (eds) *Rassismus und Migration in Europa*, Hamburg: Argument Verlag.

Guillaumin, C. (1972) *L'idéologie Raciste: Genèse et Langage Actuel*, Paris: Mouton.

—— (1980) 'The idea of race and its elevation to autonomous scientific and legal status', in UNESCO, *Sociological Theories: Race and Colonialism*, Paris: UNESCO.

—— (1988) 'Race and nature: the system of marks', *Feminist Issues*, 1988: 25–43.

Gundara, J.S. (1990) 'Societal diversities and the issue of "the other" ', *Oxford Review of Education*, 16(1): 97–109.

Hailbronner, K. (1989) 'Citizenship and nationhood in Germany', in W.R. Brubaker (ed.) *Immigration and the Politics of Citizenship in Europe and North America*, Lanham: University Press of America.

Hall, S. (1978) 'Racism and reaction', in Commission for Racial Equality, *Five Views of Multi-Racial Britain*, London: Commission for Racial Equality.

—— (1980) 'Race, articulation and societies structured in dominance', in UNESCO, *Sociological Theories: Race and Colonialism*, Paris: UNESCO.

—— (1983) 'The great moving right show', in S. Hall and M. Jacques (eds) *The Politics of Thatcherism*, London: Lawrence and Wishart.

——, Critcher, C., Jefferson, T., Clarke, J., and Roberts, B. (1978) *Policing the Crisis: Mugging, the State and Law and Order*, London: Macmillan.

Hammar, T. (ed.) (1985) *European Immigration Policy: A Comparative Study*, Cambridge: Cambridge University Press.

—— (1990) *Democracy and the Nation State*, Aldershot: Avebury.

—— and Lithman, Y.G. (1987) 'The integration of migrants: experiences, concepts and policies', in OECD, *The Future of Migration*, Paris: OECD.

Hanagan, M. (1989) 'Nascent proletarians: migration patterns and class formation in the Stéphanois region, 1840–1880', in P.E. Ogden and P.E. White (eds)

Migrants in Modern France: Population Mobility in the Later 19th and 20th Centuries, London: Unwin Hyman.

Harris, C. (1987) 'British capitalism, migration and relative surplus population', *Migration*, 1: 47–90.

Harrop, J. (1989) *The Political Economy of Integration in the European Community*, Aldershot: Edward Elgar.

Haupt, G., Lowy, M., and Weill, C. (1974) *Les Marxistes et la Question Nationale, 1848–1914: Études et Textes*, Paris: Maspero.

Hayes, P. (1973) *Fascism*, London: Allen and Unwin.

Heckmann, F. (1985) 'Temporary labor migration or immigration? "Guest workers", in the Federal Republic of Germany', in R. Rogers (ed.) *Guests Come to Stay: The Effects of European Labor Migration on Sending and Receiving Countries*, Boulder: Westview Press.

Herbert, U. (1986) *Geschichte der Ausländerbeschäftigung in Deutschland 1880–1980*, Berlin/Bonn: J.H.W. Dietz Nachf.

Hirschfeld, M. (1938) *Racism*, London: Gollancz.

Hobsbawm, E.J. (1983) 'Introduction: inventing traditions', in E.J. Hobsbawm and T. Ranger (eds) *The Invention of Tradition*, Cambridge: Cambridge University Press.

—— (1990) *Nations and Nationalism Since 1780: Programme, Myth and Reality*, Cambridge: Cambridge University Press.

Hollifield, J.F. (1986) 'Immigration policy in France and Germany: outputs versus outcomes', *Annals of the American Academy of Political and Social Science*, 485: 113–28.

Holmes, C. (ed.) (1978) *Immigrants and Minorities in British Society*, London, Allen and Unwin.

—— (1979) *Anti-Semitism in British Society 1876–1939*, London: Edward Arnold.

—— (1988) *John Bull's Island: Immigration and British Society, 1871–1971*, London: Macmillan.

—— (1991) *A Tolerant Country? Immigrants, Refugees and Minorities in Britain*, London: Faber and Faber.

Husbands, C. (1991) 'The support for the *Front National*: analyses and findings', *Ethnic and Racial Studies*, 14(3): 382–416.

Huxley, J.S. and Haddon, A.C. (1935) *We Europeans: A Survey of 'Racial' problems*, London: Jonathan Cape.

Hyman, R. (1983) 'Andre Gorz and his disappearing proletariat', in R. Miliband and J. Saville (eds) *The Socialist Register*, London: Merlin Press.

Isaac, J. (1954) *British Post-War Migration*, Cambridge: Cambridge University Press.

Ishiguro, K. (1990) *The Remains of the Day*, London: Faber and Faber.

Jackson, J.A. (ed.) (1969) *Migration*, Cambridge: Cambridge University Press.

—— (1986) *Migration*, London: Longman.

Jakubowicz, A. (1984) 'Ethnicity, multiculturalism and neo-conservatism', in G. Bottomley and M. de Lepervanche (eds) *Ethnicity, Class and Gender in Australia*, Sydney: George Allen and Unwin.

James, W. (1989) 'The making of black identities', in R. Samuel (ed.) *Patriotism: The Making and Unmaking of British National Identity Volume II: Minorities and Outsiders*, London: Routledge.

Jeffers, S. (1991) 'Black sections in the Labour Party: the end of ethnicity and "godfather" politics?', in P. Werbner and M. Anwar (eds) *Black and Ethnic Leaderships in Britain: the Cultural Dimensions of Political Action*, London: Routledge.

Jenkins, R. and Solomos, J. (eds) (1989) *Racism and Equal Opportunity Policies in the 1980s*, Cambridge: Cambridge University Press.

Jones, G.S. (1976) *Outcast London: A Study of the Relationship Between Classes in Victorian Society*, Harmondsworth: Peregrine Books.

Jordan, W.J. (1968) *White Over Black: American Attitudes Toward the Negro, 1550–1812*, Chapel Hill: University of North Carolina Press.

—— (1974) *The White Man's Burden: Historical Origins of Racism in the United States*, London: Oxford University Press.

Joshi, S. and Carter, B. (1984) 'The role of Labour in creating a racist Britain', *Race and Class*, 25: 53–70.

Kallen, E. (1982) 'Multiculturalism: ideology, policy and reality', *Journal of Canadian Studies*, 17(1): 51–63.

Kay, D. and Miles, R. (1988) 'Refugees or migrant workers? The case of the European volunteer workers', *Journal of Refugee Studies*, 1(3/4), 214–36.

—— and Miles, R. (1992) *Refugees or Migrant Workers? The Recruitment of Displaced Persons for British Industry 1946–1951*, London: Routledge.

—— and Miles, R. (1993) 'Migration, racism and the labour market in Britain 1946–1951' (in press).

Keneally, T. (1986) *Schindler's Ark*, London: Sceptre.

Kiernan, V.G. (1972) *The Lords of Human Kind: European Attitudes to the Outside World in the Imperial Age*, Harmondsworth: Penguin.

Kinchin, P. and Kinchin, J. (1989) *Glasgow's Great Exhibitions*, Bicester: White Cockade Publishing.

Knerr, B. (1990) 'South Asian countries as competitors on the world labour market', in C. Clarke, C. Peach, and S. Vertovec (eds) *South Asians Overseas: Migration and Ethnicity*, Cambridge: Cambridge University Press.

Knox, R. (1850) *The Races of Men: A Fragment*, London: Henry Renshaw.

Kohn, H. (1945) *The Idea of Nationalism: A Study of its Origins and Background*, London: Macmillan.

Korte, H. (1985) 'Labor migration and the employment of foreigners in the Federal Republic of Germany since 1950', in R. Rogers (ed.) *Guests Come to Stay: The Effects of European Labor Migration on Sending and Receiving Countries*, Boulder: Westview Press.

Kritz, M.M., Keeley, C.B., and Tomasi, S.M. (eds) (1983) *Global Trends in Migration: Theory and Research on International Population Movements*, New York: Center for Migration Studies.

Kushner, T. (1989) *The Persistence of Prejudice: Anti-Semitism in British Society During the Second World War*, Manchester: Manchester University Press.

—— and Lunn, K. (eds) (1989) *Traditions of Intolerance*, Manchester: Manchester University Press.

de Lary, H. (1989) 'Libre circulation et immigrés à l'horizon 1993', *Revue Française des Affaires Sociales*, 43: 93–117.

Layton-Henry, Z. (1984) *The Politics of Race in Britain*, London: Allen and Unwin.

—— (1987) 'The state and New Commonwealth immigration: 1951–1956', *New Community*, 14(1/2): 64–75.

—— (1990a) 'Citizenship or denizenship for migrant workers?', in Z. Layton-Henry (ed.) *The Political Rights of Migrant Workers in Western Europe*, London: Sage.

—— (ed.) (1990b) *The Political Rights of Migrant Workers in Western Europe*, London: Sage.

—— (1990c) 'The challenge of political rights', in Z. Layton-Henry (ed.) *The Political Rights of Migrant Workers in Western Europe*, London: Sage.

Lebon, A. (1990) 'Ressortissants communautaires et étrangers originaires des pays tiers dans l'Europe des douze', *Revue Européenne des Migrations Internationales*, 6(1): 185–204.

Lebselter, G.C. (1981) 'Anti-semitism – a focal point for the British radical right', in P. Kennedy and A. Nicholls (eds) *Nationalist and Racialist Movements in Britain and Germany Before 1914*, London: Macmillan.

Lecourt, D. (1980) 'Marxism as a critique of sociological theories', in UNESCO, *Sociological Theories: Race and Colonialism*, Paris: UNESCO.

Leonard, D. (1988) *Pocket Guide to the European Community*, Oxford and London: Basil Blackwell and The Economist Publications.

Lipman, V.A. (1990) *A History of the Jews in Britain Since 1858*, Leicester: Leicester University Press.

Lloyd, C. (1991) 'Concepts, models and anti-racist strategies in Britain and France', *New Community*, 18(1): 63–73.

Lorimer, D.A. (1978) *Colour, Class and the Victorians: English Attitudes to the Negro in the Mid-Nineteenth Century*, Leicester: Leicester University Press.

Lugard, F.D. (1929) *The Dual Mandate in British Tropical Africa*, Edinburgh: William Blackwood & Sons Ltd.

Lunn, K. (1989) 'The British state and immigration, 1945–51: new light on the Empire Windrush', *Immigrants and Minorities*, 8: 161–74.

Macdonald, I. (1983) *Immigration Law and Practice in the United Kingdom*, London: Butterworths.

MacDougall, H.A. (1982) *Racial Myth in English History*, Montreal: Harvest House.

Maillat, D. (1987a) 'European receiving countries', in OECD, *The Future of Migration*, Paris: OECD.

—— (1987b) 'Long-term aspects of international migration flows: the experience of European receiving countries', in OECD, *The Future of Migration*, Paris: OECD.

Malchow, H.L (1979) *Population Pressures: Emigration and Government in Late Nineteenth-Century Britain*, Palo Alto: Society for the Promotion of Science and Scholarship Inc.

Marrus, M.R. (1971) *The Politics of Assimilation: A Study of the French Jewish Community at the Time of the Dreyfus Affair*, Oxford: Clarendon Press.

—— (1985) *The Unwanted: European Refugees in the Twentieth Century*, London: Butterworths.

Martin, P.L., Hönekopp, E., and Ullman, H. (1990) 'Europe 1992: effects on labor migration', *International Migration Review*, 24(3): 591–603.

Martiniello, M. (1991) 'Racism in paradise', *Capital and Class*, 32(3): 79–84.

Marx, K. (1976) *Capital Volume 1*, Harmondsworth: Penguin.

Mayer, N. and Perrineau, P. (eds) (1989) *Le Front National à Découvert*, Paris: Presses de la FNSP.

Mehrländer, U. (1985) 'Second generation migrants in the Federal Republic of Germany', in R. Rogers (ed.) *Guests Come to Stay: The Effects of European Labor Migration on Sending and Receiving Countries*, Boulder: Westview Press.

Meillassoux, C. (1981) *Maidens, Meal and Money: Capitalism and the Domestic Community*, Cambridge: Cambridge University Press.

Melander, G. (1988) 'The concept of the term "refugee" ', in A.C. Bramwell (ed.) *Refugees in the Age of Total War*, London: Unwin Hyman.

Miles, R. (1980) 'Class, race and ethnicity: a critique of Cox's theory', *Ethnic and Racial Studies*, 3(2): 169–87.

——(1982) *Racism and Migrant Labour: A Critical Text*, London: Routledge and Kegan Paul.

——(1984a) 'Marxism versus the "sociology of race relations"?', *Ethnic and Racial Studies*, 7(2): 217–37.

—— (1984b) 'The riots of 1958: the ideological construction of "race relations" as a political issue in Britain', *Immigrants and Minorities*, 3(3): 252–75.

—— (1985) 'The relative autonomy of ideology: racism and the migration of labour to Britain since 1945', *Groupe de Recherche d'Analyse des Migrations Internationales*, Document de Travail No. 7.

—— (1986) 'Labour migration, racism and capital accumulation in western Europe', *Capital and Class*, 28: 49–86.

—— (1987a) *Capitalism and Unfree Labour: Anomaly or Necessity?*, London: Tavistock.

—— (1987b) 'Class relations and racism in Britain in the 1980s', *Revue Européenne des Migrations Internationales*, 3(1/2): 223–8.

—— (1987c) 'Racism and nationalism in Britain', in C. Husband (ed.) *'Race', in Britain: Continuity and Change*, London: Hutchinson.

—— (1987d) 'Recent Marxist theories of nationalism and the issue of racism', *British Journal of Sociology*, 38(1): 24–43.

—— (1988a) 'Beyond the "race" concept: the reproduction of racism in England', in M. de Lepervanche and G. Bottomley (eds) *The Cultural Construction of Race*, Sydney: Sydney Association for Studies in Society and Culture.

—— (1988b) 'Racism, Marxism and British politics', *Economy and Society*, 17(3): 428–60.

—— (1989a) *Racism*, London: Routledge.

—— (1989b) 'Bedeutungskonstitution und der Begriff Rassismus', *Das Argument*, 175: 353–67.

—— (1989c) 'Migration discourse in post–1945 British politics', *Migration*, 6: 31–53.

—— (1989d) 'Nationality, citizenship and migration to Britain, 1945–1951', *Journal of Law and Society*, 16(4): 426–42.

—— (1990a) 'Die marxistische Theorie und das Konzept "Rasse" ', in E.J. Dittrich and F.-O. Radtke (eds) *Ethnizität: Wissenschaft und Minderheiten*, Opladen: Westdeutscher Verlag.

—— (1990b) 'The racialisation of British politics', *Political Studies*, 38(2): 277–85.

—— (1990c) 'Whatever happened to the sociology of migration?', *Work, Employment and Society*, 4(2): 281–98.

—— (1991a) *Rassismus: Einführung in die Geschichte und Theorie eines Begriffs*, Berlin: Argument Verlag.

—— (1991b) 'Migration to Britain: the significance of a historical approach', *International Migration*, 29(4): 527–43.

—— (1991c) 'Die Idee der "Rasse" und Theorien über Rassismus: überlegungen zur britischen Diskussion', in U. Bielefeld (ed.) *Das Eigene und das Fremde: Neuer Rassismus in der Alten Welt?*, Hamburg: Junius Verlag.

—— (1991d), 'Who belongs?: the meanings of British nationality and immigration law', *Journal of Law and Society*, 18(2): 278–85.

—— (1992) 'Le racisme européen dans son context historique: Reflexions sur l'articulation du racisme et du nationalisme', *Genèses*, 8: 108–31.

—— (1993) 'Explaining racism in contemporary Europe: problems and perspectives', in A. Rattansi and S. Westwood (eds) *On the Western Front: Studies in Racism, Modernity and Identity*, Cambridge, Polity Press..

—— and Dunlop, A. (1986) 'The racialisation of politics in Britain: why Scotland is different', *Patterns of Prejudice*, 20(1): 23–32.

—— and Dunlop, A. (1987) 'Racism in Britain: the Scottish dimension', in P. Jackson (ed.) *Race and Racism*, London: George Allen and Unwin.

—— and Muirhead, L. (1986) 'Racism in Scotland: a matter for further investigation?', in D. McCrone (ed.) *Scottish Government Yearbook: 1986*, Edinburgh: Edinburgh University Press.

—— and Phizacklea, A. (1984) *White Man's Country: Racism in British Politics*, London: Pluto Press.

—— and Räthzel, N. (1992) 'Labour migration, racism and capital accumulation in western Europe', in S. Bolaria (ed.) *World Capitalism and the International Migration of Labour*, Toronto: Garamond Press.

—— and Satzewich, V. (1990) 'Migration, racism and "postmodern" capitalism', *Economy and Society*, 19(3): 332–56.

—— and Solomos, J. (1987) 'Migration and the state in Britain: an historical overview', in C. Husbands (ed.), *'Race', in Britain: Continuity and Change*, London: Hutchinson.

Miliband, R. (1972) *Parliamentary Socialism*, London: Merlin Press.

Mock, W. (1981) 'The function of "race" in imperialist ideologies: the example of Joseph Chamberlain', in P. Kennedy and A. Nicholls (eds) *Nationalist and Racialist Movements in Britain and Germany Before 1914*, London: Macmillan.

Modood, T. (1988) ' "Black", racial equality and Asian identity', *New Community*, 14(3): 397–404.

—— (1990) 'Catching up with Jesse Jackson: being oppressed and being somebody', *New Community*, 17(1): 85–96.

—— (1991) 'The Indian economic success: a challenge to some race relations assumptions', *New Community*, 19(3): 177–89.

Molle, W. and Van Mourik, A. (1988) 'International movements of labour under conditions of economic integration: the case of western Europe', *Journal of Common Market Studies*, 26(3): 317–39.

Montagu, A. (ed.) (1964) *The Concept of Race*, New York: Free Press.

—— (1972) *Statement on Race*, London: Oxford University Press.

——(1974) *Man's Most Dangerous Myth: The Fallacy of Race*, New York: Oxford University Press.

Mooers, C. (1991) *The Making of Bourgeois Europe: Absolutism, Revolution and the Rise of Capitalism in England, France and Germany*, London: Verso.
Morgan, K.O. (1984) *Labour in Power, 1945–1951*, Oxford: Clarendon Press.
Morokvasic, M. (1988) 'Cash in hand for the first time: the case of Yugoslav women in western Europe', in C. Stahl (ed.) *International Migration Today Volume 2: Emerging Issues*, Paris/Needlands: UNESCO/University of Western Australia.
Mosse, G.L. (1978) *Toward the Final Solution: A History of European Racism*, London: Dent & Sons.
Muus, P.J. (1990) *Migration, Minorities and Policy in the Netherlands*, Amsterdam: Institute for Social Geography, University of Amsterdam.
Nairn, T. (1981) *The Break-up of Britain*, London: Verso.
—— (1988) *The Enchanted Glass: Britain and its Monarchy*, London: Radius.
Newman, G. (1987) *The Rise of English Nationalism: A Cultural History 1740–1830*, London: Weidenfeld and Nicolson.
Nikolinakos, M.(1975) 'Notes towards a general theory of migration in late capitalism', *Capital and Class*, 17(1): 5–18.
Nimni, E. (1991) *Marxism and Nationalism: Theoretical Origins of a Political Crisis*, London: Pluto Press.
Noiriel, G. (1984) *Longwy: Immigrés et Prolétaires 1880–1980*, Paris: Presses Universitaires de France.
—— (1988) *Le Creuset Français*, Paris: Éditions du Seuil.
—— (1990) *Workers in French Society in the 19th and 20th Centuries*, New York: Berg.
—— (1991) *La Tyrannie du National: Le Droit d'Asile en Europe 1793–1993*, Paris: Calmann-Lévy.
Nolte, E. (1965) *Three Faces of Fascism*, London: Weidenfeld and Nicolson.
NSCGP (Netherlands Scientific Council for Government Policy) (1979) *Ethnic Minorities*, Den Haag: NSCGP.
—— (1990) *Immigrant Policy: Summary of the 36th Report*, Den Haag: NSCGP.
OECD (Organisation for Economic Cooperation and Development) (1990) *SOPEMI: Continuous Reporting System on Migration 1989*, Paris: OECD.
—— (1991) *Migration: the Demographic Aspects*, Paris: OECD.
Ogden, P.E. (1989a) 'Industry, mobility and the evolution of rural society in the Arcdèche in the later nineteenth and early twentieth centuries', in P.E. Ogden and P.E. White (eds) *Migrants in Modern France: Population Mobility in the Later 19th and 20th Centuries*, London: Unwin Hyman.
—— (1989b) 'International migration in the nineteenth and twentieth centuries', in P.E. Ogden and P.E. White (eds) *Migrants in Modern France: Population Mobility in the Later 19th and 20th Centuries*, London: Unwin Hyman.
—— (1991) 'Immigration to France since 1945: myth and reality', *Ethnic and Racial Studies*, 14(3): 294–318.
—— and White, P.E. (eds) (1989) *Migrants in Modern France: Population Mobility in the Later 19th and 20th Centuries*, London: Unwin Hyman.
Okolski, M. (1991) 'La nouvelle donne migratoire en Europe de l'est', *Revue Européenne des Migrations Internationales*, 7(2): 7–40.
Omi, M. and Winant, H. (1986) *Racial Formation in the United States: From the 1960s to the 1980s*, New York: Routledge and Kegan Paul.

Outlaw, L. (1990) 'Toward a critical theory of "race" ', in D.T. Goldberg (ed.) *Anatomy of Racism*, Minneapolis: University of Minnesota Press.

Oz, A. (1986) *A Perfect Peace*, London: Flamingo.

Palidda, S. and Campani, G. (1990) 'Italie: racisme et tiers-mondisme', *Peuples Méditerranéens*, 51: 145–69.

Panayi, P. (1988) ' "The hidden hand": British myths about German control of Britain during the First World War', *Immigrants and Minorities*, 7(3): 249–72.

—— (1989) 'Anti-German riots in London during the First World War', *German History*, 8: 184–203.

—— (1991) *The Enemy in our Midst: Germans in Britain During the First World War*, New York/Oxford: Berg.

Papademetriou, D. (1988) 'International migration in a changing world', in C. Stahl (ed.) *International Migration Today Volume 2: Emerging Issues*, Paris/Needlands: UNESCO/University of Western Australia.

Parry, C. (1957) *Nationality and Citizenship Laws of the Commonwealth and the Republic of Ireland*, London: Stevens and Sons Ltd.

Peach, C. (1968) *West Indian Migration to Britain*, London: Oxford University Press.

Penninx, R. and Muus, P. (1989) 'No limits for migration after 1992? The lessons of the past and a reconnaissance of the future?', *International Migration*, 27(3): 373–88.

PEP (Political and Economic Planning) (1948) *Population Policy in Great Britain*, London: PEP.

Perrineau, P. (1991) 'Le Front National: du desert a l'enracinement', in P.-A. Taguieff (ed.) *Face au Racisme Tome 2: Analyses, Hypothèses, Perspectives*, Paris: Editions La Découverte.

Petri-Guasco, R (1989) 'Les Français a l'étranger', *Problèmes Economiques*, 2150: 14–17.

Phizacklea, A. (Ed.) (1983) *One-Way Ticket*, London: Routledge and Kegan Paul.

—— and Miles, R. (1979) 'Working class racist beliefs in the inner city', in R. Miles and A. Phizacklea (eds) *Racism and Political Action in Britain*, London: Routledge and Kegan Paul.

—— and Miles, R. (1980) *Labour and Racism*, London: Routledge and Kegan Paul.

Pilkington, E. (1988) *Beyond the Mother Country: West Indians and the Notting Hill White Riots*, London: I.B. Tauris.

Plender, R. (1988) *International Migration Law*, Dordrecht: Martinus Nijhoff.

Poliakov, L. (1974) *The Aryan Myth: A History of Racist and Nationalist Ideas in Europe*, London: Heinemann.

Pollak, M. (1992) *Vienne 1990: Une Identité Blessée*, Paris: Gallimard.

Pollard, S. (1981) *The Integration of the European Economy Since 1815*, London: George Allen and Unwin.

Pooley, C.G. and Whyte, I.D. (1991) *Migrants, Emigrants and Immigrants: A Social History of Migration*, London: Routledge.

Porter, B. (1979) *The Refugee Question in Mid-Victorian Politics*, Cambridge: Cambridge University Press.

Price, C.A. (1989) 'Long term immigration and emigration: its contribution to the developing world (with particular reference to movement between Australia and Asia and the Pacific)', in R. Appleyard (ed.) *The Impact of International Migration on Developing Countries*, Paris: OECD.

Ramdin, R. (1987) *The Making of the Black Working Class in Britain*, Aldershot: Gower.

Rath, J. (1990) 'Voting rights', in Z. Layton-Henry (ed.) *The Political Rights of Migrant Workers in Western Europe*, London: Sage.

Räthzel, N. (1991) 'Germany: one race, one nation', *Race and Class*, 32(3): 31–48.

Reeves, F. (1983) *British Racial Discourse*, Cambridge: Cambridge University Press.

Rex, J. (1970) *Race Relations in Sociological Theory*, London: Weidenfeld and Nicolson.

—— (1983) *Race Relations in Sociological Theory*, London: Routledge and Kegan Paul.

—— (1986) *Race and Ethnicity*, Milton Keynes: Open University Press.

Rich, P.B. (1986a) *Race and Empire in British Politics*, Cambridge: Cambridge University Press.

—— (1986b) 'The politics of "surplus colonial labour": black immigration, Britain and governmental responses, 1940–1962', in C. Brock (ed.) *The Caribbean in Europe: Aspects of the West Indian Experience in Britain, France and the Netherlands*, London: Frank Cass.

Richmond, A.H. (1988a) 'Socio-cultural adaptation and conflict in immigrant-receiving countries', in C. Stahl (ed.) *International Migration Today Volume 2: Emerging Issues*, Paris/Needlands: UNESCO/University of Western Australia.

—— (1988b) *Immigration and Ethnic Conflict*, London: Macmillan.

Riggs, F.W. (1991) 'Ethnicity, nationalism, race, minority: a semantic/onomantic exercise (part two)', *International Sociology*, 6(4): 443–63.

Robinson, C.J. (1983) *Black Marxism*, London: Zed Press.

Robinson, V. (1986) *Transients, Settlers and Refugees: Asians in Britain*, Oxford: Oxford University Press.

Rogers, R. (1986) 'The transnational nexus of migration', *Annals of the American Academy of Political and Social Science*, 485: 34–50.

Roseman, M. (1988) 'Refugees and Ruhr miners: a case study of the impact of refugees on post-war German society', in A.C. Bramwell (ed.) *Refugees in the Age of Total War*, London: Unwin Hyman.

Royal Commission on Alien Immigration (1903) *Report*, London: HMSO (Cd. 1741).

Royal Commission on Population (1949) *Report of the Royal Commission on Population*, London: HMSO (Cmd. 7695).

Rozat, G. and Bartra, R. (1980) 'Racism and capitalism', in UNESCO, *Sociological Theories: Race and Colonialism*, Paris: UNESCO.

Runnymede Trust (1987) *Combating Racism in Europe: A Summary of Alternative Approaches to the Problem of Protection Against Racism and Xenophobia in Member States of the European Communities*, London: Runnymede Trust.

Rushdie, S. (1982) 'The new empire within Britain', *New Society*, 62: 417–21.

Said, E. (1985) *Orientalism*, Harmondsworth: Penguin.

Salt, J. (1984) 'High level manpower movements in northwest Europe and the role of careers: an explanatory framework', *International Migration Review*, 17: 633–52.

—— (1988) 'Highly-skilled international migrants, careers and internal labour markets', *Geoforum*, 19: 387–99.

—— and Clout, H. (1976) *Migration in Post-War Europe: Geographical Essays*, London: Oxford University Press.

—— and Findlay, A. (1989) 'International migration of highly-skilled manpower: theoretical and developmental issues', in R. Appleyard (ed.) *The Impact of International Migration on Developing Countries*, Paris: OECD.

—— and Kitching, R. (1990) 'Foreign workers and the UK labour market', *Employment Gazette*, 98: 538–46.

Sassen, S. (1988) *The Mobility of Labor and Capital: A Study in International Investment and Labor Flow*, Cambridge: Cambridge University Press.

Satzewich, V. (1991) *Racism and the Incorporation of Foreign Labour: Farm Labour Migration to Canada Since 1945*, London: Routledge.

Schierup, S. (1990) *Migration, Socialism and the International Division of Labour: The Yugoslavian Experience*, Farnborough: Avebury.

Schnapper, D. (1992) *l'Europe des Immigres*, Paris: Francois Bourin.

Seccombe, I.J. (1988) 'International migration in the Middle East: historical trends, contemporary patterns and consequences', in R. Appleyard (ed.) *International Migration Today Volume I: Trends and Prospects*, Paris/Needlands: UNESCO/University of Western Australia.

Seidal, G. (1986) 'Culture, nation and "race", in the British and French New Right', in R. Levitas (ed.) *The Ideology of the New Right*, Cambridge: Polity Press.

Shaw, A. (1988) *A Pakistani Community in Britain*, Oxford: Basil Blackwell.

Shaw, C. (1988) 'Latest estimates of ethnic minority populations', *Population Trends*, 51: 5–8.

Silverman, M. (1991) 'Citizenship and the nation state', *Ethnic and Racial Studies*, 14(3): 333–49.

—— (1992) *Deconstructing the Nation: Immigration, Racism and Citizenship in Modern France*, London: Routledge.

Simmonds, K.R. (1988) 'The concertation of community migration policy', *Common Market Law Review*, 25: 177–200.

Simon, G. (1987) 'Migration in southern Europe: an overview', in OECD, *The Future of Migration*, Paris: OECD.

—— (1991) 'Une Europe communautaire de moins en moins mobile?', *Revue Européenne des Migrations Internationales*, 7(2): 41–62.

Singer-Kérel, J. (1991) 'Foreign workers in France, 1891–1936', *Ethnic and Racial Studies*, 14(3): 279–93.

Sivanandan, A. (1982) *A Different Hunger: Writings on Black Resistance*, London: Pluto Press.

——(1983) 'Challenging racism: strategies for the '80s', *Race and Class*, 25(2): 1–12.

——(1985) 'RAT and the degradation of the black struggle', *Race and Class*, 26(4): 1–34.

—— (1988) 'The new racism', *New Statesman and Society*, 1(22): 8–9.

—— (1990) *Communities of Resistance: Writings on Black Struggles for Socialism*, London: Verso.

Smailes, H. (1981) *Scottish Empire: Scots in Pursuit of Hope and Glory*, Edinburgh: HMSO.

Small, S. (1991a) 'Racialised relations in Liverpool: a contemporary anomaly', *New Community*, 17(4): 511–37.

—— (1991b) 'Attaining racial parity in the United States and England: we got to go where the greener grass grows', *Sage Race Relations Abstracts*, 16(3): 3–55.

Smith, A.D. (1979) *Nationalism in the Twentieth Century*, Oxford: Martin Robertson.

—— (1983) *Theories of Nationalism*, London: Duckworth.

—— (1991) *National Identity*, Harmondsworth: Penguin.

Smith, S.J. (1989) *The Politics of 'Race' and Residence*, Cambridge: Polity Press.

Smith, T.E. (1981) *Commonwealth Migration: Flows and Policies*, London: Macmillan.

Social Europe (1988) *The Social Dimension of the Internal Market*, Brussels: Commission of the European Communities.

Solomos, J. (1986) 'Varieties of Marxist conceptions of "race", class and the state: a critical analysis', in J. Rex and D. Mason (eds) *Theories of Race and Ethnic Relations*, Cambridge: Cambridge University Press.

—— (1990) *Race and Racism in Contemporary Britain*, London: Macmillan.

SOPEMI (1990) *Continuous Reporting System on Migration: 1989*, Paris: OECD.

—— (1991) *Continuous Reporting System on Migration: 1990*, Paris: OECD.

Soulis, S. (1987) 'Illegal immigration to Greece', in OECD, *The Future of Migration*, Paris: OECD.

Sponza, L. (1988) *Italian Immigrants in Nineteenth-Century Britain: Realities and Images*, Leicester: Leicester University Press.

Stadulis, E. (1951/2) 'The resettlement of displaced persons in the United Kingdom', *Population Studies*, 5: 207–37.

Stahl, C. (ed.) (1988) *International Migration Today Volume 2: Emerging Issues*, Paris/Needlands: UNESCO/University of Western Australia.

Stepan, N. (1982) *The Idea of Race in Science: Great Britain, 1800–1945*, London: Macmillan.

Straubhaar, T. (1984) 'The accession of Spain and Portugal to the EEC from the aspect of the free movement of labour in an enlarged common labour market', *International Migration*, 22(3): 228–38.

Summers, A. (1981) 'The character of Edwardian nationalism: three popular leagues', in P. Kennedy and A. Nicholls (eds) *Nationalist and Racialist Movements in Britain and Germany Before 1914*, London: Macmillan.

—— (1989) 'Edwardian militarism', in R. Samuel (ed.) *Patriotism Volume I: History and Politics*, London: Routledge.

Swift, R. and Gilley, S. (eds) (1985) *The Irish in the Victorian City*, London: Croom Helm.

—— and Gilley, S. (eds) (1989) *The Irish in Britain 1815–1939*, London: Pinter.

Sword, K. (1988) 'The absorption of Poles into civilian employment in Britain, 1945–1950', in A.C. Bramwell (ed.) *Refugees in the Age of Total War*, London: Unwin Hyman.

—— Davies, N., and Ciechanowski, J. (1989) *The Formation of the Polish Community in Great Britain, 1939–50*, London: School of Slavonic and East European Studies.

Szymanski, A. (1985) 'The structure of race', *Review of Radical Political Economics*, 17(4): 106–20.

Taguieff, P.-A. (1987) *La Force du Préjugé: Essai sur le racisme et ses doubles*, Paris: Editions La Découverte.
—— (1990) 'The new cultural racism in France', *Telos*, 83: 109–22.
Tannahill, J.A. (1958) *European Volunteer Workers in Britain*, Manchester: Manchester University Press.
Todorov, T. (1989) *Nous et les Autres: La Réflexion Française sur la Diversité Humaine*, Paris: Seuil.
UNESCO (1980) *Sociological Theories: Race and Colonialism*, Paris: UNESCO.
Venturini, A. (1991) 'Immigration et marche du travail en Italie: données recentes', *Revue Européenne des Migrations Internationales*, 7(2): 97–114.
Venturini, P. (1989) *1992: The European Social Dimension*, Brussels: Commission of the European Communities.
Verhaeren, R.-E. (1990) *Partir? Une Theorie Economique des Migrations Internationales*, Grenoble: Presses Universitaires de Grenoble.
Vichnevski, A. and Zayontchkovskaia, J. (1991) 'L'émigration de l'ex-union sovietique: premices et inconnues', *Revue Européenne Des Migrations Internationales*, 7(3): 5–29.
Visram, R. (1986) *Ayahs, Lascars and Princes: The Story of Indians in Britain 1700–1947*, London: Pluto Press.
Wallerstein, I. (1979) *The Capitalist World-Economy*, Cambridge: Cambridge University Press.
—— (1988) 'Universalisme, racisme, sexisme: les tensions ideologiques du capitalisme', in E. Balibar and I. Wallerstein, *Race, Nation, Classe: Les Identités Ambiguës*, Paris: Editions La Découverte.
Walvin, J. (1973) *Black and White: The Negro and English Society, 1555–1945*, London: Allen and Unwin.
—— (1984) *Passage to Britain*, Harmondsworth: Penguin.
Watson, J. (ed.) (1977) *Between Two Cultures*, Oxford: Basil Blackwell.
Watson, M. (ed.) (1990) *Contemporary Minority Nationalism*, London: Routledge.
Webber, F. (1991) 'From ethnocentrism to Euro-racism', *Capital and Class*, 32(3): 11–17.
Weber, E. (1977) *Peasants into Frenchmen: The Modernisation of Rural France 1870–1914*, London: Chatto and Windus.
White, P.E. (1989) 'Internal migration in the nineteenth and twentieth centuries', in P.E. Ogden and P.E. White (eds) *Migrants in Modern France: Population Mobility in the Later 19th and 20th Centuries*, London: Unwin Hyman.
Wieviorka, M. (1991) *L'Espace du Racisme*, Paris: Seuil.
—— (1992) *La France Raciste*, Paris: Seuil.
Wihtol de Wenden, C. (1988) *Les Immigrés et la Politique*, Paris: Presses de la Fondation Nationale des Sciences Politiques.
—— (1990) 'The absence of rights: the position of illegal immigrants', in Z. Layton-Henry (ed.) *The Political Rights of Migrant Workers in Western Europe*, London: Sage.
—— (1991) 'Immigration policy and the issue of nationality', *Ethnic and Racial Studies*, 14(3): 319–32.
Wilpert, Z. (1988) 'Migrant women and their daughters: two generations of Turkish women in the Federal Republic of Germany', in C. Stahl (ed.) *International Migration Today Volume 2: Emerging Issues*, Paris/Needlands: UNESCO/University of Western Australia.

Wilson, T. (1952) 'Manpower', in G.D.N. Worswick and P.H. Ady (eds) *The British Economy 1945–1950*, Oxford: Clarendon Press.

Wolpe. H. (1980) 'Capitalism and cheap labour-power in South Africa: from segregation to apartheid', in H. Wolpe (ed.), *The Articulation of Modes of Production: Essays from Economy and Society*, London: Routledge and Kegan Paul.

——(1986) 'Class concepts, class struggle and racism', in J. Rex and D. Mason (eds) *Theories of Race and Ethnic Relations*, Cambridge: Cambridge University Press.

Womack, P. (1989) *Improvement and Romance: Constructing the Myth of the Highlands*, London: Macmillan.

Wood, E.M. (1986) *The Retreat from Class: A New 'True' Socialism*, London: verso.

Woods, D. (1992) 'The centre no longer holds: the rise of regional leagues in Italian politics', *West European Politics*, 15(2): 56–76.

Wright, P. (1985) *On Living in an Old Country*, London: Verso.

Yarrow, S. (1989) 'The impact of hostility on Germans in Britain, 1914–1918', *Immigrants and Minorities*, 8: 97–112.

de Zayas, A.-M. (1988) 'A historical survey of twentieth century expulsions', in A.C. Bramwell (ed.) *Refugees in the Age of Total War*, London: Unwin Hyman.

Zolberg, A. (1981) 'International migrations in political perspective', in M.M. Kritz, C.B. Kelley and S.M. Tomasi (eds) *Global Trends in Migration: Theory and Research on International Population Movements*, New York: Center for Migration Studies.

—— (1989) 'The next waves: migration theory for a changing world', *International Migration Review*, 23(3): 403–30.

—— , Sergio, A., and Astri, S. (1989) *Escape from Violence: Conflict and the Refugee Crisis in the Developing World*, New York: Oxford University Press.

Zubryzcki, J. (1956) *Polish Immigrants in Britain: A Study of Adjustment*, The Hague: Martinus Nijhoff.

Name index

Subject index

Act of Union (1707) 78
Africa 67, 89, 113, 114, 119, 129, 154, 184, 195, 199
Africans 82, 93
Afro-American 48
Albania 200
aliens 37, 132–4, 134–49, 150–69, 185; *see also* foreigner
Aliens Act (1905) 141, 143–8, 154
Aliens Order (1920) 154, 155
Aliens Restriction Act (1914) 138
Aliens Restriction (Amendment) Act (1919) 138
Anglo-Saxon 65–6, 69
anti-semitism 85, 86, 104, 144
apartheid 6
assimilation 20, 91–2, 140–43, 161, 165
aussiedler 202, 205–6, 207
Australia 110, 123, 188, 205, 209
Austria 156, 199

Baltic states 140
Belgium 157, 187, 188, 199, 202, 203, 208
'black' 4, 18, 149; 'black/white' relations 12, 13–14, 18, 38, 212–13; and immigration 128–30, 206
Black Sections 4
'black' struggle 30, 37
blasphemy 4
Blue Danube scheme 156
Boers 68

bourgeoisie 32, 90–2, 95
breeding 66, 94, 103; codes of 95–6
Britain 6, 9, 10, 14, 19, 22, 36, 37, 39, 43, 49, 60, 83, 85, 94–5, 98, 102, 176, 199, 201, 205; and business migration 186–7; emigration from 110, 130; and European migration 11, 12, 110, 111–12, 117, 121, 130–4, 128–49, 150–69; and history of migration 107–27, 128–49; and migration of managerial, technical and professional labour 186–7; as a multicultural society 209; and New Commonwealth migration 11, 12, 15, 35, 37, 108, 109, 125–6, 128–30, 132–4, 150–69, 206; and politics of integration 174–5; as a society of immigration 109–110
British Nationality and Status of Aliens Act (1914) 153
British Nationality Act (1948) 133, 153–4, 159, 160–3, 164
British Nationality Act (1981) 76
British subjects 37, 132–4, 150–69
Britishness 56, 74, 76, 160, 169; *see also* Englishness
Brixton 42

Canada 110, 123, 153, 181, 187, 188, 203, 205, 209
capital accumulation 36, 39, 51, 112–13, 118, 121, 124, 125, 127, 192, 205